DA.

❧ Música Tejana

Number One:

University of Houston Series
in Mexican American Studies

Sponsored by the Center
for Mexican American Studies

Tatcho Mindiola,
Director and General Editor

Música Tejana

The Cultural Economy of Artistic Transformation

MANUEL PEÑA

Texas A & M University Press
College Station

The paper used in this book meets the minimum
requirements of the American National Standard for
Permanence of Paper for Printed Library Materials,
z39.48-1984. Binding materials have been chosen
for durability.
∞

This book is sponsored and partially funded by the Center
for Mexican American Studies, University of Houston.

Library of Congress Cataloging-in-Publication Data

Peña, Manuel H., 1942–
    Música tejana : the cultural economy of artistic
transformation / Manuel Peña.
        p.   cm. — (University of Houston series in Mexican
American studies : no. 1)
    Includes bibliographical references (p.   ) and index.
    ISBN 0-89096-877-2 (cloth). — ISBN 0-89096-888-8 (pbk.)
        1. Tejana music—Texas—History and criticism.
    2. Mexican Americans—Texas—Music—History and
    criticism.   I. Title.   II. Series.
    ML3481.P45   1999
    781.64'089'68720764—dc21   98-47951
                                                         CIP
                                                          MN

For Emilio, Alyssa Lynn, and Maxwell——

So near to and yet so far from the events
described in this book.

Contents

Illustrations

Preface

This book represents several years of research on Texas-Mexican music, or *música tejana,* as it is sometimes called. Música tejana is not one single music but several musical and musico-literary genres, ensembles, and their styles. It encompasses the major musico-literary genres covered in this book—the *corrido, canción,* and what I call the *canción-corrido.* It also includes two major regional ensembles and their styles—the *conjunto,* a close cousin of *música norteña,* and the Texas-Mexican version of the *orquesta,* a multi-styled wind ensemble patterned after the American swing band. Lastly, música tejana also includes yet another, more recent crop of synthesizer-driven ensembles and their styles, known since the mid-1980s as "Tejano."

Despite their diversity, the various ensembles, genres, and styles collectively known as música tejana share one fundamental characteristic: they are all homegrown, and they all speak after their own fashion to fundamental social processes shaping Texas-Mexican society. As I explain in later chapters, they speak to a transforming economy and its associated culture, and their effects on the Texas-Mexicans. In recognition that economy, or the social organization of productive activity, and culture, the social organization of communication, are intricately related, throughout the book I use the term "cultural economy" as an organizing principle to elucidate the relationship between music as a form of artistic culture and the social processes out of which it emerges. As will become clear later, *música tejana* is very much a product of a transforming "cultural economy."

As this preface is written, música tejana is undergoing what appears to be another major shift. The big recording labels, whose full-force intervention in the mid-eighties substantially transformed the process of music making, evidently are retreating from their previously aggressive promotion of Tejano

(Arista [BMG] closed its Latin branch in Austin on May 1, 1998). Perhaps they discovered that the music was not as profitable in the long run as they initially had anticipated. In any case, the major labels' hesitation seems to have reinvigorated local tejano (Texas-Mexican) labels, or "indies," as small-time operations are called. The lower profile of the majors and the rejuvenation of the tejano indies may signal a commercial setback for Tejano, since the indies lack the economic reach of the Aristas (BMGs) and EMIs. Yet the commercial contraction of música tejana may help reground it to its original tejano base, thus reversing a recent trend toward full-scale commodification and a concomitant loss of symbolic charge. In short, Tejano may be compelled by market forces to return to its "roots." Such an outcome could restore some of the organic quality música tejana had lost through large-scale commodification. Only time will tell whether such a retrogressive result is possible, however.

I mentioned at the outset that this book represents several years of research. I would like to single out a couple of individuals whose help was crucial in bringing the work to fruition. First, my thanks go to Doug Foley, who over the years has been both trusted friend and uncompromising critic. As usual, he helped me to rethink my approach on several issues and thus to bring my main arguments into better focus.

Second, I owe a debt of gratitude to Tatcho Mindiola, director of Mexican American Studies at the University of Houston, who bailed me out of a difficult academic situation back in the summer of 1992. He offered me a visiting scholarship at the University of Houston, which helped immensely to jump-start the research on this project, after years of sporadic activity. As the first in a series of publications cosponsored by Mexican American Studies and Texas A&M University Press, this book will hopefully pay back a little of Tatcho's generosity.

Last, I am deeply indebted to the countless individuals—musicians, promoters, record-label executives, and everyday fans—who shared their thoughts on Texas-Mexican music with me over the years. To them all, I dedicate this book. I hope that my own evaluation of the music and musicians does not violate their expectations or diminish the historical value of what is undeniably the great record of musical innovation *música tejana* represents.

Música Tejana

❧ Introduction

Music as Culture and as Spectacle

Symbolic and Commercial Aspects of Música Tejana

Music may be universal, but, as ethnomusicologists have repeatedly demonstrated, its social significance is not (Slobin and Titon 1996). It is only in specific social settings, when activated in a communicative process through performance, that music attains meaningful status as a part of culture. Strictly speaking, a musical item—the score or a recording of Beethoven's Fifth Symphony, for example, or a specific instrument such as the violin—is not a part of musical culture, at least not as long as it remains unperformed.[1] It becomes culture, or socially communicative activity, when it is brought to life in performance—a live concert or other communal event, a televised program, or even as a recording played on a home audio system.

Following Dan Ben Amos (1972), we may propose that, as long as an instrument or musical composition (a symphony, song, fiddle tune, lament, etc.) remains an inert object in more or less permanent disuse (a recording, a score, a trombone in its case, a scribbled tune on a piece of paper, a memorized song in someone's head), it should be considered a "superorganic" cultural phenomenon. By *superorganic* we mean, in the first instance, that it exists as an artifact (or *mentifact,* in Ben Amos's terminology) but is not engaged in communication. As an object or concept, it can be widely dispersed; and, like other cultural artifacts and mentifacts, it "can shift media, cross language boundaries, pass from one culture to another" (Ben Amos 1972:4). Indeed, it can even outlive its original creators. But the object remains inert, a bit of "potential" culture. It becomes active (or, to borrow a term from physics, "kinetic") culture only when it passes from the superorganic to the "organic" realm—when it becomes subject to "social context," "cultural attitude," "rhetorical situation," or, in short, when it is performed as an integral part of a communicative event in a culture-specific context (ibid.; see Abrahams 1977 on folklore as cultural "enactment").

But the activation or enactment of music through performance is only a starting point, insofar as its status as organic cultural activity is concerned. Other matters immediately intervene in determining its potential for context-specific meaning. As Slobin and Titon (1996) point out, who performs the music, who listens to it, and the circumstances under which it is performed all are critical considerations in determining a music's social significance. Beethoven's Fifth, performed by the Chicago Symphony Orchestra, may generate tumultuous applause in a concert hall, but it would be out of place at the Tejano Rose Nightclub in San Antonio—and even more so in a ritual among the Kaluli of Papua–New Guinea (see Feld 1990).[2] By the same token, a Tejano Rose act such as Ram Herrera and the Outlaws would create a scandal were it to appear, say, during the intermission of a Chicago Symphony concert. The two types of music represent incompatible forms of artistic culture. The Chicago Symphony Orchestra and its music epitomize the apex of Western elite or "high" culture; they are associated historically with the most dominant classes in Europeanized capitalist societies. Ram Herrera represents a music subculture historically stigmatized in American society and confined to certain segments of a marginalized ethnic class.

Further complicating what we may call the organic/superorganic dichotomy in this moment of "late capitalism" (Jameson 1984b) is the increasing influence on musical performance that the technology of musical production and reproduction has exerted since the second decade of the twentieth century (Frith 1988; Gronow 1983; Robinson, Buck, and Cuthbert 1991). Especially critical, in terms of the link between music and its makers and sponsors, is the appropriation of music by the mass-communication industry and its media—radio, film, television, and audio-video technology in general. In particular, the recording industry's splitting off of production from performance and performance from transmission—what Steve Feld (after composer Murray Schafer) has called "schizophonia," or the "splitting of sounds from sources"—ruptures what we might call the "first-order" link between music and its immediate social context (Feld 1994:259 passim; see Attali 1985 on "repeating").

By "first-order," we mean those situations in which musical performance forms an indispensable element in some larger face-to-face cultural enactment—a rite, festival, dance, game—in short, a performance of an organic, deeply symbolic nature that brings groups of people together in common and earnest celebration (in festival, for example; see Stoeltje 1992). Since the advent and expansion of recording technology, music increasingly has been performed in "second-order" or—what we may consider the second instance of the superorganic—acontextual or weakly symbolic settings, such as commercial studios, where performance is converted into a commodity, then packaged and warehoused until ready for marketing to an absent, anonymous audience. That audience may be the isolated individual, a "partying" group, or no one in particular (as in the case of "supermarket music," or Muzak). As a superorganic phenomenon, music is substantially emptied of its symbolic load.

Increasingly, this superorganic, second-order form of performance has affected the status of music in and *as* culture. Except during unique and isolated events, such as ceremonials, religious rituals, and, occasionally, some communal forms of celebration, we do not regularly use music to negotiate in-the-flesh, face-to-face social commitments or obligations.[3] Rather, we are just as likely to consume it in private "rituals," as an atomized commodity that cuts us off from the rest of society. Or, we may use it as we do other commodities, such as cosmetics, jewelry, cars, or any of a wide array of products—as "surface" markers for our shifting individual "personalities" in a "decentered" society of faceless strangers. The performance and (re)enactment of music thereby are splintered from active social interaction. Instead of serving primarily social imperatives (for example, reinforcing community ties through close social interaction), music serves primarily individual ends (e.g., a jogger marking time while listening to Mariah Carey on a "Walkman").[4]

In arguing that "repetition" in music creates a new and atomized "network" of social relations (as mediated through the economy of music), Attali echoes our concerns here about the transformation of music from a first-order to a second-order phenomenon (from organic to superorganic) by the capitalist market. In the network of repetition (music in the service of profit accumulation, as assembly-line commodity):

each spectator has a solitary relation with a material object; the consumption of music is individualized, a simulacrum of ritual sacrifice, a blind spectacle. The network is no longer a form of sociality, an opportunity for spectators to meet and communicate, but rather a tool making the individualized stockpiling of music possible on a large scale. Here again, the new network first appears in music as the herald of a new stage in the organization of capitalism, that of the repetitive mass production of all social relations. (Attali 1985:32)

And this schism, between the production of music as a mass commodity and its consumption as an individualized act of stockpiling, lies at the heart of the difference between music as organic cultural performance and music as super-organic or "blind" spectacle.

The difference between cultural performance and spectacle is critical. Music-as-cultural-performance speaks powerfully to politico-aesthetic issues that "re-center" a social group, thus contributing to a shared, reciprocating identity. As I am conceptualizing it here, spectacle is inescapably tied to the tendency of late capitalism to transform social relations into commodity rela-tions. Spectacle involves, centrally, the surface play of signifiers qua com-modities to create a "detached" form of "entertainment" (Manning 1992: 295). Of the various commentators on spectacle, Guy Debord (1994) most closely approximates my own view of music-as-spectacle. For Debord, "spec-tacle is not a set of images, but social relations mediated by images" (p. 12); it is action not "directly lived" but "mere representation" (ibid.), in which "all community and critical awareness have ceased to be" (p. 21). Or, as Man-ning interprets Debord, spectacle is "a pathological condition that preempts valid social discourse" (1992:295). In short, spectacle is quintessentially rep-resentative of the "postmodern condition" (Lyotard 1984)—a concatenation of fragmented images, packaged and sold as commodities, that creates a fleet-ing sense of sociability, only to confirm the detachment and alienation of the spectators, who remain "individuated" and "uncommitted" (Manning 1992:295).

The mass-commodification of music sets the stage for its function as spec-tacle. As a mass-commodity—a CD, cassette, video, or even a concert—its production may be socially generated, in that many people's work is coordi-nated in the manufacturing process, but it remains an inert object, a com-modity in which are invested the producers' hopes for capital accumulation. Commodified music is a superorganic artifact—even when activated through performance. That is, as a commodity consumed atomistically—even in large public events—the music fails to bridge, and may even widen the gap between, the superorganic and the organic. To borrow terminology from Marxist theory, as a superorganic phenomenon music-as-commodity yields to the reifying tendencies of exchange-value. To become organic cultural activity, music first must be transformed by use-value.[5]

The schism between socialized production and atomized consumption inevitably is implicated in the opposition between use- and exchange-value. Just as the difference between music-as-cultural-performance and music-as-spectacle is critical, so is that between use- and exchange-value. Use-value is a unique *quality* inherent in all objects of purposeful, concrete human labor, particularly as they are transformed into symbolic forms with the power to fulfill direct and "transparent" social obligations—for example, of reciprocity (see Mauss 1954 on the symbolic [use-]value of the "gift"). In the medieval practice of *corvée,* for instance, "every serf [knew] that what he expend[ed] in the service of his lord [was] a specific quantity of his own personal labour-power" (Marx 1977:170). As mediated by the use-value of the serf's labor, the social relations between serf and vassal were "personal" and "not disguised as social relations between things, between products of labor" (i.e., commodities; ibid.).

Exchange-value is the use-value of commodities abstracted from its immediate social-interactionist context and transferred onto an anonymous marketplace. Exchange-value is "human labor in the abstract"; it is not a quality but a *quantity,* which is best represented by the universal equivalent of exchange-value: money. When a cultural economy becomes dominated by exchange-value—that is, when money becomes the universal equivalent through which all products are exchangeable—a complex social change is set in motion that works, ultimately, to undermine the "transparency" of cultural communication mediated by use-value (see Sapir 1949 on "genuine" versus "spurious" culture). A Pandora's box of social antagonisms is unleashed, culminating in the "decentering" of society and the estrangement of human beings from their own labor and from each other.

In a well-argued article on the performance of *Los Pastores,* an old Spanish-Mexican Christmas play that also includes music, Richard Flores (1994; see also Flores 1995) illustrates the difference both between cultural performance and spectacle and between use- and exchange-value. Flores draws a distinction between the performance of *Los Pastores* in a Mexican *barrio* and its performance at one of San Antonio's historic missions. According to Flores, in the barrio the play constitutes the "gifting of performance," or a freely proffered act of personal labor. As enacted in the *barrio, Los Pastores* is a communal event designed to cement reciprocal relations between the members of the cast, who themselves are barrio residents, and their audiences, usually home gatherings where a religious "promise" is being fulfilled. For Flores, this "labor as free activity," or labor as "gift-giving," constitutes an act of "sociability" wherein social relations arising from a common ethnic/class bond are re-negotiated and thereby reaffirmed.

In our terminology, the barrio performance constitutes an act motivated by the principle of use-value. As an act of use-value, *Los Pastores* becomes an "organic" form of cultural performance, what I call a "strong" symbol whose principal function is to "re-center" the community in a common gesture of cooperation and reciprocity, free of the coercion that underlies social relations under wage-labor (i.e., the exchange-value underwriting the relation between an employer and employee). In the mission, on the other hand, the play is "displaced," transformed into a form of contracted wage-labor, or work as "commodity exchange." Staged before an anonymous audience as an exchanged commodity (the group is paid one hundred dollars for the performance), the play loses its organic quality. No longer is it hard-wired into the innermost circuits of barrio communication. Instead, it is treated as an *object* of tourist attraction, as the performers are uncomfortably aware.

In short, in the mission setting, *Los Pastores* becomes a superorganic spectacle of desultory social value. It is a "weak" symbol, a touristic token of San Antonio's imaginary and romanticized "Spanish heritage." And although Flores does not distinguish between the two performances precisely in terms of use- versus exchange-value (or cultural performance versus spectacle), he clearly has this distinction in mind when he assigns a labor-gifting (use-value) function in the barrio and a commodity-exchange (exchange-value) function in the mission.[6]

Examples more closely related to our argument on the use-value versus exchange-value of music (and, hence, on its "organic" versus "superorganic" function) may be drawn from a form of entertainment widespread in American life—the public concert and/or dance. Popular-music concerts large and small are common in American cities, where performers ranging from Reba McEntire to Julio Iglesias are featured. The price of admission to these events can be quite high, but multitudes of people attend, nonetheless, to see and hear their favorite performers in person. But these events are a function of market forces and the profit motive that drives them. Far more than *Los Pastores* at the mission, they are spectacles driven by the principle of exchange-value. The performers are glamorized commodities no different, really, from a coveted sports car or expensive watch, perfume, or other market product that stimulates our desires and buys for us our sense of individuality. Moreover, while an ephemeral sense of sociability may emerge during the concert or dance, no lasting bonds are established. No deeply cultural or ideological purpose issues forth from such gatherings. The spectators remain "detached" and "uncommitted."

Certain communitarian music-dance events, on the other hand, can generate a strong sense of community. They can be driven by cultural or ideological imperatives that result in bold statements of identity and communal obligations and goals. They can, in short, be driven by the principle of use-value.

A good example of such events is the kind of dance in which I participated while a member of a Mexican American dance band, or *orquesta*,[7] in the city of Fresno, California (see Peña 1980; 1999). During the 1960s and 1970s, as a member of "La orquesta de Beto García y sus GGs," I played regularly for Saturday-night dances sponsored by a Mexican American organization, the Veterans of Foreign Wars (VFW), Post 8900. These Saturday dances, held as frequently as once a month, contained a number of distinctive features that marked them strongly as ethnic, *mejicoamericano* celebrations. A deeply felt sense of sociability was present, such that, in their totality, the events evoked a spirit of community, of people engaged in what Clifford Geertz has called "deep play" (Geertz 1973). Through the dance as a form of deep play, social bonds based on ethnicity and class were reinforced, enabling the participants to reclaim their sense of communal identity in a society in which Mexicans historically have occupied a position subordinate to that of the dominant Anglos. In sum, while the musicians did not play for free and a token admission fee was paid to join the celebration, the principal factor at work in these celebrations was use-value, not exchange-value.[8]

The Saturday-night dances were, in fact, a form of ritualized play (Peña 1980; 1999), in which the principle of use-value finds its consummate expression. Music in such contexts acquires an indexical status as an emblem of the group's most basic sense of communal identity and purpose. (See Titon 1996 for examples of the use-value of music-as-ritual in Africa, South America, and other regions.) Through the activation of numerous symbolic cues, participants in the VFW Post 8900 dances invoked a strong and romanticized sense of their *mexicanidad* (Mexicanness), or, better yet, of their Mexican Americanness, marshaling these cues to affirm to themselves and to the world their cohesiveness as a group with common aesthetic and community interests. As I wrote elsewhere, "In returning again and again to the dance, the participants demonstrated their wish to engage in a communal experience, a cultural reality that in its distinctive ethnic difference effectively contested the homogenizing power of the dominant society" (Peña 1999). That communal experience was made possible through the use-value function of the music performed by Beto García y sus GGs. It was a music of and by the community, a music whose symbolic power emanated from the deepest levels of that community's artistic culture.

To summarize this necessarily brief overview of music-as-culture, we may propose two major distinctions and their respective functions with respect to music and its performance in this epoch of "late capitalism." These are: organic, culturally meaningful performance based on use-value; and superorganic commodity production driven by exchange-value. In its use-value context, music projects an aesthetic principle deeply embedded within the core of a group with an identifiable sense of community. In a world driven by massive commodity exchange, with its tendency to alienate people from each other, music animated by use-value resists such alienating or reifying tendencies, becoming an effective medium by which people can express their sense of commonality, whether this commonality be ethnic, class, gender, or generational. Bonds of social reciprocity are enacted through this type of musical performance.

In its exchange-value context, on the other hand, as a superorganic mass commodity bought and sold in an anonymous market, music tends to lose its power to strengthen social relations. As George Lipsitz has written about mass culture generally, commoditized music is part of an "ever expanding supply of free-floating symbols only loosely connected to social life" (1990:134). It is either a personalized object of consumption or a performance spectacle. In either case, it satisfies personal aesthetic desires through individualized "rituals" disconnected from any larger social purpose. Yet, perhaps because humans are inescapably social beings, except under extreme circumstances—say, as background for supermarket shopping—music always retains some measure of social significance. Even in the most commodified of contexts, such as the spectacle, it constitutes cultural—or, more accurately, ideological—activity, however attenuated it may be from a symbolic standpoint (Frith 1988; Hebdige 1979).

Música Tejana: Organic Symbol or Superorganic Commodity?

Notwithstanding the highly organic and symbolic quality of performances by musicians such as Beto García y sus GGs, much of the music that defines the Mexican American experience in the southwestern United States since the rise of the recording industry has been commercially generated—that is, subject to the alienating tendency of exchange-value. This has been particularly true of Texas-Mexican music. Does this, then, make música tejana a superorganic artifact—a commodity lacking in cultural significance? Nothing could be further from reality. As indicated above, commercialization, in and of itself, does not necessarily strip music of its symbolic power—its capacity to communicate deeply felt aesthetic and other social meanings. This is especially true of such musics as música tejana, which historically are "hard-wired" into their indigenous cultures. Thus, in the case of the styles and forms most intimately associated with tejanos, such as the accordion ensemble known as conjunto, the orquesta, and the narrative ballad known as corrido, commercialization did not transform these into pure commodities, nor did it strip them of their use-value. On the contrary, the commercial market actually intensified the symbolic power associated with their use-value.

How did this seemingly paradoxical turn of events come about—how did música tejana respond to the pressures of exchange-value yet retain intact, for the most part, the power of its use-value? The key to the capacity of música tejana to remain a viable symbol of tejano identity and solidarity—and, hence, to retain its cultural power—lies in the locus of control and distribution in the production of the music. The first efforts at commercialization took place in the mid-1920s, when the large American recording companies—Columbia, Victor, Decca, Brunswick, Vocalion—discovered the abundance of native talent and stylistic diversity. However, as ethnomusicologist Bruno Nettl has said of the major labels' early relationship to localized, indigenous musics generally, "the aim of the record industry was to provide each culture and subculture its own, local music" (Nettl 1985:62). In other words, at least prior to World War II, the major labels were not interested in controlling talent or musical style. They allowed local markets, through indigenous intermediaries, or brokers, to dictate what music would be recorded.

In the Southwest, entrepreneurs like the Acostas in San Antonio and Felipe Valdez Leal in Los Angeles played key roles in brokering arrangements between the recording industry and local musicians. Beyond that, however, these entrepreneurs were cultural "insiders," individuals whose aesthetic and ideological views had been molded within the confines of an ethnic mejicano (Mexican) culture. Moreover, the roots of that culture were embedded solidly in a rural, pastoralist environment, although a more refined and urban sensibility had been in evidence since the turn of the century. The local entrepreneurs were no strangers to musical tastes as they had evolved in the Southwest—tastes solidly grounded within the bedrock of regional Hispanic cultures such as that of the Texas-Mexicans. Here a wealth of musical talents and styles flourished. These styles ranged from the duet tradition and the emergent conjunto ensemble to the more genteel *orquesta de cuerda* (string orchestra).

What commercialization by the major labels did, then, was to cement hitherto diffuse styles, such as the conjunto and the duet (both male and female), which, under the impetus of the commercial market, gained cultural power as organic cultural icons, rather than being cast adrift as superorganic commodities with no specific cultural base. In other words, what we might identify as the capitalist market's *centrifugal* tendency to disperse and dilute musical symbols and to transform them into reified commodities did not achieve its full effect in the Southwest. The market was unable to overcome the *centripetal* tendency of contextualized, group-centering performance to spawn strong, organic musical symbols. Thus, in the case of the conjunto, for example, its commercialization within a tightly circumscribed and more or less homogeneous social context not only did not dislodge the music from its central position in tejano culture, but actually helped to certify it as *the* music of the tejano (and northern mejicano) working class.

Events after World War II did not appreciably change the commercial climate, insofar as the music of the Hispanic Southwest was concerned. While the major labels abandoned their regional operations in Texas and elsewhere, local companies such as Ideal, from Alice, Texas, and Imperial, from Los Angeles, filled the gap. Owned by local entrepreneurs like Ideal's Armando Marroquín, individuals who were intimately familiar with the music and musicians, these labels helped the Mexican music of the Southwest remain bounded by its regional, ethnic geography. The limited circulation in turn contributed to the music's autonomy.

Armando Marroquín, for example, whose Ideal label became one of the most influential in the Southwest during the 1940s and 1950s, was raised, as he once said in an interview, in a social environment in which folk music close to the hearts of the common people reigned. He was introduced early to such powerful musical forms as the corrido (see chapter 1). In sum, Marroquín was closely attuned to the musical tastes of the everyday people—tastes produced by local conditions dictating the direction of change within the various musical traditions. In this sense, Marroquín was very much an "insider," someone whose cultural interests transcended purely economic motives. Thus, despite his obvious goal of exploiting tejano music for economic gain, he also valued the music as an expression of "his people" and their cultural aspirations. In his mind, economic and cultural interests coincided, and he was able to form partnerships with the artists who recorded for Ideal for the purpose of promoting musical styles ultimately crucial to the ethnic interests of tejanos.

As we shall see, it was in the limited commercial context in which Ideal and other regional companies operated that the conjunto, the orquesta, and musical forms indigenous to the Hispanic Southwest proliferated.[9] This context, subject to the limitations that an ethnic, regional market imposes, prevented the various musics from spinning out of the organic orbit into which they were launched. They thus retained the power to speak to the most basic aesthetic and ideological impulses of their given constituencies and "to shout their sufferings," to co-opt Attali's phrase about music of the "exploited" (1985:8). Naturally, in time these constituencies became more diversified, as Mexican Americans began to experience disparate rates of upward mobility and assimilation into American culture, particularly after World War II. Given the emerging social differences within the Mexican American community in the Southwest, it was inevitable that these differences would find expression at the level of musical activity. The chapters on the conjunto and the orquesta—as these evolved contemporaneously with social change, "technological developments in the music industry[,] and the pressures of commercialization" (Mitchell 1996:10)—explore the relationship between music and what Richard Bauman (1972) has called "differential identity."

The 1980s introduced a new musical climate in Texas, as well as a major transformation of música tejana. Tejano,[10] as a collection of diverse styles came to be known, diverged sharply, both stylistically and commercially, from earlier forms of Texas-Mexican music. I shall address this divergence at length in chapter 6; here it suffices to say that Tejano was the product of what we may call the "postmodernist" moment in Texas-Mexican society, when the major labels—active once more in tejano music—and a social formation transformed by the principle of exchange-value had considerably (though not totally) changed the process of music making. Caught between a persistent "residual" culture still grounded on music-as-organic-performance and a new network driven by the surging popularity of music-as-spectacle, Tejano of the 1990s equivocated. In some instances it claimed to—and perhaps did—represent the aesthetic interests of Texas-Mexicans, but on the whole it moved inexorably toward the status of a full-fledged market commodity driven by the alienating principle of exchange-value.

Tejanos and Their Music: A Thematic Summary

Among the Mexican Americans who inhabit the American Southwest—the states of California, Arizona, New Mexico, Colorado, and Texas—one group has distinguished itself for its strongly innovative musical spirit: the Texas-Mexicans, or tejanos, as they sometimes call themselves. Historically, tejanos have been the principal innovators in the three musical forms and styles treated in the bulk of this book (chapters 2, 3, 4, and 5). These are the corrido, the conjunto (known more generically as música norteña), and an orchestral ensemble patterned after the big American swing bands, known in the Southwest as orquesta. Moreover, the tejanos remained in the musical vanguard in the Hispanic Southwest in the waning years of the twentieth century, as the newer musical forms known as Tejano continued to expand their influence. This latter development is treated more fully in chapter 6.

A question logically arises with respect to the tejanos' dominance in the musical culture of the Southwest. What sociohistorical circumstances have come into play in installing the Texas-Mexicans as musical leaders among their regional peers in the Hispanic Southwest? Why not the New Mexicans, who have a longer and more stable historical presence in the region? Or, for the twentieth century, why not the Mexicans of Los Angeles, whose numbers exceed those of any concentrated metropolitan area where tejanos predominate? In fact, the Angelenos have made major contributions in the latter part of the twentieth century, most notably through the explosive growth of *banda,* a musical form with great ethnomusicological potential. Yet banda, a latter-day reincarnation of an old military-band tradition known as *banda sinaloense,* remains a localized phenomenon. It has been unable so far to duplicate the enormous historical influence of the Texas-Mexican conjunto and its offshoot, música norteña, or that of the orquesta during its years of peak popularity, when it went by the label *La Onda Chicana.*

It is to the tejanos, then, that musical supremacy must be ceded and with whom the answer to the above questions resides. So—to repeat the key question—what are the sociohistorical circumstances that have generated such intense and creative musical activity among the Texas-Mexicans?

To begin with, let me state a basic thesis of this work—namely, that, as James Ackerman once proposed, stylistic breakthroughs in artistic culture may be thought of as a "class of related solutions to a problem—or responses to a problem" (Ackerman 1962:228). To view the matter from a different angle, throughout this work I am concerned to "make intelligible for us why a certain [musical] style [or styles] may have emerged in the social and cultural structure of a given period, and thus clarify the sociological pre-requisites and conditions involved" (Serauky, quoted in Etzkorn 1973:9). My position, then, is that influential musics do not emerge in a sociocultural vacuum. Rather, culturally powerful styles—that is, "strong" musical forms driven by the principle of use-value—are always responses to equally powerful movements at the "base" of the social structure—especially fundamental shifts in the processes of production, or, in other words, at the level of economic activity. Such shifts often are accompanied by social and cultural turmoil and subsequent attempts at its resolution.

In the Southwest, fundamental changes in economic production and an aftermath of turmoil and conflict begin with the Anglo-American invasion of the territory, with Texas the first area to feel the pressure. The American invasion began in 1821, when Stephen F. Austin obtained permission from the Mexican government to resettle a group of American immigrants in the province of Tejas. Austin and his compatriots revolted in 1832, and they achieved independence from Mexico in 1836. Meanwhile, Americans in mushrooming numbers were streaming into other regions of the Southwest, heightening tension between Mexico and the United States. That tension finally erupted into war in 1846. When the war ended in 1848, California, New Mexico, Arizona, *and* Texas (whose independence Mexico never had recognized officially) were ceded to the victorious Americans. The Treaty of Guadalupe Hidalgo, signed in early 1848, granted American citizenship to the native Spanish Mexicans of the Southwest, but the rights of those citizens were violated often in the years that followed, as the new Mexican Americans eventually were reduced to the status of peons and lowly workers (Barrera 1979; Foley 1988; Taylor 1971 [1934]).

The Mexican American War, then, marks a turning point in the social, cultural, and economic transformation of the Southwest. Thereafter ensued a lengthy history of interethnic conflict between Anglos and Mexicans. The subordination of the latter within the new social order forced the Mexicans into a process of cultural and economic adjustment. In their effort to adapt to the sometimes harsh conditions imposed upon them, the Mexican Americans, as well as the waves of Mexican immigrants who came later, ultimately forged a unique expressive culture, ranging from bilingualism to the musical forms that are our concern here. As folklorist Américo Paredes correctly observed in explaining the uniqueness of one form of this expressive culture, "A purely Mexican American folklore must be sought in the conflict of cultures" (1993a:13).

The conflict between Anglos and Mexicans was particularly violent in Texas; understandably, it spawned a number of cultural responses among the Texas-Mexicans. The tejanos were at ground zero, so to speak, in the explosion set off by the clash of social systems in the Southwest. This explosion eventually installed the Anglos and their capitalist system as lords over not just Texas, but all the territory acquired from Mexico. It was in the Lone Star State, however, that open conflict first broke out, as the Anglo-Texans began to assert their dominance over the Texas-Mexicans following their victory over Santa Ana's army and their subsequent declaration of independence from Mexico. Flush with victory, the Anglo-Texans saw the Mexicans as inferiors with no claim to citizenship in the new order. Gradually the Mexicans were reduced to the status of second-class citizens, as *peones* and (later) proletarian workers (De León 1983; Foley 1988; Montejano 1987; San Miguel 1987; Taylor 1971 [1934]).

The tejanos responded with characteristic vigor to their changing circumstances. Despite their subordination in the new social order, they waged, first, a "war of maneuver," to borrow a phrase from the Marxist political theorist Antonio Gramsci (1971; cf. Limón 1994), in which they openly defended their

sovereignty against the Anglo invaders. This pattern of intense conflict, sometimes marked by bloodshed, did not cease with the conclusion of the Mexican American War of 1846–48. Rather, as historians have confirmed, the
"war" continued into the early twentieth century, in the form of skirmishes
and quasi-guerrilla tactics, such as Catarino Garza's raids in the 1910s (Paredes
1995 [1976]). After about 1920, a war of maneuver no longer was possible; in
Gramscian terms, a "war of position" then ensued—one that, despite sharp
attenuation, continued to the end of the twentieth century.

The "war of position" is important more for its verbal ammunition—including artistic ammunition—than for any form of firepower. For it is in the
trenches of this war of position that the problems mentioned earlier give rise
to artistic "solutions." We should add here that this war of position is dominated by the Anglos and their hegemonic order; moreover, it is encumbered
by numerous contradictions, as increasingly the combatants and battle lines
become blurred by interethnic class affinities and by the very nature of the
capitalist system within which the struggle is carried on. Even as Anglos and
Mexicans represent two discrete ethnic and, at least initially, unequal class
groups, the hegemonic ideology of "equaliberty," as Balibar (1994) calls notions of equality in liberal democracies, complicates matters as the twentieth
century wears on. Driven by what I have called the "dialectic of conflict"
(Peña 1999), ethnic and class relations in the Southwest evolved in a dynamic
fashion, so that by the end of the twentieth century those relations had been
transformed substantially in the direction of equaliberty.

The initial clash of cultures, though, cannot be characterized as anything
other than explosive. Despite (or perhaps because of) the eventual triumph of
Anglo capitalism over the subsistence economy that had prevailed in the Hispanic era, racial and cultural conflict reverberated well into the twentieth century. To begin with, the new system abolished the social relations based on
use-value and its myriad reciprocal obligations and responsibilities, which
were the norm in the subsistence economy prevailing in Texas and elsewhere.
These were replaced by the relations of exchange-value prevalent under capitalism. The switch in economic systems and their respective social relations
was so radical it forced the native Mexicans to restructure their whole way of
life from top to bottom. In time, the new system inescapably forced tejanos
(as well as other Mexicans in the Southwest) to adapt to the social relations
governed by a capitalist economy.

For example, in the old subsistence economy, *patrón-peón* relationships were common, in which social ties and obligations were cemented by communal cultural practices that ranged from religious ceremonial to community festivities and the system of *compadrazgo* (N. Gonzales 1969; Briggs 1988; R. Gutiérrez 1991; Paredes 1958). The latter was a fictive kinship system based on Catholic ritual, whose effect was to bind diverse members in a community—such as *patrones* and *peones*—into communitywide networks of mutual obligations. These networks were a logical outcome of the subsistence economy underpinning life in the Hispanic Southwest (see León-Portilla 1972). Although social relations were not necessarily egalitarian, the relative isolation of the far-flung communities and the harsh climatic environment fostered interdependence and cooperation among the different segments. As Briggs wrote about Cordova, New Mexico:

> The most important feature of this era [before the twentieth century] is the high degree of cooperation. The work of the community was a communal enterprise. Individuals assumed various roles—as farmers, hunters, and guards—in accordance with the needs of the settlement as a whole. Each family received an equal portion of what the community produced. Unlike the present, there was no monetary remuneration for services: "they didn't pay them anything, they just helped. Nowadays there is no one who would help out anyone else." . . . Although the settlers are seen as having been extremely poor, their lot was made easier by an abundance of natural resources and a strong communitarianism. (Briggs 1988:31)

Briggs's comments on the communitarian nature of Hispanic society—especially as these apply to conditions prior to the 1840s—echo those of American travelers and settlers who observed first hand the Spanish Mexican society of the Southwest, as well as natives such as Guadalupe Vallejo of California (Zavalishin 1973; Bell, 1927; A. Robinson 1925). For example, while some land was owned privately, legal titles were rarely used, and the general community usually enjoyed access to most land. "Fencing in the range" (Taylor 1971 [1934]) was a practice alien to the Hispanic communities. American capitalism changed that, often to the plight of the original Mexican owners. The case of Mariano Vallejo, a member of one of the Spanish Mexican families who first settled California, is instructive. One of his sons, Guadalupe

Vallejo, in the late nineteenth century recalled an incident in which his father had given an American squatter permission to occupy a tract, only to see the squatter gain possession when the elder Vallejo could not produce a deed. A bitter Vallejo related the following:

> In many similar cases, American settlers in their dealings with the rancheros took advantage of laws which they understood, but which were new to the Spaniards, and so robbed the latter of their lands. Notes and bonds were considered unnecessary by a Spanish gentleman in a business transaction, as his word was always sufficient security. (Vallejo 1890)

The net effect of the new economy was not only to disfranchise the Hispanic communities, but to force upon them an alien system and its social relations and cultural practices. This system, capitalism, coupled with the harsh discrimination against Mexicans which it fostered, imposed great hardships upon the new Mexican Americans, hardships they only gradually overcame. In the process of adapting, the tejanos in particular continued to practice many of their former customs, in this way resisting the culture of the capitalist Anglos. Based on a subsistence economy, these customs—what the English writer Raymond Williams in another context has called "residual culture"[11]—corresponded to the social relations obtaining under the old subsistence economy. As Briggs (1988) observed of the *mexicanos* of Cordova, New Mexico, these forms often clashed with the new cultural economy introduced by the Anglos.

In the clash of cultural economies and their changing course, several musical forms have been enlisted—some harking back to an earlier existence based on subsistence agriculture and ranching, some representing responses to the new capitalism, and still others representing contradictory adaptations. In short, each of the major musical forms examined here, beginning with the corrido and extending to contemporary Tejano music, represents some form of response to the clash of cultural economies, as well as the changing nature of the conflict between Anglos and Mexicans. Each of these developments, then—the corrido, the conjunto, the orquesta, and even late-twentieth-century Tejano, to a certain extent—represents a unique adaptation to the evolving nature of the conflict and the numerous attempts that both groups, Anglos and Mexicans, made over time to mitigate the grossly unequal relationship following the American victory.

Let us consider first the corrido—or, more precisely, a subtype known as the "corrido of intercultural conflict" (Paredes 1995 [1976]). No other regional group of Mexicans in the Southwest exploited this quintessentially Mexican ballad to the extent the tejanos did in staking out a position vis-à-vis the Anglo-Americans. As Américo Paredes has demonstrated convincingly (Paredes 1958; 1995 [1976]), this narrative ballad functions historically as an expression of stark cultural contrasts in the conflict surrounding Anglo-Mexican relations in Texas. It flourished at a time when that conflict was intense and not yet mediated by the gestures of intercultural accommodation that emerged much later. The corrido of intercultural conflict is a product of an early historical era Paredes has labeled the "open hostility" stage in Mexican folklore in its encounter with the Anglo. This was a time, roughly from the second half of the nineteenth century until the early twentieth, when the Mexicans of the Southwest still entertained hopes—however those hopes may have diminished with time—that they might yet reclaim the sovereignty they had enjoyed before the territory was annexed by the United States.

Thus, in the corrido, the Anglo is seen as "the enemy" who is valiantly confronted by a Mexican hero—usually a man armed only "with his pistol in his hand" (Paredes 1958). A narrative typically depicting actual events, the corrido nonetheless is not neutral: it invariably portrays the Texas-Mexican protagonist as a fearless, larger-than-life hero, while reducing his Anglo adversaries, usually Texas Rangers, sheriffs, or other lawmen, to smaller-than-life cowards. I shall have more to say about these portrayals in chapters 1 and 2; here it suffices to say that, in the intense conflict accompanying the initial interethnic encounter, the corrido functioned as a powerful symbolic response by the Texas-Mexicans to their oppression under the new system installed by the Anglos throughout the Southwest.

Clearly, to judge by the number of corridos and certain variants I have labeled *canciones-corridos* (Peña 1999, especially ch. 2), the Texas-Mexicans resisted their subordination much more vigorously, at least from the standpoint of expressive culture, than did their counterparts elsewhere in the Southwest. The proximity of a vibrant culture in northeastern Mexico helped, particularly as this culture was transported by norteños and tejanos back and forth across the border. The tejanos' ties to norteño culture emboldened them to challenge the victorious Anglos. And, although the interethnic match overwhelmingly favored the new rulers of the territory, on occasion the tejanos engaged their Anglo adversaries in successful armed skirmishes (as in the case of

Juan Cortina and Aniceto Pizaña; see Paredes [1995 [1976]]. More important, verbal warfare, in the form of folklore such as the corrido, emerged as a potent expression of resistance, even if in time the goal of political emancipation became increasingly unrealistic (Paredes 1966, 1995 [1976]).

But the corrido is not, historically, the only symbolic resistance the Texas-Mexicans offered. Like the corrido, the Texas-Mexican conjunto represents a powerful oppositional form of culture, except that, by the 1930s, when it emerged as an identifiable style, the interethnic relationship had been altered by changes in the economy, by shifts in the ideology of citizenship (who was and was not an "American"), and by the increasing diversity within the tejano community. In other words, while the conjunto approximates the oppositional character of the corrido, in important respects it also reflects the changed struggle from a "war of maneuver" and armed confrontation to a "war of position" and expressive-cultural resistance. The conjunto also reflected other emergent forces, such as class friction within Texas-Mexican society itself, that demarcate a different symbolic territory for the conjunto and its constituents. In sum, the conjunto is enlisted in the conflict between Anglos and Mexicans, but, as an expression of working-class people, it also plays a role in differentiating them from other Texas-Mexicans, whom the working class generally considered to be more *agringados* (Anglicized) (Limón 1978) and more "high-class" and snobbish (in the regional idiom, more *jaitones*—from the English *high-toned* [see Peña 1985a, 1985b]).

The other major musical genre to emerge among Texas-Mexicans, the orquesta, represents yet another cultural strategy in the protean interethnic conflict that energizes artistic culture among Texas-Mexicans. Like the conjunto, it is a response to the "problems of an age," to recall Ackerman. However, unlike the conjunto and the corrido, the orquesta represents the forces of acculturation, interethnic accommodation, and upward mobility. Particularly after World War II, when the orquesta emerged as an influential artistic expression, Texas-Mexican society had split irreversibly into working and middle classes, with the latter evincing a much more assimilative stance vis-à-vis what we may call "mainstream" American culture.[12] The middle class was much more accommodationist toward Anglo-Americans, just as it aspired to become more like them in everyday practice. The orquesta responded to the assimilationist impulse, and it acquired at least a partial American identity. In short, like its subscribers, it became bicultural, or bimusical.

In the twentieth century, especially in urban areas, the clash of cultures was complicated by developments within the Mexican American community itself. As indicated above, *intra*ethnic fissures emerged within Mexican American society as upwardly mobile people began to distance themselves from the lifestyle of their less economically mobile peers, both native and immigrant. These peers continued to practice a wider range of expressive culture, from medical beliefs to kinship arrangements, based upon the earlier, subsistence mode of existence. As the upwardly mobile began to gravitate toward forms of expressive culture more aligned with what they perceived to be a "mainstream" American lifestyle, a clear-cut cultural wedge opened between them and their (usually) less acculturated working-class peers (again, both Mexican Americans and more recent immigrants from Mexico). The cleavage between the two groups gave rise to incipient (and sometimes open) dissension within the Mexican American community, a dissension articulated in various realms of expressive culture, including musical preference.[13]

For example, besides endorsing the ranchero and working-class conjunto, the more traditional Mexican Americans continued to subscribe to the medicinal tenets of *curanderismo,* a form of folk medicine overlaid with magical elements believed to cure diverse illnesses (see Paredes 1993c). This whole complex of medical practices corresponded to the type of culture and technology associated with subsistence economies, where the empiricist practices of capitalism have not yet taken root. Other Mexican Americans, particularly in the twentieth century, inevitably succumbed to the power of American capitalist culture and its emphasis on "science" and the "rational" or "modern." A fissure thus emerged between these acculturative Mexican Americans and their more traditional Mexicanized peers—a fissure skillfully described by Américo Paredes in his landmark article, "Folk Medicine and the Intercultural Jest" (1993c).[14]

In "Folk Medicine and the Intercultural Jest," Paredes describes the effects that partial cultural assimilation had on upwardly mobile individuals, particularly as these individuals found themselves torn between a mainstream, middle-class American culture very compatible with their social status, and an ethnic culture whose stubborn presence in their lives complicated their sense of "cultural citizenship."[15] The prevalence of *curanderismo* among many of their proletarian peers frustrated these middle-class tejanos. As subscribers to the rationalist and empiricist ideology that goes by the name of "science" in American life, Paredes's collaborators told jests that parodied the belief tale (*caso*) among traditional Mexicans, by way of poking fun at what they perceived to be a backward and superstitious belief system.

Being caught in the schism between two dissimilar cultural economies, however, the jest tellers could not help betraying the contradictions attending their lives. Thus, on the one hand they could ridicule the outmoded beliefs of the poorer Mexicans, but on the other they were acutely aware of the subordinate status occupied by all Mexicans in the American social order. The jests necessarily became a vehicle for the critique of American capitalism and its Anglo proponents—hospitals and the medical profession in particular—who emerged as the real "bad guys" in this clash of ideologies.

Divisions between more and less acculturated tejanos also found expression in musical practice. After World War II, in particular, when tejanos began to mount a more successful drive against an entrenched Anglo power structure, an upwardly mobile middle class emerged with greater force. As Rubel and others correctly observed (Howard 1952; O. Simmons 1974 [1952]), members of this class aspired to be more like their Anglo counterparts in cultural matters ranging from household furniture to musical tastes (Rubel 1966:11 passim). It was at this moment that the Mexican American orquesta (described in chapter 4) burst upon the scene. Again, however, caught between the cultural economy of their predecessors, whose residual cultural effects lingered in the Mexican American community, and the pressures of the modernistic capitalist economy and its culture, these middle-class Mexican Americans found themselves on the horns of a dilemma. Wanting to claim American cultural citizenship but thwarted by Anglo discrimination, they equivocated and in the end settled for a type of biculturalism that included the bimusical orquesta—one capable of playing both Mexican and American music, both *ranchero* ("country") and *jaitón* (sophisticated).

So far I have outlined the main sociohistorical trends of an evolving musical culture among Texas-Mexicans. It is worth reiterating that this culture was forged in the crucible of an intense intercultural conflict between Anglos and Mexicans. Caught at the epicenter of the powerful clash between two disparate cultural economies and ethnic/racial groups, as these collided in the Southwest, the tejanos seized the historical moment to create musical forms that installed them as leaders among their regional Hispanic peers in the realm of artistic culture.

Even at the end of the twentieth century, Texas-Mexicans were still busy propagating their homegrown creations, although by this time the "post-modernist" moment in "late capitalism" had succeeded in taking a good deal of the ideological edge off what by then was known widely as "Tejano music" (see chapter 6). Quite simply, this music had become more commoditized and "superorganic," having loosened in the process its organic connection with its tejano social base. Nonetheless, true to its historical wellspring, Tejano at the end of the twentieth century continued to resist total commodification, as the Texas-Mexicans insisted on stamping their unique identities on their latest musical creation. The remainder of this book, then, explores the particularities of these Texas-Mexican identities and their relationships to a transforming música tejana and its cultural economy.

Notes

1. A discussion between two musicians in the Western "classical" tradition on the merits of this or that phrasing nuance, as it relates to a passage in the score, constitutes cultural activity, but that is another matter.

2. A story circulated some years ago about an experiment in which a European musicologist played Beethoven's Fifth Symphony to a group of African "natives" in order to gauge their interest. After listening to the tape recorder for a few polite minutes, one by one they began to disperse. The music was absolutely meaningless to them.

3. Public dances and concerts are common enough, but see below.

4. On the social significance of the Walkman, see Negus (1992:35): "The Walkman enables its user to take music wherever they [sic] go and exclude the external world and other human beings."

5. My use of the concepts "use-value" and "exchange-value" derives from Marx. See, especially, Marx 1977, ch. 1, "The Commodity," 1:163–77.

6. It is this distinction—artistic expression motivated by use-value versus artistic expression driven by exchange-value—that Mitchell overlooks when he denies any "truth value" to African American "roots music" (e.g., the blues) after its appropriation by whites (1996:10). In the white market, the derivatives of this music (e.g., rock-and-roll) have been driven from the beginning by the principle of exchange-value, although occasionally rock music has been "hijacked" by various segments of the white population and reconverted into an "organic" expression. In the black communities, blues, rhythm-and-blues, hip-hop, and other varieties of music have tended to retain their use-value, even in the face of commodification.

Therein lies their symbolic power, if not their "authenticity." See the discussion of Tejano music in chapter 6 of this book.

7. Spanish words (for example, *orquesta* and *conjunto*) and phrases (such as *música tejana*) that are used repeatedly throughout the text will be italicized only the first time they appear.

8. The token fee of five dollars per person went to a fund that members of VFW Post 8900 created for the purpose of building their own hall. Enough funds had been raised by 1981 to build the hall.

9. I use the term *indigenous* to acknowledge the originality of the conjunto, orquesta, and other musical forms or styles popular among tejanos. I do not mean to imply that these musics were "pure," "authentic," and without antecedents. The accordion is a widely dispersed instrument, and the tejano orquesta owed much to both American and Mexican dance bands. Despite Mitchell's skepticism, which questions the existence of "traditional" music possessed of any "originality" or "inherent value" (1996:10), tejano forms and styles do possess such value historically, and at least two, the conjunto and canción-corrido, are unique enough to be considered "indigenous."

10. I shall capitalize the label "Tejano" to distinguish its designation of contemporary musical groups from other referents of the word "tejano."

11. For Williams, "residual culture" may be rooted in past social formations, but it is an "active . . . effective element of the present" (1977:122). Residual culture "may have an alternative or even oppositional relation to the dominant culture" (ibid.).

12. The term *mainstream* is rather imprecise, since it implies that some form of monolithic culture defines a core American experience. This, of course, is not the case. However, there are certain definable ideological tendencies that develop historically as a kind of "glue" holding together the unwieldy frame of American capitalism. These tendencies revolve around the many shared values of an American middle class that crystallized rapidly during the twentieth century. These values are visible enough to motivate at least one writer to identify them as part of the "American national character" (Inkeles 1979). Others have identified these values as part of what McLemore (1980) called the "Anglo-conformity" ideology.

13. This is not to suggest that some form of "class warfare" was waged among the various sectors of Texas-Mexican society. The relationship between upwardly mobile tejanos and their less affluent compatriots was too complex for any clear-cut divisions to exist. See my statements below on the intercultural jest (Paredes 1993c).

14. Limón has faulted Paredes for glossing over this very fissure, an error that he attributes to Paredes's "rhetorical erasure" (1994:89) of *fuereños* (immi-

grant "outsiders"). The most serious flaw in Limón's criticism of Paredes—and this undermines much of his own interpretation of Texas-Mexican expressive culture—is his confusion concerning *fuereños* and his apparent ignorance of immigration patterns prior to the 1970s. Until the seventies, *fuereños*—immigrants from the interior of Mexico—constituted a small minority of the Mexican-descent population in Texas. The vast majority of immigrants were *norteños*—people from the border states of Coahuila, Nuevo León, Tamaulipas, and Chihuahua, who already shared in great part the regional mejicano culture of the Texas-Mexicans (Taylor 1968; Foley 1988) and who can hardly be considered *fuereños*. Thus, while disagreements between tejanos and norteños surfaced often enough, the real rift, as Paredes recognized, was between the upwardly mobile Texas-Mexicans and their less affluent peers—both tejano and norteño (see Paredes 1993c). The true *fuereños*, upon whom Limón stakes his criticism of Paredes, played an insignificant role in this rift.

15. My view of cultural citizenship is based partly on that elaborated by Ong. Like Ong, I see the process of cultural citizenship in contemporary nation-states as "dialectically determined" and thus shaped by the contradictory forces of identity and difference—the ceaseless effort by the state and its accomplices, the dominant classes, to create malleable subjects who share an equalized "identity" (e.g., as "Americans"); as against hierarchical arrangements based on class, gender, and "race," which inevitably create difference and inequality. It is, ultimately, a matter of hegemony and its challenges. In the United States, the search for cultural citizenship for ethnic/racial minorities like the Mexicans pits both external pressures to "be American" *and* their internal desire to share in the "American dream" against the reality of ethnic/racial discrimination and the minorities' efforts to re-center their identity—to ground it in their "roots" through ethnocentrist acts of reaffirmation. The outcome of all of these seemingly irreconcilable realities is a chain of "contradictory experiences" (Ong 1996:737).

1 ❧ Music of the Nineteenth Century

An Overview

Despite important differences between Texas-Mexican music in the nineteenth century and in the twentieth, the basic outlines of the latter, both stylistic and social, were laid out clearly in the earlier century. In other words, while sociomusical discontinuities exist between the two historical periods, certain continuities persist as well. It is therefore worthwhile to provide at least an overview of musical developments in the tejano communities of the earlier period. Tracing the "roots" of contemporary Texas-Mexican music may enable us to understand better the basic dynamics that to some extent continue to drive musical developments even on the eve of the twenty-first century.

"The Fandango Is Their Prime Joy"

Tejanos have always been avid dancers. Visiting San Antonio in 1837, Andrew F. Muir was impressed by the number of *fandangos* he observed. "There are seldom less than three or four during the night in different portions of the city," he wrote (1958:104). Muir's is not the only account we have of the proliferation of music and dance in nineteenth-century San Antonio. In their profile of the Alamo City, De la Teja and Wheat inform us that, based on licenses issued by the *ayuntamiento,* seventy-two private dances were held in the city in 1827, in addition to numerous public balls (1991:6). And in 1847, San Antonio authorities collected a total of $560, at the rate of $1 per dance (Downs 1971:77).

Mexican San Antonians were not unique in their love of dancing. Accounts from other areas of South Texas indicate just how devoted Texas-Mexicans were to music and dance. On numerous occasions in the late nineteenth century, the *San Antonio Express,* historically the most influential newspaper in South Texas, carried stories of dancing activities in the Mexican communities beyond San Antonio. For example, on November 10, 1880, the paper reported on a dance in San Diego; and on June 18, 1881, on a "fandango" in Del Rio. On August 20, 1881, another article on fandangos in the Rio Grande Valley was headlined "The Fandango Is Their Prime Joy." In the edition of September 12, 1882, we read about "fandango halls" in Laredo. Other sources provide additional accounts of the dancing activities of the Mexicans in South Texas. For example, in her master's thesis, folklorist Jovita González describes some of the more elite functions:

> The dances which were given by the owners of the ranches marked the social feature of the year. To these functions were invited all the landed aristocracy from the surrounding country as well as from the towns. The ladies came in the family coach escorted by mounted cavaliers who rode by the side of the carriage. The dances gave occasion to the ladies to display their finery and their charm. An orchestra from town furnished the music, waltzes, polkas, schottishes. A midnight dinner was served, wine was drunk, and toasts were offered the ladies, and a convivial atmosphere prevailed throughout the evening. (1930:62)

Basing her report on a diary kept between 1850 and 1904 by a woman of the border region (a descendant of the settlers of Nuevo Santander), amateur historian Adeline Dinger wrote of "Carnival time" surrounding Mexican Independence Day, September 16. "It was a period of merrymaking," wrote Dinger, "which continued, in some cases, for three or four weeks" (1972:39). All classes from neighboring communities gathered to participate: "The carnival was always ushered in with a 'formal' dance. It mattered not that the dance floor was only the hard-beaten ground, or, at best, a platform of rough boards. The formality of the 'first night dance' was indicated by an elegance of costume that must have been wonderful to see" (ibid.)

Another leading South Texas newspaper, the *Corpus Christi Caller,* informs us in its edition of March 23, 1884, that "the regular Sunday night fandango at Santa Cruz [near Brownsville] passed off quietly, and was enjoyed by all that participated. Dancing, gambling, drinking bad mescal, and the shooting of fireworks constituted the main features of amusement." And the edition of Sunday, May 27, 1883, carried a story on "a popular string band from Laredo." According to the *Caller,* "every night since early last week sweet strains of music have been heard in our city. Serenading has been the order of the night. . . . When it was announced that Gloria's Band would play at Herdic Park, Thursday night, the crowd which gathered there was extraordinary [sic] large."

Music and Social Difference: Fandango versus Baile

It is important to note that the accounts by Anglo travelers, newspapers, and other observers do not portray an undifferentiated musical scene. In fact, these accounts alert us to important distinctions present in Texas, as elsewhere in the Hispanic Southwest. Sometime in the nineteenth century, the dance, if not the music, became divided along socioeconomic lines. The term *fandango,* which in an earlier period had been used to designate any form of public dance, around the 1830s began to designate the celebrations of the lowest segments of Mexican society. The term *baile,* meanwhile, increasingly was reserved for celebrations of the more affluent sectors of the society.

For example, in his early (1828) account of life in Texas, J. C. Clopper mentions his Mexican "landlady" and her two "pretty" daughters, whom he accompanied on several occasions to the "fandango," which was held on the street and was attended by all members of the community (1929:71). By 1837, however, William Ballaert was making a distinction between the fandango and the *bayle* [*sic*]. "In [high] society," he wrote, "the fandango is not introduced; their dancing is called Bayle or a ball—there is only to be seen the madamas of the city" (1956:218).

George W. Kendall, a member of the notorious Santa Fe Expedition, described a fandango he attended in 1841:

> As I entered the room, which was destitute of other floor than the hard earth, and lighted by two or three coarse tallow candles, a single couple were shuffling away, face to face, and keeping time to a cracked violin. . . . The woman was as destitute of beauty as an Egyptian mummy . . . her partner was even more ugly. Some half dozen slovenly, badly-dressed Mexican girls were sitting upon benches at either end of the room, while an old woman in one corner was selling paper cigars and vile whiskey. (1935:46)

In a footnote, Kendall's betrays his class prejudices: "This was but a fandango of the lowest order. The reader must not suppose that there is no better society among the Mexicans of San Antonio than I found at this place" (ibid.).

The distinction between fandango and baile, especially as promoted by Anglos, alerts us to the social differentiation that existed within Texas-Mexican society in the nineteenth century, a distinction made in other regions of the Hispanic Southwest as well (see Bell 1927, for distinctions in California; Davis 1973 [1857], for a similar assessment of dances in New Mexico). While the An-glo invaders of the Southwest saw Mexican society generally as backward, idle, and lacking in industry and enterprise (De León 1983; Foley 1988; Kenneson 1978), nonetheless they were sensitive to the social differences present in the region. Thus, in their judgments of the native Mexicans, the Anglos did make a few exceptions—exceptions they saw manifested in the fandango-baile dis-tinction. Moreover, the Anglos judged social and musical differences through the lens of race; they conceived of the "better class" of Mexicans as "Spaniards," even entertaining a grudging admiration for this class's way of life. As the his-torian William Goetzmann wrote of the "Texians" (Anglo-Texans) and their myth of cultural superiority:

> In fact, a good many aspects of Hispanic culture actually appealed to the
> Texians. Thus, endemic to the Texian myth is the love-hate relationship
> with the Spanish [Mexican] people. For example, the Texian admired life
> on "the Big Hacienda". . . . He also thrived on the food, the fandangos,
> vaquero-cowboying, the violent macho lifestyle, and especially the Span-
> ish sense of pride. Love and hate made the Texian myth complex from
> the beginning. (Goetzmann 1985:31; material in brackets added)

The "love-hate" relationship Goetzmann proposes between Anglos and Mexicans in Texas is in fact an important element in the evolution of both cultures, not only in Texas but also elsewhere in the Southwest (see McWil-liams 1948 on the Anglos' "fantasy heritage"; see also C. Robinson 1992). It is a key component in what I have elsewhere called the dialectic of conflict that drives the relationship between the two groups (Peña 1999; see below), a di-alectic particularly important in the emergence of one major tejano musical style, the orquesta. I shall have more to say in chapter 4 about the dialectic of conflict and its influence on interethnic relations and the orquesta.

Meanwhile, despite the complex relationship evolving historically between Anglos and Mexicans, and the former's admiration for things "Spanish," in the nineteenth century the attitude of Anglos toward the Mexican "riff raff"—peons, peasants, and other lowly workers—was nothing short of contemptuous and racist to the core. In reporting on the fandangos of the proletarian masses, the *San Antonio Express,* for example, could be harshly judgmental. The following reports—the first from Cameron County, located along the Texas-Mexico border; and the second from Laredo, also on the border—are typical of the newspaper's attitude:

We want men [i.e., European immigrants] of capital, and men that can and will work to increase our progress. The prevailing class of population [the Mexicans] might hold the country a thousand years, and it would still present the homely picture as when Alva first looked upon it. The comforts of industry are closed to their sight; no ambition can rouse their lethargy to excel the customs of their fathers; it is all *dolce far niente*— sweet idleness! The fandango is their prime joy. For days and nights they beat their drums and whirl in the dance. These fandangos are a great curse to the country; the respectable class of Mexicans do not attend them. (August 20, 1881; material in brackets added)

And, on the dancing activities of the "motley crowd of the lowest order" in Laredo, the *Express* reported with its customary indignation:

The evening's amusements open by the almost ceaseless beating of a large, loosely strung drum on one of the plazas in front of a fandango house. Presently the band, consisting of two instruments and a half, and a snare and bass drum, starts on the march about the streets, producing a confusion of sounds that suggests a fair idea of the hideous noises of Bedlam itself. The musicians are all Mexicans, whose uniforms look as if they had been raked from the dump of a scavenger cart. After parading an hour or so . . . they wind up in front of the dance hall, where a motley crowd is gathered, and then the hall opens. Women of the lowest order, and men after their kind, are the chief patrons of this place. . . . There is but one fandango hall conducted here now, and it is run by an ex–San Antonian, a couple of others having just been suspended on account of their disorderly character. (September 12, 1882)

In contrast to their harsh treatment of the celebrations of the impoverished classes, the *San Antonio Express* and other chroniclers of Mexican American musical life could be effusive in their praise when it came to the celebrations of the more affluent. Attracted to cultural expression that approximated their own sense of what was "tasteful" or properly aesthetic, the Anglo chroniclers— themselves members of, or at least aspirants to, the middle class—were favorably impressed by the celebrations of the Mexican elite, small as this group may have been by the end of the nineteenth century. For example, during the 1880s and 1890s, the *Express* often reported the activities of the Alamo City's *Club Social Mejicano* (Mexican Social Club), obviously a group with middle-class pretensions. The first of these reports is dated Saturday, September 22, 1883: "Last evening the elite of Mexican society were gathered at the Turner Hall where was given a ball by the Mexican Social Club of this city." The *Express* reporter was especially attentive to the dress of those in attendance: "The toilettes of the ladies were elegant and tasteful," while the "gentlemen were attired in full dress suits." All in all, according to the *Express,* "it was a very pleasant affair."

Like other such clubs in the Hispanic Southwest (see M. García 1981; Sheridan 1986), the Club Social Mexicano obviously was composed of the more affluent members of Mexican American society. In the latter part of the nineteenth century, such individuals comprised a small but evidently influential class of merchants, professionals, and white-collar workers. The *Express* and other Anglo observers took great pains to distinguish this class and its celebrations from those of a despised underclass of workers, peasants, and other marginal people (see Kendall's remarks above). The *Express* devoted space to a number of the club's celebrations in the last years of the nineteenth century. On February 24, 1884, the *Express* followed up on the previous year's report with one headlined "A Brilliant Fete Attended by a Galaxy of Beauty and Chivalry":

> Last evening at the Casino occurred the inaugural ball of the Mexican Social Club, to which they had invited a great many lovely ladies and distinguished gentlemen. The ball was tastefully decorated, the American and Mexican colors being intertwined, symbolic of the amity between the sister republics. The 8th Cavalry brass band furnished a number of orchestral selections. . . . A string band furnished the music for dancing. . . . It was an elegant evening.

On July 13, 1891, the *Express* again devoted coverage to one of the club's events. As on previous occasions, the tone of the report was enthusiastic, taking care to describe the constituency of the club as "a very fine class of Latin Americans":

The Mexican Social Club, composed of a very fine class of Latin-Americans, had an anniversary entertainment at Convention Hall last night, at which were present, on invitation, the members of the French Day Association. Mr. Claudon made an address in behalf of the latter, and Messrs. Rivas, Cardenas and others spoke for the former, eulogizing the society which was celebrating its anniversary, and the president and other officers who had done so much to make it a success. (July 13, 1891)

As had become typical at elite celebrations by the end of the nineteenth century, an orchestra, or orquesta, provided the music for the dancing segment of the celebration. On this occasion, the orquesta was that of Pablo Persio, a name mentioned on other occasions by the *Express* in connection with the club's social events.

Lastly, I cite an extended passage by A. D. Richardson, who spent time in Texas in 1859–60. During the course of a single evening, he attended two dances in El Paso—one a fandango and the other a baile—and described both in some detail. Unlike his fellow Anglos, Richardson betrays a certain attraction to the fandango, which he found "lively." His impression of the baile was less complimentary; he found it "heavy" and "stupid." In Richardson's own words:

The first evening's duty was to attend a fandango. When we entered, the dancing had begun. . . . The faces of dancers and spectators in the low basement, lighted by tallow candles, made up a medley of hues from dark Indian to fairest Saxon. On the platform at one end, three musicians without coats were hard at work. All entered into the amusement with enthusiasm; and participants and lookers on of both sexes were smoking. . . . The women were coarse-featured and homely, but their voices low and pleasing as they chattered in liquid Spanish. Many had beautiful, luminous eyes, and all a grace of motion rarely seen in their English or American sisters.

At ten o'clock we left the lively fandango for a ball of "the first society"—a few families who claim that their pure Castilian blood has never mixed with that of the native Indians. They were not wont to associate with Americans, but to-night a few Texans were invited.

I found this patrician *baile* in an ancient family mansion. . . . There were no chairs, but stationary benches against the walls. . . . The dancing had already begun, but it was listless; and like most aristocratic affairs this proved heavy and stupid. Among the thirty or forty guests I saw no Indian features. The ladies were no darker than our own brunettes. (1867:242)

In general, such were the attitudes evinced by Anglos toward the Mexicans and their musical activities. The most egregious of these attitudes did not go unchallenged, however; both in their musical communication and in other forms of expressive culture, the tejanos responded decisively to the Anglos' often negative reactions and to the new system engulfing them in the nineteenth century.

Anglos, Mexicans, and Intercultural Contact: Expressive Culture as Mediation

Chicano scholars (and a few others) have written extensively about the Anglos' racist attitudes toward the Mexicans they defeated in the struggle for control of the Southwest territory (Acuña 1972; Barrera 1979; Camarillo 1979; Foley 1988; Sheridan 1986). Particularly during the early days of Chicano scholarship (the 1960s and most of the 1970s), exclusive emphasis was placed on what Alex Saragoza has called the "us-versus-them" paradigm (1987; see also D. Gutiérrez 1989; Muñoz 1983), or the "internal colony" model (Acuña 1972; Barrera 1979).[1] Viewed through the prism of this model, the interethnic relationship was defined in terms of a dominant Anglo majority exploiting a subordinate Mexican minority amid a static, unchanging state of conflict perpetuated by the Anglos' unreconstructed racism (Acuña 1972; Barrera 1979).

As persuasive as the internal-colony model appeared initially, it eventually came under criticism for failing to capture the complex interplay among class, race, and gender inequalities and what, after Etienne Balibar, we may call the ideology of "equaliberty" (Balibar 1994)—American capitalism's peculiar insistence that all its citizens are born "free" and "equal." In this interplay among contending forces, mammoth contradictions arise historically, contradictions that constantly are being negotiated, only to resurface as new points of tension appear along the various social fault lines. In short, the relationship between Anglos and Mexicans is better understood if conceived within the framework of what I have previously described as a "dialectic of conflict." Within this dialectic, relations between the two groups respond in progressive stages to the contradictions generated by an evolving capitalist system and its dialectical logic (see Peña 1999).

A more nuanced, dialectical view of Anglo-Mexican relations conceives of expressive culture, including music, as a symbolic mechanism that in complex ways mediates the evolving relationship between Anglos and Mexicans. Conceiving of expressive culture as a form of mediation enables us to capture the multiple contradictions built into the interethnic relationship, as it is buffeted by the clash among ideologies of racial superiority, "equaliberty," and the economic imperatives of capitalism. The more nuanced conception of Anglo-Mexican relations advanced here is confirmed by the reports of Anglo chroniclers themselves. The distinction they drew between baile and fandango illustrates their ambivalence toward the people they had conquered (see Goetzmann's "Texian myth," above), just as it confirms the power of the political economy and its class ideologies to shape aesthetic perception. The Anglos' approach to Mexicans and their culture was thus never one-dimensional, despite early Chicano scholars' temptation to characterize it monolithically in terms of unmediated racial hatred and exploitation.

Despite their generalized feelings of racial and cultural superiority, the Anglos clearly recognized differences within the Mexican community (just as they recognized differences within their own communities), and they made the appropriate communicative distinctions, especially toward those they perceived as "Spaniards"—people who to some extent approximated their heightened notions of Europeanness. In sum, as Goetzmann implies, while a racist climate predominated among Anglos, the variety of phenotypes among the Texas-Mexicans (as elsewhere in the Southwest) modulated the Anglos' attitudes; moreover, class differences within the Mexican American community, attenuated as these may have been, further complicated the interethnic relationship. Finally, ever sensitive to the continually evolving climate of interethnic relations, Mexican expressive culture generally, the major musical forms examined here specifically, responded to the unfolding dialectic of conflict, reflecting contemporary patterns and even adumbrating the shape of things to come.

To begin with, the Texas-Mexicans did not passively accept Anglo characterizations of them and their culture, just as they did not passively accept their subordination after defeat at the end of the Mexican American War. As folklorist Américo Paredes has demonstrated so brilliantly (1958, 1995 [1976]), both armed resistance and various forms of expressive culture were marshaled by the tejanos in their efforts to counteract open violence, as well as a steady stream of denigrative expressive culture, directed against them from the Anglo camp (Paredes 1966, 1993c; see also De León 1983).

In a well-documented work, historian Arnoldo De León catalogued the litany of nineteenth-century Anglo-Texan stereotypes of the Mexican. A couple of citations may illustrate these Anglo views. A visitor in Brownsville in the early 1860s, Gilbert D. Kingsbury, had this to say about the local Mexicans: "They are of mongrel blood[,] the Aztec predominating. These degraded creatures are mere pilferers, scavengers and vagabonds, downright barbarians but a single remove above the Digger Indians, hanging like vermin on the skirts of civilization—a complete pest to humanity" (quoted in De León 1983:15).

And the following quote is from a letter by George L. Robertson, a soldier stationed on the Texas-Mexico border, to his sister, dated March 26, 1864: "There is a report in camp that our company has been ordered to Corpus Christi which I hope is so. I am getting rather tired of the Rio Grande and the *greasers,* of all the contemptable [*sic*], despecable [*sic*] people on Earth the greasers are the lowest, meaner even than the Cummanche [*sic*]. They are ugly, theiving [*sic*], rascally in every way" (De León 1983:xiv).

The Mexicans responded more or less in kind. Indeed, as armed struggle became less and less an alternative to their subordination, the tejanos relied more and more on expressive culture to articulate their response to intercultural conflict. The corrido and (to a lesser extent and in later years) the canción became vehicles for this response; however, from rather early on, nonmusical verbal expression also played a key role. In "The Anglo-American in Mexican Folklore" (1966), Paredes concisely summarizes the critical role that artistic verbal communication played in voicing the Mexican Americans' attitudes toward the Anglo in the conflictual relationship. For Paredes, that relationship has gone through three more or less distinct stages: an early one that he labels "open hostility" (roughly from the Mexican American War period to the early twentieth century); a middle stage he calls "veiled hostility" (a period, from the early twentieth century to World War II, when armed retaliation had become impossible for the Mexicans); and, finally, a period of self-criticism that Paredes labels the "self-satire" stage of folklore development (1966).

The first two stages are especially important for the way folklore articulates the Mexican American response to Anglo domination. A number of stereotypes emerged among the Mexicans of the Southwest to challenge a rival repertoire circulating among Anglos. Responding to such Anglo derogatory terms as "greaser," "spic," and "Meskin," the Mexicans rose to the challenge with their own epithets: *gringo, patón* ("Bigfoot," from the Anglos' allegedly oversized and smelly feet), *gademe* and *sanavabiche* (from the Anglos' habitual use of "goddammit" and "son-of-a-bitch"), and *gabacho*. The latter originally was used by the Spanish against the troops of Napoleon; the Mexicans used it later against Maximilian's forces, and, finally, the Mexican Americans appropriated it for use against the Anglo-Americans. Other stereotypes related to Anglo dietary habits: *repollero,* referring derisively to the Anglos' taste for boiled cabbage; and *jamonero,* indexed to what the Mexicans saw as the Anglos' "strange, almost sybaritic habit—that of the ham sandwich" (Paredes 1966:115).

If verbal art served generally as an effective medium for addressing the interethnic encounter and its conflict, music played its own key role. As genres tapping both the verbal and musical domains, the corrido, the canción, and the canción-corrido (a hybrid that emerged early in the twentieth century) came to articulate this conflict more forcefully than any other forms of expressive culture. All three flourished extensively in the twentieth century; however, the corrido and the canción have their origins in the nineteenth, and here we at least can profile their development in the earlier period.

Vocal Music: The Canción and the Corrido

Two genres predominated in the vocal music of the Texas-Mexicans of the latter years of the nineteenth century—the canción, or lyrical song, and the recently emerged corrido. Historically, the canción is a rather diffuse genre that seems to be in perpetual hybridization. It subsumes a broad array of forms and themes (Mendoza 1961), just as it often merges with other genres—especially dance genres such as the *habanera,* the *bolero,* and even the *vals* (waltz). We thus see such hybrids as *canción-bolero, canción-vals,* and *canción-huapango.* The thematic treatment of intercultural conflict within the canción genre actually did not begin until the twentieth century, particularly in its canción-corrido variant; but other themes, such as that of unrequited love, were common enough by the late nineteenth century. In any case, as an identifiable genre, however diffuse, the canción had made a deep and lasting impact on tejano musical life by this time, and it merits discussion here.

In his folksong collection from the lower Texas-Mexico border region, Américo Paredes includes a motley group of "songs," all of anonymous origin, that at one time or another had belonged to different generic categories (*romances, danzas,* and even schottishes). By the end of the nineteenth century, however, they were far along the continuum of hybridization, their original characteristics cohering around the native category *canción* (Paredes 1995 [1976], parts 1, 3, 4, and 5). Examples of hybridization collected by Paredes include "La pastora" and "La ciudad de Jauja," both originally *romances* brought to New Spain by the Spaniards but, by the end of the nineteenth century, transformed into canciones. Two other canciones compiled by Paredes, "El borrego gordo" and its close cousin "El marrano gordo," originally were "tall tales in ballad form" (6), while "Dime sí, sí" was sung in the form of a *canción-schottishe* (146).

By the end of the nineteenth century, a rapidly developing canción subtype was taking root among Texas-Mexicans, as it had generally among Hispanic peoples around the globe—the Italian-inspired *canción romántica* (romantic song). With a firmly entrenched love theme that ranged from unrequited love to betrayed passion, the canción romántica rapidly was becoming dominant at the end of the century. Paredes collected a few canciones románticas popular along the border, where many anonymously composed songs from greater Latin America were in circulation (see Robb 1980). Many canciones of known authorship not collected by Paredes enjoyed wide circulation among Texas-Mexicans, and most of these came from Mexico, where, according to Juan Garrido (1974), the canción romántica had begun to flourish toward the latter part of the century.

According to Paredes, the social function of the canción varied with type. Fiestas and family gatherings could include almost any type of song, except for erotic pieces such as the traditional "La pastora," about a beautiful young woman who in very explicit terms (and in vain) offers her body to a naïve shepherd (Paredes 1995 [1976]:xxi). The *style* of singing also could be affected by context. Thus, for example, boisterous singing, with interspersed *gritos* (Mexican shouts peculiar to certain song-performance contexts), was taboo in family-oriented fiestas. The canción romántica was particularly appropriate for lovers' serenades, at which (usually) young men approached a young woman's window late at night and sang (or hired someone to sing) appropriately amorous canciones románticas.

Among Texas-Mexicans, most singing took place in family celebrations. Salons and concert halls, typical bourgeois occasions for public song making in Europe (Attali 1985) and Mexico (Mayer-Serra 1941), were missing from Texas-Mexican musical life, although the working-class cantina, or "fandango house," apparently was common in cities and towns by the late nineteenth century. Here, as in the French *caf' conc'*, an "unrestricted atmosphere" prevailed (Attali 1985:75), with drunkenness, loud singing, and other boisterous behavior common. And, in a telling parallel suggesting how class power regulates social relations in similar ways across time and space, the Anglo middle class in Texas, like its counterpart in France, "directed much more criticism toward the [fandango house =] *caf' conc'*, the 'place of debauchery,' than toward the [social club =] cabaret" (ibid.).

In its most fundamental aspects, the canción represents the internal evolution of Mexican American society, as it does a more global Mexican and, ultimately, Latin American musical sensibility. As a form of vocal music, in the nineteenth century it was part of the slow cultural change going on throughout Latin America—enunciating, for example, the increasing importance of romantic love in the courtship between two individuals unbeholden to the marriage rules (such as arranged marriages) of earlier cultural economies. On the whole, however, the canción tended to reflect the continuity of traditional Mexican agrarian culture in the Southwest, rather than to mediate the deeper transformations being wrought within that culture by the modernizing impact of a capitalist political economy. Only later, during its development in the twentieth century, would the canción begin to symbolize the polarization of cultural economies. In a new variant, the *canción ranchera,* it would speak poignantly to the harsh conditions of the working class while evoking a vanishing pastoral economy; by contrast, the canción romántica would invoke the modernizing power of capitalism. I shall address this issue more extensively in chapter 2.

Meanwhile, the corrido of the nineteenth century responded far more vigorously than the contemporaneous canción to the intercultural encounter and its conflict—particularly the subtype Paredes has labeled the "corrido of intercultural conflict" (1995 [1976]). Like the traditional canción, the corrido was rooted inescapably in the cultural economy of the agrarian Texas-Mexicans. As a rapidly developing narrative form, however, it was in a strategic position to respond to the turbulence fomented by economic transformation *and* intercultural conflict. The corrido of intercultural conflict thus emerged as the most symbolically effective artistic expression forged by the tejanos in their struggle to negotiate both economic upheaval and conflict with the aggressive Anglos.

In chapter 2, I shall trace the development of the corrido in greater detail; here it suffices to reiterate that this important ballad type emerged as a potent form of cultural mediation in the early stages of interethnic contact, when relations between Anglos and Mexicans had not yet been modulated by the dialectic of conflict, and when open and sometimes bloody strife was still common. Finding themselves at a disadvantage in the conflict, the Texas-Mexicans relied increasingly upon symbolic expression, such as the corrido, to voice their deepening disempowerment.

Thus, although it was not until the first half of the twentieth century that the corrido reached its culmination, its form and function already were firmly established by the end of the nineteenth century. Américo Paredes, again, has documented the sudden and dramatic appearance of the corrido along the Texas-Mexico border during the latter third of the nineteenth century. An incipient musical narrative until this historical moment (a few proto-corridos date to the Mexican wars of independence, 1810–21; see Paredes [1993d]), in the 1860s the corrido suddenly burst forth as a dynamic expression of intercultural conflict (Paredes 1958; 1995 [1976]).[2] Indeed, Paredes has raised the possibility that this quintessentially Mexican expressive form—a descendant of the Spanish *romance* brought to Mexico by the original conquistadors— may have been created along Mexico's northern border, and not in Michoacán or Guanajuato, as others previously had assumed (Paredes 1993d:139ff.).

Paredes bases his argument for a border genesis on the fact that the oldest corrido to be collected in its entirety, "El corrido de Kiansis," apparently was composed by a border *corridista* (balladeer). It describes the actions of *vaqueros* engaged in cattle drives from Texas to Kansas stockyards, common in the 1860s and 1870s. More important, in "El corrido de Kiansis" the theme of intercultural conflict is fully adumbrated; unlike in later corridos, however, here the theme surfaces in subtle portrayals: experienced, dependable Mexicans contrasted with clumsy, timid Anglos. As Paredes remarks, "There is intercultural conflict in 'Kiansis,' but it is expressed in professional rivalries rather than in violence between men" (1995 [1976]:26). The following stanzas illustrate the ethnic contrasts:

Quinientos novillos eran,	Five hundred steers there were
todos grandes y livianos,	all big and quick;
y entre treinta americanos	thirty American cowboys
no los podían embalar.	could not keep them bunched together.
Llegan cinco mexicanos,	Then five Mexicans arrive,
todos bien enchivarrados,	all of them wearing good chaps,
y en menos de un cuarto de hora,	and in less than a quarter-hour,
los tenían encerrados.	they had the steers penned up.

(Paredes 1995 [1976]:55)

Corridos expressing full-blown conflict were not long in making their appearance, however. By the end of the nineteenth century, "El General Cortina," a corrido well known in South Texas even during the early part of the twentieth century, had gone through several variants to assume the prototypical form of the corrido of intercultural conflict. This corrido documented the exploits of border raider Juan Nepomuceno Cortina, who began his campaign against the Anglo-Americans when he intervened on behalf of a ranch hand who worked for his mother, in the process wounding a Brownsville city marshal. His "war of protest" (Paredes 1995 [1976]:23) carried over into the Civil War, when he aided the Union cause against Confederate forces (with which Anglo-Texans were allied). Eventually, Porfirio Díaz, in a gesture of cooperation with the United States, had Cortina exiled to Mexico City, from whence he returned to the border but once, in 1890. He died in 1892. According to Paredes, "Cortina and his rancheros briefly occupied Brownsville, won a few engagements, and finally gave way to superior force. The people who sympathized with him were subjected to reprisals; others suffered merely because they were of the same origins as he. Cortina, meanwhile, escaped across the newly created border, establishing a pattern that would be followed by others during the next three-quarters of a century" (1958:134).

The following are the key stanzas in the corrido about Cortina, in which the theme of intercultural conflict is expressed unequivocally:

Ese General Cortinas	That General Cortinas
es muy libre y soberano	is very sovereign and free;
han subido sus honores,	the honor due him is greater
porque salvó a un mexicano.	for he saved a Mexican's life.
Los americanos hacían huelga,	The Americans made merry,
borracheras en cantinas,	they got drunk in the saloons,
de gusto que había muerto	out of joy over the death
ese General Cortinas.	of that General Cortinas.

(Paredes 1995 [1976]:48)

Among the forms of expressive culture that define continuities between the nineteenth and twentieth centuries, the corrido is one of the most compelling. Although still in the process of crystallization, the theme of intercultural conflict is clearly discernible in such early corridos as "Juan Cortina." In the next century, this theme would become central to the corrido tradition in Texas, a key element at the extreme pole of cultural opposition in the unfolding dialectic of conflict. In other words, at the same time that it represented the residual influence of an earlier Mexican culture based on a subsistence mode of economic activity, the corrido functioned as an antithetical, counter-cultural response to the dominant power of Anglo culture and its accelerating impact on the lives of the subordinated Texas-Mexicans. With respect to Cortina's exploits and their subsequent distillation as the theme of conflict within the corrido tradition, Paredes has traced their unfolding course: "The corrido of border conflict follows a general pattern, out of which emerges the Border concept of the hero. It is a concept that is reflected in other corrido themes as well, because border conflict dominated Border balladry for almost a century. Basically the pattern is that established with Cortina in 1859. It is always expressed in corrido form" (1958:148–49).

As we shall see, however, consistent with the dialectical nature of the intercultural conflict itself, in time the corrido did shift its focus: instead of portraying larger-than-life heroes like Cortina, it began in the 1930s to depict helpless victims of Anglo injustice. I shall have more to say about this shift. Meanwhile, it is important to reiterate that hero corridos typified by "El General Cortina" are traceable to the nineteenth century, and to point out that they offer graphic testimony to the resistive bent of the Texas-Mexicans even during this period, when they and their whole way of life were still reeling from the catastrophic defeat at the hands of the Anglos and their powerfully ascendant economic order.

Instrumental Dance Music

If vocal music (principally in the form of the corrido) emerged in the latter nineteenth century to articulate in dramatic fashion the harsh realities of conflict and subordination for the Texas-Mexicans, instrumental music experienced less drastic—though no less important—developments. More than the corrido, however, which represented an ecumenical response by the total ethnic group to the pressures of intercultural conflict, instrumental music in its increasing variety represented the incipient differentiation of Texas-Mexican society, particulary during the latter part of the century. It was at this historical juncture that the soon-to-be-dominant accordion ensemble increasingly became associated with the fandango—although small, makeshift violin ensembles retained their presence in fandangos and other working-class dances until the 1920s. The baile, meanwhile, became the principal site for the development of a variety of orchestralike ensembles, most notably the string band but also wind ensembles of various configurations.

The first appearance of the accordion in Texas-Mexican musical culture never has been adequately documented. Invented in Vienna in 1829, this bellows-driven, diatonically tuned reed instrument seems to have attached itself to peasant and working-class traditions wherever it took root. This is as true of ethnic groups such as the Czechs, Poles, and Germans as it is of Louisiana Creoles and Arizona Apaches (Keil and Keil 1992). The Mexicans were no exception; from perhaps the 1860s, when it made its first appearance in northern Mexico, the accordion was immediately adopted by the *peones, campesinos,* and other low-level workers. It is uncertain whether, in Texas, the instrument was introduced to the tejanos by European ethnics such as the Czechs and Germans, or whether it came to the tejanos from northern Mexico after its introduction there (see Peña 1985a; Strachwitz 1974).

In any case, there is little doubt that, by the end of the nineteenth century, a tradition of accordion music was rapidly taking root among tejanos and establishing itself as the premier expression of a rural, working-class aesthetic.

We get an inkling of its popularity from an early report in the *San Antonio Express,* dated June 18, 1881, which describes a fandango in Del Rio, "where the natives chased the merry hours with flying feet." According to the reporter, "The orchestra was an accordeon [*sic*] and the engineer was muscularly developed. . . . About forty couples participated." An account by Capt. John G. Bourke, anthropologist and soldier (see Limón 1994), further confirms the presence of this instrument among tejanos by the early 1890s. Writing for *Scribner's Magazine,* Bourke brings to our attention festival days along the lower Rio Grande, such as St. John's Day, when the "peons" and "pelados" (low-class scum) congregated to celebrate. "On these occasions," wrote Bourke, "there is always music of some kind—it may be nothing more than an accordion or a mouth-organ, but it is music" (1894:604).

More important, as the accordion took on an increasingly norteño-tejano stylistic identity, it assumed a stronger symbolic association with the predominantly rural masses on both sides of the border. Aiding in forging a norteño identity for the instrument, as well as strengthening its symbolic standing, was the union of the accordion with the *bajo sexto* and a quasi-native drum known as the *tambora de rancho* (as well as, of course, the ubiquitous guitar). The bajo sexto is a bass-like, twelve-string instrument with a strong mejicano identity of its own. It was originally crafted—or at least popularized—in the west-central states of Michoacán and Guanajuato, but at some point during the latter half of the nineteenth century, it migrated to northern Mexico and South Texas. The *tambora* has an interesting history in the music of Texas-Mexicans and norteños. It merits further comment here.

The tambora de rancho evidently was an improvised and rather primitive "native" drum, fashioned out of whatever materials might be available (see fig. 1). According to two pioneer conjunto musicians, accordionists Pedro Ayala and Narciso Martínez, it had a long history in Texas, stretching back, perhaps, to the earliest Spanish-Mexican colonies. Pedro Ayala recalled how the tambora was made in the second decade of the twentieth century, when he was a young boy (Ayala was born in 1911):

> The tambora de rancho was a makeshift drum that people made with wire and rope. They would stretch the goatskins. The body was made of wood, held together with wire and rope. We would fasten it to the waist—a medium-sized drum, not too large. We used two different drumsticks—one was a mallet with a large ball at the tip and a hole in

Figure 1 Los Hermanos Chavarría at a *matachines* celebration, 1927. *Courtesy Arhoolie Records, El Cerrito, Calif., 94530.*

the handle, through which we ran a string that we wrapped around the wrist. The other was a drumstick something like those we use nowadays. You could hear the *tamborazo* [drumbeats] for miles. There were dances by the river—about seven miles from here, and you could hear the sound of the drum. Of course, in those days there were hardly any cars, there wasn't much noise. You could hear the drumming. (Personal interview, June 29, 1979, author's translation)

The popularity of the tambora de rancho among the Texas-Mexican folk is fundamentally related to the political economy of subsistence. Its very name— tambora de rancho—evokes a pastoral image; indeed, the name epitomized a pastoral people unaccustomed, as Ayala implies, to the noise and the hustle and bustle of modern industrial life. It was an instrument attuned to the life-rhythms of an agrarian people.

Until the 1920s, however, no conventional conjunto ensemble had materialized. Despite the increasing union of accordion with the bajo sexto (or guitar) and/or tambora de rancho, performance practice during the nineteenth century was far from standardized. No permanent arrangement among any of the instruments—accordion, tambora, bajo, guitar—had been forged. Indeed, the accordion often was played as a solo instrument. In other words, a fixed relationship among instruments (such as that of the classical string quartet)—one that would focus symbolic attention upon an ensemble with the power to speak aesthetically for the ideological interests of a tejano (or norteño) working class—still was missing. Nonetheless, by the 1890s, an incipient ethnic, working-class identity had coalesced around the accordion-tambora combination (the bajo sexto remained an irregular addition until the 1920s). This combination was stable enough to prompt Anglo observers to make connections—usually unflattering—between these two instruments and their working-class, Texas-Mexican enthusiasts. Thus, for example, when the *San Antonio Express* condemned the Mexicans for beating their drums (see quotation above), it is likely that the reference was to the tambora, which, according to don Pedro Ayala, was a very "ancient instrument" *(instrumento anciano)*—one that had been popular well before his time.

Meanwhile, among the more affluent tejanos, orquestas of different varieties were common, as were brass bands, although the string orquesta seems to have been favored. Here it should be noted that, even among the most affluent patrons, orquestas could not have attained the refinement of the truly elite ensembles common in the Anglo-American upper class. The disparity in quality reflected the lack of elite musical conservatories among the Texas-Mexicans. There is no evidence that Texas-Mexicans participated in the musical training offered by educational institutions controlled by Anglos, either in Texas or in the more established centers of the East. As was the case elsewhere in the Southwest (see, for example, the case of Federico Ronstadt and the Club Filarmónico in Tucson [Sheridan 1986]), tejano musicians typically were self-taught or were recipients of performance practices transmitted informally through oral and aural means within the various subgroups that made up Texas-Mexican society.

We should note, however, that, toward the end of the century, an increasing number of *profesores de música* from the more cosmopolitan Mexican city of Monterrey, Nuevo León, had begun to migrate toward South Texas. Many an aspiring young tejano violinist, for example, received the benefit of instruction by a *profesor* trained in Monterrey. Monterrey by this time was a well-known center of elite musical activity, ranging from salon performance to opera (Vizcaya Canales 1971); documentation exists to demonstrate that Monterrey and its culture exerted considerable influence as far north as San Antonio (Vizcaya Canales 1971). Moreover, information from my own informants and other sources indicates that it was not uncommon for musically trained individuals who found life in Monterrey unsatisfactory to migrate to South Texas, where they offered musical instruction (Peña 1985a: ch. 1).

The availability of *profesores* created a pool of more or less trained musicians, a pool that remained at the disposition of the more affluent segments of tejano communities for their celebrations. It is evident from descriptions offered by contemporary reports (e.g., the *San Antonio Express*) that the music provided by middle-class-oriented orquestas (e.g., Pablo Persio's) was of exceptional quality. In this respect, El Paso, isolated as it may have been from the rest of Texas (but not from Chihuahua; see M. García 1981), presents an interesting case. As in other cities (Brownsville, Laredo, San Antonio), well-organized orquestas and even brass bands were in evidence early on in this border city, and by the end of the century, a number of these groups were providing music for the genteel members of the Mexican American community.

For example, according to historian Mario García, an erstwhile member of Porfirio Diaz's administration, Trinidad Concha, organized an orchestra in 1896, whose music was "intended to appeal to Mexican as well as American bourgeois tastes" (1981:207). I shall have more to say about the development of the orquesta in chapter 4. Here it is worth noting that, if the commercial recordings available from as early as the 1920s are any indication, the level of proficiency evident in the best orquesta recordings was attributable to a sufficiently large pool of trained musicians. Finally, this pool itself was evidence of a rather lengthy formative period for the orquesta in Texas, one extending back to the nineteenth century.

Conclusions

Several conclusions can be drawn from the data available on Texas-Mexican music of the nineteenth century. First, much of the musical activity remained a function of the musical economy that had prevailed throughout the Southwest in an earlier period, and as such, it contributed to the continuity of cultural forms antedating the American invasion. It was this continuity that lent musical and other cultural practices a nativistic character—a character that jaundiced Anglo eyes viewed as exotic and even savage (see, for example, the descriptions in Bourke 1894). The canción and its performance context represented one aspect of this continuity. Also contributing to the cultural continuity were the small, makeshift ensembles built around the violin; these were still prevalent toward the end of the century. Finally, even the fledgling accordion ensemble, novel as it may have been, was inserted into a musical context still grounded in a pastoral culture and its attendant economy.

Texas-Mexican society was swept inexorably into the system transforming the land and people in the Southwest in the latter part of the nineteenth century, and some aspects of tejano music did respond—vigorously—to this transformation. The corrido is a case in point. Its rapid development in the last quarter-century attests to the resistive efforts of the tejanos, just as it demonstrated their capacity to adapt, however torturously, to the Anglo conquerors and their system. Lastly, the growing sophistication apparent in the urban orquestas provides an indication of how the more affluent Mexicans in cities like Brownsville, Corpus Christi, El Paso, and San Antonio were adapting to the middle-class culture of an American capitalism surging in these population centers. The better organized orquestas provided a musical repertoire commensurate with the tastes of these affluent people.

Finally and most important, instrumental music at the end of the nineteenth century, more than vocal music, was adumbrating the social direction that Texas-Mexican music would take in the twentieth century. The accordion ensemble, tentative as it may have been, already was aligning itself with the aesthetic and ideological interests of a large mass of proletarian and subproletarian workers. The orquesta, meanwhile, was emerging as the artistic voice of a nascent but increasingly influential and upwardly mobile class. In the twentieth century, these two types of ensemble and their styles would blossom as powerful voices for the divergent aesthetic interests of the middle and working classes in Texas-Mexican society. Each ensemble would also play a crucial mediative role in the continuing dialectic of conflict that historically marks Anglo-Mexican relations.

Notes

1. The internal-colony model is a variation on the classical colonial model developed by writers like Memmi (1965), Cabral (1979), and Fanon (1965) in relation

to European domination of Africans. In the colonial model, the colonized are in the majority; in the internal-colony model, they are in the minority (see Blauner 1972).

2. The question of corrido origins has not been without debate. See the exchange between Paredes (1958, 1963) and M. Simmons (1963).

2 ❧ Vocal Music of the Twentieth Century

The Canción Before Mid-Century

By the end of the nineteenth century, the Mexican canción had begun to divide itself into two broad stylistic categories—the traditional *canción mexicana* (Mendoza 1961) of long-standing circulation, sometimes known as *canción típica;* and the *canción romántica*. The former was generally of a folk nature—with simple tune and lyrics, anonymous in composition, and often of antiquarian origins. The latter was more specifically associated with modern Latin American urban culture and its attraction to European importations, especially Italian music (Garrido 1974:16; see Burns 1980).

No documentation exists on the social contrasts implied by the labels *típica* and *romántica,* as applied to the canción in the latter part of the nineteenth century; but it is reasonable to infer that the labels encoded such contrasts, particularly as these may have been indexed to parallel distinctions communicated by the two ideologically charged terms "the country" and "the city," and the host of oppositions and contradictions attached to them (Williams 1973; discussed below).[1] In other words, the *canción típica* evoked attributes associated with an agrarian economy and its culture, while the canción romántica symbolized the whole process that goes by the label "modernization" (Burns 1980).

The distinctions inherent in the *típica/romántica* contrast remained more or less submerged among Texas-Mexicans in the nineteenth century, perhaps because ethnic subordination overshadowed all other social differences that may have been present within tejano society. However, after about 1920, ingroup disparities emerged with greater clarity and force, and the canción began to address such disparities. Meanwhile, the greater Mexican *canción típica* acquired a new name in the 1920s—*canción ranchera* (Garrido 1974). Despite intensive commercialization, the new *ranchera* became the property of the disfranchised masses on both sides of the border, for whom it served both as ideological shibboleth in a latent but persistent class struggle and as a "residual" form of expression (Williams 1981) invoking a vanished cultural economy and its social relations (particularly gender relations; see the discussion below). The ideological function of the canción ranchera was particularly robust in Texas and the Hispanic Southwest. Here a wealth of commercially recorded canciones exists that enables us to draw some conclusions about what is essentially a use-value function extracted from the exchange-value commercial context in which the ranchera flourished.

There is little doubt that, in the twenties, thirties, and forties, the canción ranchera of the Southwest became powerfully charged with class and gender implications. Indeed, these two types of social relations became intertwined in the ranchera. As we shall see, the lyrics of representative songs reveal latent but powerful social forces in the poetic consciousness of the vernacular song makers of the Southwest (as in Mexico), forces that shaped the aesthetic sensibilities of a whole generation of working-class Mexicans in Texas and elsewhere in the Hispanic Southwest. The harsh economic climate of the Great Depression no doubt contributed to the heightened class and gender sensibilities expressed in the canción ranchera, but it is also possible that its generic contiguity to the corrido, especially as bridged by the canción-corrido, infused the canción ranchera itself with the corrido's grasp of the consciously political.

When the major American recording labels—Decca, Okeh (Columbia), Bluebird (RCA Victor), Brunswick, and Vocalion—arrived in the Southwest, they discovered a wealth of musical talent. A wide assortment of preexisting ensembles and styles, ranging from the string orquestas to vocal duets, was swept into the commercial web. The duets especially became a focus of commercial exploitation, and they were the most popular form of musical expression in the commercial market of the Hispanic Southwest. Judging from the ledgers left by the major labels (and compiled into a comprehensive discography by Richard K. Spottswood [1990]), we can estimate that perhaps two-thirds of the music popularized by the labels was of the vocal duet variety.

Texas is well represented in this discography. Indeed, along with Los Angeles, the cities of San Antonio and Dallas became the principal centers of

Figure 2 Lydia Mendoza recording at the Texas Hotel, San Antonio, 1936. *Courtesy U.T. Institute of Texan Cultures, The San Antonio Light Collection.*

recording activity. As pointed out earlier, Mexican American brokers arranged for musicians to travel to these cities and perform for the phonograph, usually in makeshift studios set up in local hotels (see fig. 2). As a rule, these recording sessions were set up in assembly-line fashion, with one musician after another brought in for one or two quick "takes" before the final version was approved for release. On any given day, as many as a dozen or more musicians would pass through the "studio." But no matter how makeshift or mechanical the operation, the performers were immortalizing their traditions through the magical wax disc, even as they were inventing new ones. Moreover, as contributors to musico-historical traditions forged in the crucible of class-mediated interethnic conflict, the performers seemed compelled to create forms and styles with an ideological edge. In short, Texas-Mexican music was an organic expression laden with use-value.

Such, at any rate, was the case with the canción, the corrido, and the canción-corrido hybrid. In Texas, the best-known exponents (popular singers such as Lydia Mendoza, Los Hermanos Chavarría, Gaitán y Cantú, and Rocha y Martínez) all recorded their share of canciones—again, mostly rancheras, though the songs were not necessarily so labeled. And, although a large portion of the repertoire concentrated on what was by then a conventionalized theme of exalted love, many canciones took on a decidedly "materialist" perspective, in which the theme of betrayed love looks suspiciously like an alibi or a symbolic front for something hidden in the folds of what Fredric Jameson (1981) has called the "political unconscious." [2] In other words, as Texas-Mexicans were more and more socialized within a capitalist system that seemed increasingly immutable, "normal," and beyond challenge, the injuries of class and racial oppression that tejanos experienced daily were more and more driven underground, their force deflected in random symbolic directions, such as that of the canción and other aesthetic expression.

Nonetheless, the canción ranchera (although less so than the corrido and canción-corrido) certainly was capable, especially during the critical years of the twenties, thirties, and forties, of articulating the concerns of a society in transition from a rural, subsistence-type economy to the urban capitalist culture in whose webs the Texas-Mexicans were inescapably caught. Thus, materialist themes related to wealth and poverty, power and dispossession, did invade the consciousness of the ranchera, even if these themes often were couched in the symbolic language of love—particularly betrayed love.

In reference to the latter, it is of crucial import that the betrayer almost always was the woman, seldom the man. This gender bias, which coalesced around the theme of the treacherous woman (see Herrera-Sobek 1993; Peña 1991), raises a fundamental issue with respect to the manner in which concrete social relations—class and gender, specifically—were transfigured in the symbolic language of the canción (ranchera). One glaring contradiction stands out: the theme of the treacherous woman perversely inverted a norm that was more or less inviolable in Mexican society—the faithful wife or sweetheart. In fact, men were far more likely to be unfaithful than women. The treacherous-woman theme in the canción thus *reversed* gender norms, it did not *reflect* them.

Since the theme of the treacherous woman of the canción does not in any way index actual gender roles, it becomes necessary to look behind the surface message. First, however, we should be aware that, until the 1940s, when Carmen y Laura made female duets fashionable in Texas, men dominated vocal music, as they did the field of musical performance generally.[3] Male domination clearly had an impact on the themes that found their way into the canción, and this may explain why women's viewpoints seldom were represented. Before the 1940s, professional female performers were rare, and nonexistent as instrumentalists. The legendary Lydia Mendoza—La Alondra de la Frontera (The Lark of the Border)—was undoubtedly the best-known tejana singer, perhaps because her canciones, leaning toward a ranchero sensibility, resonated strongly with her tejano public. Only two other women achieved any degree of prominence—San Antonians Eva Garza and Rosita Fernández, both of whom recorded extensively for the major labels (as did Mendoza). But neither approached the popularity of La Alondra, possibly because both leaned toward the canción romántica with full orchestration, which was less appealing to tejanos than the simple ranchera. In any case, Lydia Mendoza's 1934 hit, "Mal hombre" ("Evil Man"), was the only canción to buck the overwhelming practice of casting women as deceitful lovers. But, as I have indicated, this practice had deeper roots.

I have analyzed elsewhere a parallel form of expressive culture, the folklore of *machismo,* which, like the canción ranchera, serves as a forum for the disparagement of women, specifically through the theme of the treacherous woman (Peña 1991). I suggest the analysis of the folklore of *machismo* applies also to the canción ranchera. Thus, the theme of the treacherous woman in both folklore and canción may be conceived as a form of ideological displacement, in which resentment arising out of class oppression is repressed by the masking strategies of capitalist ideology, only to find an outlet in another sphere of social conflict—gender relations. A conflation of the two types of conflict ensues, in which women, more accessible targets in both real and symbolic terms than the dominant classes, emerge as substitute "oppressors."

Take, as a first example, the old and well-traveled canción, "Las gaviotas," recorded by (among others) Los Hermanos Chavarría in 1930. It is one of several canciones focusing on the theme of betrayed love included in an LP, *Los Hermanos Chavarría,* reissued by Folklyric Records in its *Texas-Mexican Border Music* series. The song is in *tempo di polka,* in four-line strophes, and has the simple melody and harmony of the garden-variety ranchera, or the *típica* of an earlier era. "Las gaviotas" opens with the ubiquitous question—"Why can't (or won't) you love me?"—and follows with a hyperbolic (though quite poetic) description of the woman's beauty. However, it abruptly turns bitter, thematically linking the woman's treachery with the evils of money. The injured—and, presumably, economically disadvantaged—lover accuses her of cruelty, treachery, and an opportunistic desire for wealth, which the narrator cannot satisfy. Unlike many rancheras, however, the song ends on a rather hopeful note. Here are the pertinent verses:

Ay, dime negra, pórque no me amas,	Oh, tell me, dark girl, why you don't love me,
tú ya en mi vida, mi bien, estás.	you are already part of my life.
Dame un abrazo, dame un besito,	Give me a hug, give me a kiss,
vente conmigo, vamos al mar.	Come with me, let's go to sea.
Ay, como brilla tu pelo negro	Oh, how your black hair shines
como las flores al reventar;	like the flowers about to burst [into bloom];
miles de conchas tiene la arena,	thousands of shells has the sand,
miles de perlas tiene la mar.	thousands of pearls has the sea.
. . .	
No cabe duda que eres ingrata,	There's no doubt that you are cruel,
no cabe duda que eres infiel;	there's no doubt that you are unfaithful;
amas el oro, amas la plata,	you love gold, you love silver,
eres amiga del interés.	You are a friend of opportunism.
Si quieres niña venir conmigo,	If you want to come with me, little girl,
en mi barqilla te llevaré.	I'll take you in my little boat.
Ya cuando estemos en otra orilla,	And when we're on another shore,
nuevas canciones te cantaré.	new songs I'll sing for you.

From another LP in the Texas-Mexican Border Music series, Cancioneros de Ayer—Part 3, comes another and quite typical canción, also dwelling on the theme of betrayal. "Lágrimas lloro," originally recorded in 1936 by the duet (Juan) Gaitán y (Timoteo) Cantú, is, like many rancheras, structured in four-line stanzas, with the second and fourth lines rhyming (abcb scheme). Sung in a fast waltz tempo, the song laments the loss of a beloved but treacherous woman, who has driven the man to a state of abject deprivation in which liquor alone affords relief. The following are the most poignant verses:

Lágrimas lloro cuando me acuerdo	I shed tears when I recall
de una mujer que yo amaba tanto.	a woman that I loved deeply.
Nomás me acuerdo y verla quisiera	When I remember I wish I could see her
para adorarla y calmar el llanto.	to adore her and soothe the grief.
Yo no comprendo cual es el odio	I can't understand the hate
ni por qué causa me despreció;	nor why she rejected me;
yo la quería más que a mi madre,	I loved her more than my own mother,
pero la ingrata me traicionó.	But the cruel woman betrayed me.
. . .	
Tú bien lo sabes que yo te amaba	You know full well that I loved you
como se quiere con fe y lealtad.	as one should love, with faith and loyalty.
Fuistes ingrata y mal pagadora,	You were cruel and deceitful
y amaste siempre la libertad.	and always yearned to be free.
. . .	
Tú destrozaste toda mi vida,	You wrecked my whole life,
y hasta mis hijos también perdí.	I even lost my children.
Tú eres la causa de mi desgracia,	You are the cause of my misfortune,
y a nadie culpo nomás a ti.	and I blame no one but you.
'Ora las copas son mis quebrantos,	Now the bottle is my downfall,
y el sentimiento me hace llorar;	and the grief makes me weep;
pues las botellas son mi esperanza,	Now the bottle is my only hope,
y siempre borracho me has de encontrar.	and drunk, always, is how you will find me.

These two examples are not in the least out of the ordinary, when compared with the canciones most popular among the Mexican masses in the thirties and forties. To be sure, a surprising variety of themes may be found in the canciones of the period, ranging from exalted love to critiques of the various ways of modern life (new modes of dress, for example). Yet, again and again, the theme of the treacherous woman appears, and again and again the crushed male victim finds refuge from his grief in the bottle. In some canciones, the deceitful woman stands alone as the culprit responsible for the man's downfall; however, in a significant number, the subtheme of wealth and poverty appears as a factor contributing to the woman's desertion (as in "Las gaviotas"). In any case, the sheer volume of canciones dominated by the theme of the treacherous woman far exceeds anything seen in other historical periods, and this inordinate preoccupation with what was after all the exception (most women clearly were not unfaithful) demands explanation. Interpreting the treacherous-woman theme as a form of ideological displacement is one alternative.

It is worth noting, by way of comparative analysis, that the themes of female betrayal and drunken oblivion dominating the canción ranchera of the thirties and forties also predominated in the folk blues of African Americans (Evans 1986), and they were common as well in white "country" music, especially the honky-tonk variety (Malone 1985). Blacks and honky-tonk whites differed in many cultural respects from Mexican Americans, but they shared one characteristic—class. Bill Malone referred to honky-tonk whites as "plain . . . working-class folk" (1985:153). The phrase applies equally to blacks and Mexican Americans. Not surprisingly, the songs of the three groups shared many themes, including that of the treacherous woman. In his study of folk-blues, David Evans tells us that the blues "have commented on almost every major aspect of daily life for blacks" (1986:564). Moreover, "the man/woman relationship is by far the most important subject in the blues," with the singers (usually male) "presenting themselves as victims of mistreatment or unfaithfulness by a [usually female] lover" (ibid.:566).[4] These comments are entirely applicable to the ranchera, as they are (if to a lesser extent) to the honky-tonk song.

An interesting question arises in connection with this remarkable thematic correspondence. Is the presence of the treacherous woman in the blues, the ranchera, and honky-tonk songs simply the result of commercial diffusion, a popular theme inevitably crossing market boundaries? Or is there a structural correspondence among the three groups that in some way predisposed them toward a common goal in symbolically articulating a shared status? Although the first alternative is plausible, the latter seems more compelling. Mexicans, blacks, and poor honky-tonk whites may have been culturally different in many ways, but economically they shared many attributes, including the pervasive alienation that comes with the hard-core poverty all three groups experienced, especially during hard times such as the Depression.

I propose that, in all three communities, the structural inequalities inherent in the class relationships among males were transferred to, and replicated in, the domain of gender relations. The structural arrangements and their transposition from the class to the gender domain are schematized in the diagram below. The upper members of the equation are dominant, the lower members subordinate. These arrangements transcend and are independent of other variables, such as region, race, and ethnicity:

CLASS RELATIONS   GENDER RELATIONS

$$\frac{\text{ruling-class men}}{\text{working-class men}} \longrightarrow \frac{\text{working-class men}}{\text{working-class women}}$$

In the domain of class relations, the men from the three groups—Texas-Mexicans, blacks, poor whites—were in a subordinate status vis-à-vis male members of the dominant classes (particularly the capitalist class). In the case of the Mexicans and blacks, their race or ethnicity may have heightened the sense of oppression, but *structurally* their subordinate status was a function of class, not racial/ethnic factors. In the domain of gender relations, men in all three groups were in a dominant relationship to the women of their group, and they exercised the same authority over women that their superior-class antagonists exercised over them. However, in the transfer of authority from the public to the domestic domain—from the level of class to the level of gender—its symbolic articulation ran amok. In the domestic sphere, the resentment arising from class domination exploded with a vengeance. The perennial conflict between men and women was reinforced by the resentment these working-class men harbored as a result of their economic oppression; in a gender relation in which, historically, they had enjoyed overwhelming dominance, working-class men were free to unleash their frustrations upon more or less defenseless women.[5] The theme of the treacherous woman, common to the ranchera, the blues, and honky-tonk, played a role in this clash of genders.

The canción romántica, meanwhile, had a rather meager impact on Texas-Mexican music in the first half of the century. According to the observations of Américo Paredes, Octavio García (informal conversations with author), and other observers of the musical scene in the 1920s and 1930s, the romántica was popular mainly in the small circles of the musically sophisticated. The masses preferred the *canción típica* (ranchera). Most significant, in terms of the nascent sensibilities distinguishing an emergent middle class from its working-class counterpart, the romántica was far more muted in its treatment of female betrayal than was the ranchera. The harsh indictments of the latter were far less prevalent in the romántica. Equally important, in terms of the lack of a robust middle-class aesthetic that could support a more sophisticated music, was the dearth of native interpreters of the romántica genre, at least in the commercial arena dominated by the big labels. The few who won acclaim were foreigners like Guty Cárdenas, Pedro Vargas, José Mojica, and others—performers whose songs subscribed to the more delicate and refined poetics of the canción romántica. These performers and their songs eschewed the vituperative treatment of women found in the ranchera.

Consider the *canción-danza*, "Júrame," composed by María Grever about 1935 and popularized by Mojica (among others). According to Octavio García, who began his career as an orquesta musician in the late twenties, it was widely appreciated among lovers of *"música buena"* in his native Rio Grande Valley in deep South Texas (personal conversation with author). Typical of the extreme romanticism of this genre, its message of unbounded love is blemished only by the bitterness expressed at the end. Here are some representative stanzas:

Júrame—	Swear to me—
que aunque pase mucho tiempo	that no matter how much time passes
no olvidarás el momento	You will not forget the moment
en que yo te conocí.	when I first met you.
Mírame—	look at me—
pues no hay nada más profundo	for there's nothing more profound
ni más grande en este mundo	nor greater in this world
que el cariño que te di.	than the love I gave to you.
Bésame—	Kiss me—
con un beso enamorado,	with an impassioned kiss,
como nadie me ha besado	as no one has kissed me before
desde el día en que nací.	since the day I was born.
Quiéreme—	Love me—
quiéreme hasta la locura:	love me into madness:
Así sabrás la amargura	then you'll understand the bitterness
que estoy sufriendo por ti.	that I'm suffering for you.

The Canción after World War II

World War II introduced important sociological changes in Texas-Mexican society, and these changes were reflected in the canción, insofar as the ranchera and the romántica solidified their positions within their respective niches in the social-class structure. The years following the war are significant, too, for the increased participation of women in the field of vocal (though not instrumental) music. That participation may have been related to the beginnings of change in the relationship between Texas-Mexican men and women, as the latter began their long road toward gender equality through increased education and work experience. One or two women were prominent singers prior to World War II, of course; but, beginning in the late 1940s, a number of female singers made their mark, including the aforementioned duet of Carmen y Laura, romántica singer Chelo Silva, and many others (fig. 3).

Figure 3
Carmen y Laura. *Courtesy Arhoolie Records, El Cerrito, Calif., 94530.*

I shall discuss social change and diversification in Texas-Mexican society more extensively in connection with the conjunto and orquesta. Here I want to stress that, despite social distinctions, no rigid dichotomy ever governed the circulation of the two canción subtypes. Indeed, except for the treacherous-woman theme of the ranchera, with its caustic denunciations, they shared a common set of lyrical conventions. Moreover, even as the ranchera became increasingly attached to the repertoires of certain "grassroots" ensembles (the working-class conjunto, for example), it acquired the status of an icon among all classes, representing a vanishing and romanticized pastoral way of life. In its celebration of this life as simple and wholesome (even if menaced by treacherous women), the ranchera triggered a deep sense of nostalgia among Texas-Mexicans, regardless of gender and social status.

Although never as popular as the ranchera, the canción romántica was endorsed by many people of both working and middle-class leanings. However, as it became identified with sophisticated urban groups—the orquesta, for one—it did tend to acquire a middle-class gloss, and many working-class people, especially rural workers, never developed a preference for it. For example, many of the farm workers among whom this writer lived as a music-loving youngster saw the canción romántica as an effete artistic form, the property of snobbish, pretentious people—*jaitones,* as they were called derisively.[6]

But the incipient opposition between the ranchera and the romántica among Texas-Mexicans was actually a localized expression of much larger social and ideological forces clashing within Latin American societies. These forces are related to the "heterodoxical" nature of capitalism (LaCappra 1983)[7] and its struggle to eradicate "residual" forms of cultural communication from rival economies that challenge from the past, as well as emergent forms that may threaten from the future. The clash of economically motivated ideologies has a long history in Mexico and Latin America (see, e.g., Zea 1963), as it does, for that matter, in the global system of capitalism. Often couched in terms of "country" versus "city" (Williams 1973), or "tradition" versus "modernity," at its most basic level this clash represents the disjuncture between capitalism and its organization of production and earlier forms of political economy (see Burns 1980; Taussig 1980; Thompson 1965).

In the march of capitalism, the city and modernity came to be seen as emblems of middle- and capitalist-class "progress" and the whole way of life organized around technology, while the country and the "traditional" (the "folk") became markers for earlier forms of life—"survivals" of earlier stages in sociocultural evolution.[8] In fact, much of the significance of the "carnivalesque," a social process that has aroused great interest in the recent past, revolves around this disjuncture between capitalism and earlier forms of social organization, with the erosion of the carnivalesque seen generally as indicative of the final defeat (or repression, in some instances) of older forms of "moral economy" and the transformation of peasants and artisans into industrial workers (see, e.g., Attali 1985; Bakhtin 1984; Stallybrass and White 1986; Thompson 1965).

In Texas-Mexican society, the disjuncture between earlier and newer forms of economic and social life took on local characteristics. As elsewhere in the Southwest (and in South America: see Taussig 1980), there was a struggle between the subsistence-type forms and capitalism (see the introduction to this book). This struggle was reinforced by the racial/ethnic differences represented by Mexicans and Anglos. The latter were "white" and entrepreneurial ("modern"), the former were "Indian" ("Mexican") and economically stagnant ("backward" or "traditional"). As the Mexican Americans were swept into the net of capitalism, they were forced to adapt to the culture imposed on them by a triumphant capitalism (as had European artisans, of course; see Thompson 1965). For the Texas-Mexicans, their racial/ethnic difference complicated matters, and, as they struggled to adapt to the new system, they necessarily created new, sometimes hybrid cultural forms, just as they accepted, rejected, and transformed others—both of American and Mexican/Latino derivation (Peña 1999). The canción was one form linking them to their greater Mexican history, just as it articulated incipient social differences among them.

With respect to the ranchera and the romántica, and the ideological poles they represented, they were illustrative, as noted, of a much larger relationship between the country and the city and its ideological articulation. I would like to explore this articulation a bit further, while at the same time demonstrating the role that the concepts "country" and "city" played in the two key labels ultimately indexed to the canción among Texas-Mexicans: *lo ranchero* and *lo jaitón*.

As the English cultural critic Raymond Williams has shown, throughout Europe's long history, the country and the city have been seen as spaces endowed with contrasting—and sometimes contradictory—ideological attributes. According to Williams, the country is conceived as a "natural way of life: of peace, innocence and simple virtue" (1973:1). The city, on the other hand, is the place of achievement: "of learning, communication, light" (ibid.). But, as Williams reminds us, each has also attracted unfavorable responses: "Powerful associations have also developed: on the city as a place of noise, worldliness and ambition; on the country as a place of backwardness, ignorance, limitation" (ibid.).

For Williams, these contradictory attitudes toward both country and city have their origins in the initial challenge that capitalism, centered in the cities, posed against feudalism, centered in the countryside (1973:280ff.). As capitalism gained the upper hand and its affluent, elite culture was concentrated in cities, the urban way of life became an index for the highest stage of civilization—hence the prestige attached to the metropolis. The country, with its vestiges of an earlier, less developed civilization, lost status. Yet the seamy underside of capitalism—its social fragmentation, poverty, and squalor—also festered in the city, while the countryside remained, seemingly, a more tranquil, more ordered space—hence its romanticization. But, as Williams makes clear, the two spaces are indissolubly linked, and the contrasts ultimately are a function of a singular ideology—the search for Utopia amid the harsh realities of capitalism's social inequalities and exploitation of workers.

The ideological contradictions analyzed by Williams are graphically encapsulated in the tejano labels, *ranchero* and *jaitón*. However, within the semantic field of these labels, the original country/city dichotomy is further complicated by the racial and class inequalities experienced by the Texas-Mexicans. Let us address, first, the concept of *lo ranchero*. The tejanos inherited its ideological baggage from Mexico and Latin America—its romanticized images existing side-by-side with its liabilities. On the one hand, among tejanos the term *el rancho* signified the purity and simplicity of rural life, as it did for Latin Americans and Europeans generally. The dashing *charro* of the popular *comedia ranchera* ("ranch comedy," a movie genre; see Saragoza n.d.) was its shining icon, just as the canción ranchera was the *charro's* most poetic form of communication. As conveyed by the *comedia ranchera*, both *charro* and *rancho* represented an idealized rural, communitarian experience, where the workings of capitalism and its harsh organization of production were erased from view.

Yet, of course, by the 1930s, the Mexican rancho—not to mention the American ranch (or, actually, farm), where most Texas-Mexicans toiled—was deeply enmeshed in the world system of capitalism. More important for the ideological construction of the rancho, however, this place also harbored, along with the dashing *charro,* the backward, uncivilized *peón,* or *campesino,* popularly seen in the United States as a lazy Mexican sleeping under the cactus. The two images—*charro* and *campesino*—could only collide in the consciousness of the Texas-Mexicans, creating ambiguous feelings toward the rancho. However, thanks to the power of the canción ranchera (and the *comedia ranchera*), the *charro* and other rural-type heroes emerged as the dominant images of the rancho. The lowly *peón* remained repressed—only to reemerge as the hard-luck lover betrayed by the treacherous woman of the ranchera.

In the meantime, influenced as they were by urban life and its amenities, upwardly mobile Texas-Mexicans, at least, had ready recourse to musical culture that signified the urban modernity they sought—*música romántica* generally, and the canción romántica specifically. For it was during the period after World War II, with its modernizing influence, that música romántica emerged in full force, as Mexico and the Hispanic Southwest enjoyed an unprecedented spell of economic prosperity. Indeed, at this time música romántica acquired the label *música moderna.* The orchestra, or orquesta, patterned after American middle-class swing bands, came of age during this historical moment, and in the Southwest it became the principal purveyor of the canción romántica, most notably through its newly dominant genre, the Cuban-Mexican bolero. In short, for Texas-Mexicans generally, the *canción-bolero* became the epitome of both *lo romántico* and *lo moderno* in the postwar years. Lastly, the whole música romántica/música moderna complex became inseparably linked with the sophisticated climate of urban life and its middle-class comforts.

It was in this climate of urban modernity that tejana and tejano singers of the canción romántica first gained popularity. Foremost among these was Chelo Silva, who eventually became well known in Mexico as well as Texas and the Hispanic Southwest. Chelo Silva deserves special recognition because she is arguably the most distinguished of a now extensive historical line of tejana singers, including such notables as Lydia Mendoza, Eva Garza, Laura Canales, and Selena Quintanilla-Pérez. Most important, Silva was the only one to gain fame exclusively as an interpreter of the canción romántica (fig. 4).

Silva began her singing career in the 1930s in her native city of Brownsville, Texas, with her husband, the guitarist-singer Américo Paredes. Paredes served in the U.S. Army as a war correspondent during World War II and eventually

Figure 4
Chelo Silva, ca. 1950.
Courtesy Arhoolie Records,
El Cerrito, Calif., 94530.

became a distinguished public figure in his own right, as a path-breaking Chicano scholar at the University of Texas at Austin. Meanwhile, the couple eventually drifted into divorce, and Silva struck out on her own. Her fame soared in the late 1940s, when she began recording for Falcon Records of McAllen, Texas. The powerful Mexican label, Peerless, distributed her records in Mexico, and her fame then spread south of the border. Eventually Silva signed with Columbia, a move that guaranteed even greater commercial exposure. Often accompanied by romantic guitar trios (sometimes by small orquestas), Silva sang in a distinctively husky, low contralto that lent her delivery a melancholy quality perfectly suited to the canción romántica. Her peak years were the 1950s and early 1960s, although she continued to perform until the 1980s (she died in 1988).

The canción romántica may have flourished in the sophisticated climate of urban modernity, but this climate had its critics. The sophistication of city people and their *música jaitona* might instill feelings of social inadequacy in some rural, working-class Texas-Mexicans, but it also could provoke in them a sense of rejection, based on the belief that urban, Americanized middle-class status turned people into snobs and even cultural traitors—in short, *jaitones*. For lowly workers, the canción romántica and its urban sophistication at times could serve as a token for that snobbery.

Ultimately the tensions inherent in the romántica/ranchera dichotomy are traceable to the contradictions experienced by the Texas-Mexicans in their transition from earlier forms of economy to capitalism, from Mexican to American cultural citizenship, from rural to urban modes of living, and, most important, from working-class to middle-class status. These contradictions were particularly evident during the critical period of transformation—the years surrounding World War II. I shall have more to say about this transformation in my discussion of the conjunto and the orquesta (chapters 3 and 4 of this book). Here I merely want to reiterate that the romántica and the ranchera mirrored these contradictions: the former strove for a modern, sophisticated, and (usually) urban aesthetic sensibility; while the ranchera continued to represent an idealized rural existence, the province of a folk-ethnic and increasingly working-class sensibility. Paradoxically, many tejanos, particularly the upwardly mobile, found themselves embracing both.

Meanwhile, within the purview of the ranchera and its ideological horizon, a unique variant emerged among Texas-Mexicans in the postwar period. I refer to a type that glorifies what we may call a "Texo-centric" brand of *machismo*. The type shares many of the attributes of the greater Mexican canción celebrating *machismo* (Paredes 1993e); but, in its Texo-centrism, the Texas-Mexican variant also shares key elements with the Anglo-Texan "myth of bigness" (Bauman 1985)—the popular belief that things Texan are conceived not only on a grander scale but on a superior one as well. The myth has taken many forms, but it is embodied most graphically in the image of the Texan as a larger-than-life, virile, heroic, and slightly untamed man. Long considered the exclusive property of the Anglo-Texan (Texian), the myth of bigness in fact is shared by Texas-Mexican men as well. The canción ranchera subtype I am referring to is an apt example of that cultural commonality.

Consider "El tejano enamorado," a canción high on the Texas-Mexican radio popularity charts of the 1960s and 1970s. The "amorous Texan" brazenly admits to the object of his desire that he is a boozer and a womanizer—"el mil amores," as he tells her. But she cannot resist him, because, not only is he not bound by common moral restraint, he is the only lover "who can give you a great love." Here are representative verses of the canción:

En tu casa no me quieren por borracho,	At your place they don't like me 'cause I'm a drunk,
porque dicen que me gusta vasilar.	because they say I like to play the field.
Qué me importa que me acusen de esa forma,	What do I care if they accuse me that way,
si me quieres manda a todos a volar.	if you love me let them all go fly [a kite].
Si te cuentan que yo ando en las cantinas	If they tell you that I hang around the bars
Y que tomo para ahogar este dolar.	And that I drink to kill this pain.
Si me quieres como yo te estoy queriendo,	If you love me like I'm loving you,
Pues qué importa que ya sepas la verdad.	Well, who cares if you learn the truth.
Qué importa ya, que sepan mi pasado?	Who cares now if they know about my past?
Yo no me escondo en esas cosas del amor.	I don't hide when it comes to matters of love.
Es que yo soy el tejano enamorado	It's just that I'm the amorous Texan;
al fin de todo qué me han de hacer.	after all, what can they do to me?
Si te cuentan que yo soy el mil amores,	If they tell you that I am the lover of thousands [of women],
y que tengo una mujer aquí y alla,	and that I have a woman here and another one there,
si me quieres como yo te estoy queriendo,	if you love me like I'm loving you,
Qué más vale que ya sepas la verdad.	you may as well learn the truth.

Then there was the immensely popular "El troquero" ("The Truck Driver"), another of the tejano songs featuring the virile, happy-go-lucky lover who can charm any woman he wishes into submission, and who is impervious to censure because he is "like the hummingbird who feeds from flower to flower." Further, this obviously working-class "stud" has "money to spend with my friends in the bars," where none dares provoke fights with him for fear of his dominant power. The following are key stanzas:

Soy troquero y me gusta ser borracho	I'm a trucker and I like to booze it up.
Soy parrandero y me gusta enamorar.	I go on binges and I like to play the field.
Traigo dinero pa' gastar con mis amigos	I've got money to spend with my friends;
en las cantinas no me gusta panterear.	I don't like to show off [my prowess] in bars.
Allá en el valle todititos me conocen;	In the Valley everyone knows me;
Allá en McAllen voy a gozar del amor.	In McAllen I'm going to have fun with love.
En San Benito también tengo una güerita;	In San Benito I also have a fair-skinned one;
en Santa Rosa me encontré una nueva flor.	in Santa Rosa I found a new flower.
Soy troquero, soy un triste navegante;	I'm a trucker, I'm just a lonely traveler.
soy como el ave que se cría de flor en flor.	I'm like the hummingbird that feeds from flower to flower.
Gano dinero, soy feliz con mi volante.	I earn money, I'm happy behind the wheel.
Estoy engreido y peleo por un amor.	I'm crazy [about women] and I'll fight for a love.

Lastly, I cite "El rey de Tejas" ("The King of Texas"), a canción ranchera very much a part of the conjunto repertoire of the 1960s. It was thoroughly Texo-centric, extolling the potency—sexual and otherwise—of a tough te-jano on the prowl. After describing the hero's amorous conquests, the song ends with a ringing affirmation of dominant phallic Texas macho power: "Te-jas, Tejas, mi pistola es tu rey" ("Texas, Texas, my pistol is your king").

Regarding the Texas myth of bigness, folklorist Dick Bauman has written that the exaggerated notion of bigness is not unique to the Anglo-Texans—historically it is common to all Americans. As Bauman adds, however, "Whereas bigness was brought down to size fairly soon in other parts of the country, it remained a salient component of [Anglo-]Texans' sense of their environment" (1985:8). More than that, I would suggest that the exaggerated sense of bigness, especially as it relates to the Texas male and his prowess, rubbed off on the tejanos and became part of a common patrimony, one that transcends the intercultural conflict. Goetzmann suggests as much in his description of what he calls the "Texian myth" (see chapter 1 of this book). In other words, in the dialectical relationship obtaining between Anglo and Mexican in Texas, the myth of bigness is an important mediating mechanism, one through which cultural animosities are transformed into commonalities. Opposed in an epic struggle for dominance, the two peoples fashion their identities and interact with each other on the basis of difference, only to create, over time, a merging identity. The interethnic relationship is driven, in dialectical fashion, from one inadequate response, or form of consciousness, to the next, until, step by small step, a common structuring of experience results, with Anglo emulating Mexican and Mexican emulating Anglo in an infinite variety of ways. Of course, since the Mexicans are the subordinate minority, it is they who yield the most, culturally speaking.

The Texo-centric canción is but one of those cultural forms structuring a common experience. Another is the country-style "kikker" (as opposed to "kicker") music and culture, so popular among Texas-Mexicans. It was decidedly Anglo-Texan, yet also primordially tejano. This "kikker" culture eventually was absorbed by modern Tejano music and its culture, with a number of the latter's most prominent stars making continued efforts to "cross over" into the country-western musical arena, in particular (e.g., Emilio Navaira; see chapter 6 of this book). On the Anglo side, as Goetzmann points out, certain aspects of Hispanic culture attracted the Texians from early on—as they attract Anglos throughout the Southwest to this day. Thus, historically we see the Anglos gravitating toward such Mexican cultural forms as cuisine, architecture, and the whole notion of "fiesta." All of this is in addition to linguistic assimilation, as in the many loan words that exist in the English of the Southwest, not to mention the Anglos' predilection for giving an exotic twist to streets and suburban housing developments by christening them with Spanish names.

The Corrido and Canción-Corrido

Much of the materialist-ideological thrust of the Texas-Mexican canción was masked by the kind of symbolic sublimation to be found in the elaboration of themes like that of the treacherous woman (and the myth of bigness). It could not have been otherwise, perhaps, given the prevailing conventions *and* the workings of the political unconscious. However, not all canciones were symbolically deflected from their materialist content. Some, especially the canción-corrido, could be quite explicit in their treatment of poverty, work, and other frankly materialist issues. As noted earlier, what I have called the canción-corrido hybrid emerged in the 1920s as a kind of bridge between the canción and the corrido. Sharing the lyrical qualities of the canción and at least some of the narrative features of the corrido, its form was more amorphous and, in fact, never acquired a generic label, most often being classified either as a "corrido" or a "canción." But its uniquely hybrid nature merits special consideration, and that is why I have chosen to label it "canción-corrido."

Consider "El deportado" ("The Deported One"), a canción-corrido (labeled "corrido" on the original disc) recorded by Los Hermanos Bañuelos in Los Angeles but popular during the thirties along the Texas-Mexico border. It is about the indignities suffered by a Mexican immigrant upon entering the United States, but since, prior to World War II, Texas-Mexicans were virtually indistinguishable culturally from their peers across the border, the attitudes expressed in "El deportado," especially those directed at the Anglo, were common to both groups—hence its popularity on both sides of the border. The narrative organization deftly weaves the theme of interethnic conflict with the economic oppression of the honest and hard-working Mexican. After being humiliated at the border (he is told he must be washed), the immigrant finally links up with a work crew—an *enganche*—common in the 1920s, in whose company he lives through some bitter experiences:

Crucé por fin la frontera,	I crossed the border at last,
crucé por fin la frontera,	I crossed the border at last,
y en un enganche salí.	and I left with a work crew.
Ay, mis queridos paisanos,	Oh, my beloved countrymen,
Ay, mis queridos paisanos,	Oh, my beloved countrymen,
fué mucho lo que sufrí.	what I suffered was a lot.
Los güeros son muy mal horas,	the white men are very wicked,
Los güeros son muy mal horas,	the white men are very wicked,
se valen de la ocasión.	they take unfair advantage.
Y a todos los mexicanos,	And all the Mexicans,

Y a todos los mexicanos	and all the Mexicans
los tratan sin compasión.	they treat without compassion.
. . .	
Adiós paisanos queridos,	Good-bye beloved countrymen,
Adiós paisanos queridos,	Good-bye beloved countrymen,
ya nos van a deportar.	they are going to deport us.
Pero no somos bandidos,	But we are not bandits,
Pero no somos bandidos,	But we are not bandits,
venimos a camellar.	We came here to work.

Another canción-corrido, "Radios y Chicanos" (labeled "canción" on the original disc), recorded by the duet Roca y Amador in San Antonio in 1930, provides a compelling, if implicit, contrast between an older (and valued) moral economy and the culture of modernity that is seducing the naïve "Chicano." The song lampoons the "Chicano" for his easy corruptibility by the "radio"—here a symbol of the cultural economy of capitalism and its crass commercialism, or what Luis Valdez (1972) in another context called "neon gabacho culture." Fundamentally, though, the song may be considered a critique of capitalism and modernity, with the critic implicitly defending an older moral economy. In any case, in the end, the Chicano is left grabbing at cultural straws, neither in possession of his cultural patrimony nor a bona fide participant in modern American culture. Incidentally, at first glance the song's narrator might seem to be a *fuereño*—a Mexican from the interior—criticizing the native-born Chicano, but, as Américo Paredes has pointed out, "when the Border Mexican wanted to criticize American mores and *agringamiento* among his fellows, he was likely to assume the identity of a newcomer from *el interior* (1995 [1976]:154). I quote the most caustic verses here:

En estos tiempos modernos	In these modern times
de electrizar el sonido	of electrified sound
me entretengo buenos ratos	I spend some entertaining moments
componiendo este corrido.	composing this corrido.
Ver a un buen amigo mío	Seeing a good friend of mine
que al dejar mi pueblo grato	who, upon leaving my pleasant hometown,

creyó que al cruzar el río	thought that on crossing the river
se le iría lo zurumato.	he would lose his dullness [i.e.,
	become more "modern"].
. . .	
Y al sentirse con tostones,	And finding himself with coins,
se va haciendo de confianza;	he keeps gaining confidence;
y al comprar trajes rabones	and upon buying tight-fitting suits
se siente casi Carranza.	he feels almost like [President]
	Carranza.
. . .	
Se alquila un radio victrola	He rents a radio-victrola
con foquitos y botones;	with light bulbs and buttons;
pues su casa está muy sola	his house is just too lonely
sin música ni canciones.	without music or songs.
Y a la hora que transmiten	And when the time comes to
	broadcast
los conciertos al chicano	the "concerts" for the chicano
resulta que anuncian puercos	they wind up advertising pigs
y el mejor mole poblano.	and the best mole poblano.[9]
. . .	
Al fin de tres cuartos de hora	After three-quarters of an hour
nos cantan algún mariachi;	they'll play this or that mariachi;
luego anuncian la señora	then they'll advertise the lady
que fabrica buen tepache.	who brews the best tepache.[10]
. . .	
Ya terminó este corrido	Now this song is ended
poniéndole punto y coma,	by crossing all the "t's,"
dejando a mi amigo creído	leaving my gullible friend
chiflando atrás de la loma.	whistling "behind the hill" ["grabbing
	at straws"].

The canción-corrido has been a particularly effective genre in chronicling the experiences of the Mexicans in Texas and elsewhere in the Southwest— both the native-born and the immigrant. By combining the lyrical qualities of the canción and the narrative thrust of the corrido, it captures the full range of emotions and attitudes, as well as the historical perspective, of the Mexicans as they participated in the dramatic expansion of capitalism in the Southwest. The canción-corrido both documented and morally evaluated that participation, leaving a poignant record of the Mexicans' hardships and small triumphs. Its heyday was the 1920s, 1930s, and, to a lesser extent, 1940s. While subsequent eras produced their share of canciones-corridos, none captured as vividly the day-to-day adventures of a people in the process of social transformation.

Meanwhile, the corrido itself, in its now-classic narrative form, continued to play a role in documenting the history of the Mexicans in the Southwest, with tejanos leading the way in the genre's evolution. Any event could become the topic of a corrido, although those dealing with intercultural conflict provided the most symbolically charged examples. In the latter category, the heroic corrido witnessed a "golden age" in the early twentieth century. Américo Paredes, in his book, *With His Pistol in His Hand* (1958), masterfully analyzes the creation and impact of one of the all-time classics, "El corrido de Gregorio Cortez." Perfecting the structure and tone of the modern corrido begun by "A Cortina," "Gregorio Cortez" marks the high point of the corrido tradition in Texas and the Southwest. It epitomizes the ideal hero corrido, in which a common, everyday Mexican is transformed by events into a larger-than-life hero who defends his rights "with his pistol in his hand."

The heroics of Gregorio Cortez are well documented (see Paredes 1958). On an afternoon in the summer of 1901, he was sitting peacefully at his ranch home ten miles west of Kenedy when Sheriff Brack Morris came around looking for horse thieves. After several linguistic misunderstandings—including one in which Deputy Sheriff Boone Choate failed to distinguish between *yegua* (mare) and *caballo* (horse)—he mistranslated Cortez's protest upon being told that he was being arrested, "A mí no me arrestan por nada" ("You can't arrest me for nothing"), as "No one can arrest me." Sheriff Morris then drew his gun and shot Cortez's brother, Rumaldo, who attempted to intercede. Cortez drew his own gun (which he had concealed behind his back) and shot the sheriff, who died later, alone, after crawling into the brush. He had been abandoned by Choate, who fled the scene, and another deputy, Mike Trimmell, who had been left a half-mile behind to check on some horses penned up in a corral.

In the meantime, convinced that he would be lynched were the authorities to find him when they arrived, Cortez himself fled. The next ten days became an odyssey for him, as he attempted to elude his captors. The Anglo news-papers—particularly the *San Antonio Express*—whipped public sentiment into a frenzy, at one point transforming Cortez into a ruthless "gang" of Mexican killers (Paredes 1958:66 ff.). All this time, hundreds of lawmen, in-cluding sheriff's deputies and Texas Rangers, chased after Cortez, finally cap-turing him with the aid of a Mexican informer, just before Cortez had reached his destination, the Mexican border. Paredes summarized the dramatic chase: "The chase had taken ten days, during which Cortez walked at least one hun-dred twenty miles and rode more than four hundred on the brown and the sorrel mares. He had been chased by hundreds of men, in parties of up to three hundred. He had killed two sheriffs and fought off many posses" (1958:79).

"El corrido de Gregorio Cortez" followed on the heels of the actual events. But what is most important about the creation of this historic corrido is its ideological structure. Following the example set by "A Cortina," only in a more rhetorically focused manner, "Gregorio Cortez" draws a sharp contrast between the larger-than-life Mexican hero and the cowardly, smaller-than-life Anglo lawmen. Beyond that, as I have suggested elsewhere (Peña 1982), hero corridos like that of Cortez flourished at a particular historical moment, when, as Paredes has observed, the Texas-Mexicans had reached a point in the long-running intercultural conflict when any sort of political—let alone military—victory was beyond their reach (Paredes 1966). In effect, by the turn of the century, the Texas-Mexicans were caught in a hopelessly subordi-nate position, a "war of position," having been reduced by this time to an ex-ploited proletarian minority.

Lacking the means to raise their material or political status, the Texas-Mexicans turned to symbolic expression as a compensatory outlet for their sense of oppression. Corridos fulfilled that role in a powerful manner. We may suggest that, by portraying larger-than-life heroes who defied the odds against the repressive force of an overwhelming but cowardly Anglo army of law en-forcers, the corridos of the early twentieth century provided what I have else-where called (after Victor Turner 1969) a mechanism for "status reversal" (Peña 1982). Through this mechanism, the roles occupied by the two antago-nists, Anglo and Mexican, were reversed, with the "structurally weak" Mexi-cans symbolically appropriating for themselves, through the exploits of the formidable hero, the power to disarm the "structurally strong" Anglos. The process of status reversal may be schematized as follows:

ACTUAL CONTEXT	CORRIDO CONTEXT
Dominant Anglo	*Dominant Hero* (Dominant Mexican)
Subordinate Mexican	Subordinate Lawmen (Subordinate Anglo)

$\rightarrow$

The following stanzas, from "Gregorio Cortez" (7–10 and 13 of variant "X" in Paredes 1958:155), provide us with an illustration of how the contrasting portrayals are effected, while they lend rhetorical substance to the schema I have sketched above:

Venían los americanos	The Americans were coming
más blancos que una paloma,	they were whiter than a dove,
de miedo que le tenían	from the fear that they had
a Cortez y a su pistola.	of Cortez and of his pistol.
Decían los americanos,	Then the Americans said,
decían con timidez:	they said fearfully:
—Vamos a seguir la huella	"Let us follow the trail;
que el malhechor es Cortez.	the wrongdoer is Cortez."
Le echaron los perros jaunes	They set the bloodhounds on him,
pa' que siguieran la huella,	so they could follow his trail,
pero alcanzar a Cortez	But trying to overtake Cortez
era seguir a una estrella.	was like following a star.
Tiró con rumbo a Gonzales	He struck out for Gonzales
sin ninguna timidez:	without showing any fear:
—Síganme, rinches cobardes	"Follow me, cowardly Rangers,
yo soy Gregorio Cortez.	I am Gregorio Cortez."
. . .	
Decía Gregorio Cortez	Then said Gregorio Cortez,
con su pistola en la mano:	with his pistol in his hand,
—No corran, rinches cobardes,	"Don't run, you cowardly Rangers,
con un solo mexicano.	from just one Mexican."

Several hero corridos, all composed in the mold of "Gregorio Cortez," appeared in succeeding years. Among them were "Ignacio Treviño," "Jacinto Treviño," "Los Sediciosos," and a number of corridos about smugglers (such as "Los Tequileros"). In the latter, the smuggler is cast in the mold of the hero, with the Rangers again as cowards. As Paredes put it, "The smuggler was seen [by border Mexicans] as an extension of the hero of intercultural conflict" (1995 [1976]:43). One of the most enduring of these hero corridos was that of Jacinto Treviño—or, actually, a version that conflates the two Treviño corridos (Paredes 1995 [1976]:30). That version continued to be recorded by conjuntos well into the 1980s. I cite the stanzas most applicable to the theme of the hero and status reversal—that is, those in which the symbols of Anglo domination, the Rangers, are cast as puny cowards, while the symbol of Mexican resistance, the hero, is cast in potent terms:

—*Éntrenle rinches cobardes,*	Come on, you cowardly Rangers,
Que el pleito no es con un niño;	you're not fighting with a child;
querían conocer su padre,	You wanted to meet your father?
¡Yo soy Jacinto Treviño!	I am Jacinto Treviño!
—*Éntrenle rinches cobardes,*	Come on, you cowardly Rangers,
validos de la ocasión;	you always like to take advantage;
no van a comer pan blanco	this is not like eating white bread
con tajadas de jamón.	with slices of ham.

Paredes sees the 1930s as the historical limit of the corrido tradition in Texas (1958:132). Thereafter it entered a period of decadence (ibid:149). There is no question that, after the 1920s, the corrido's thematic elaboration saw a decline—a weakening of character, plot development, and even poetic vitality. In many ways, however, its cultural significance remained as strong after he 1930s as it was prior to that period. What undeniably occurred was the symbolic transformation of the corrido, particularly after World War II. After the 1920s, the larger-than-life hero began to disappear from the Texas-Mexican corrido; in corridos of intercultural conflict, he was replaced by a more or less helpless victim (or victims). Of course, the older hero corridos remained popular after 1930, but no new ones were composed after the 1920s. Instead, as new corridos that challenged the Anglos appeared, these began to take on a different tone. In short, the hero corrido was replaced by the victim corrido. Most important, in the latter, the principle of status reversal was absent or at least attenuated.

The absence of status reversal in the victim corridos begs for an explanation, and, as I have contended elsewhere (Peña 1982), that explanation lies in the transformation of Texas-Mexican society itself. Despite the ravages of the Great Depression, the 1930s were watershed years for Texas-Mexicans, in terms of their shift from a Mexican to a more American orientation, from a rural to an urban existence, and from a rather homogeneous culture to a more socially (class) differentiated one (see Barrera 1979). As a result of their differentiation and increasing mobilization, the Texas-Mexicans in the 1930s began to challenge the dominance of Anglos—particularly through such civic-political organizations as the League of United Latin American Citizens (LULAC, founded in 1929). The challenge was tentative at first, but it became more aggressive after World War II.

The changes overtaking the Texas-Mexicans beginning in the thirties had repercussions at the aesthetic level, as my discussion of the orquesta will demonstrate (chapter 4). As an aesthetic expression, the corrido of intercultural conflict responded as well; moreover, endorsed by a more ecumenical charter than either the conjunto or the orquesta, the corrido proved a more effective tejano response to the challenge of interethnic conflict. Beginning in the 1930s, this response was communicated through the victim corrido, then bursting upon the social consciousness. By way of explaining how the victim corrido superseded the hero corrido, I suggest the latter was the product of a subordinate society whose only means of empowerment was symbolic, as in the case of the corrido hero who single-handedly redeemed his people. As Texas-Mexican society was transformed, the victim corrido emerged to articulate the aspirations of a people with an increasing sense of empowerment. By portraying helpless victims rather than potent cultural heroes, the newer corridos aroused sympathy for the victim and spurred Texas-Mexican communities to take *collective* action for the benefit of all. The real hero turned out to be the collectivity.

Two corridos written after World War II may illustrate the new politico-cultural climate: "Discriminación a un mártir," composed by *corridista* José Morante in 1949; and "Los rinches de Tejas," composed by disc jockey Willie López in 1967. Incidentally, the attributable authorship of the newer corridos marks another point of divergence from the hero corridos of old, which generally were anonymous in origin. This difference is at least partly explainable by changed commercial realities. Like the older corridos, the newer ones were swept into the commercial market; however, ever since the big recording labels had injected the profit principle into Texas-Mexican music, composers (including *corridistas*) had become acutely aware of the potential for royalties from their compositions (meager as those royalties may have been). In short, music inevitably was produced with its exchange-value in mind. As I argued earlier, however, the presence of exchange-value did not cancel the cultural work of use-value, and it is in the operation of the latter that the corrido's significance lies.

"Discriminación a un mártir" selectively narrates events surrounding the death and burial of Pvt. Félix Longoria, a soldier from Three Rivers, Texas. Longoria had been drafted into the U.S. Army in 1944, and he was sent to the Philippines to fight. According to Si Dunn, writing for *Scene,* the *Dallas Morning News Sunday Magazine* ("The Legacy of Pvt. Longoria," April 6, 1975), as the Americans were advancing against the Japanese on Luzon, "somewhere in the gathering American assault, a sergeant called for some volunteers. . . . Félix Longoria was as weary of battle as others in his company. But he had never turned his back on work, and somebody, he thought, had to go. He picked up his rifle. . . . Suddenly, there were loud, short pops: Small arms fire. The patrol took what cover it could find and fought the ambush, but enemy bullets struck and Félix Longoria was among those killed" (Ibid.:7).

Longoria's body was not immediately shipped home to Three Rivers, however. Along with many other American soldiers, he was buried temporarily in the Philippines, and his body was not exhumed for shipment until 1949. When the family started making preparations for burial, they were shocked by the Rice Funeral Home's refusal to accept the slain soldier's body. According to Dunn, the reason for the funeral home's refusal was that "whites would object" (1975:7; see also the *Corpus Christi Caller-Times,* January 12, 1949, p. I-1). "Mortified and hurt" by the blatant act of discrimination, the soldier's widow, Beatrice, turned to Dr. Héctor García, head of the G.I. Forum, for help.

Dr. García fired telegrams of protest to various individuals in influential positions, including U.S. Sen. Lyndon B. Johnson, who at the time represented Texas in Washington. He also mobilized the Mexican American community in the Three Rivers–Corpus Christi area; eight hundred people attended one meeting, for example, and, according to *La Prensa,* a San Antonio newspaper, "numerous calls from neighboring cities have been received [by Dr. García], protesting against the act of discrimination" (January 13, 1949, p. I-1). The Mexican community's protests had a salutary effect: the incident attracted national and international attention. Johnson acted quickly, and a short time later he had the body flown to Washington, D.C. Private Longoria was buried at Arlington National Cemetery with full military honors.

In Texas, meanwhile, the state legislature appointed a commission to investigate the incident. Hearings at the Rotary Club in Three Rivers provoked a hostile reaction from local Anglos. According to Tom Sutherland, a member of the Good Neighbor Commission (a group formed to promote good relations with "Latin Americans"), the atmosphere at the hearings "was like high noon in a Western movie": "That's how ugly the attitude of the hangers-around was. One man showed a bowie knife. And other men said in loud voices so they could be overheard: 'You know, really, this Longoria bunch, they're just a bunch of lowdown greasers'" (quoted in Dunn 1975:9).

The commission absolved the Rice Funeral Home and the people of Three Rivers of all charges of discrimination. But the Mexican Americans had won a moral victory: their protest had led to an honorable solution to the victimization of the slain soldier and his family. More important, as Dr. García observed years later in recalling the incident, "It was a catalyst for the cause of Mexican American civil rights" (Dunn 1975:9). The corrido that followed, "Discriminación a un mártir," kept the incident alive in the social memory, while it contributed to raising the level of political consciousness and activity within the Texas-Mexican community at large.

In studying the structure of "Discriminación," we immediately are struck by its rhetorical economy. Unlike hero corridos like "Gregorio Cortez," this narrative lacks an epic tone. The corrido moves quickly from the announcement of Longoria's death to the lament regarding discrimination against "a poor human being"—that is, the Mexican. In quick order, the corrido moves to the key stanza, where we learn that, through the resolute efforts of the collectivity, the crisis has been resolved. This stanza details how "nuestras quejas" ("our complaints"), directed at Sen. Lyndon Johnson, prompted his heart to "soften" so that he intervened swiftly to redeem the victim's honor, as well as that of the Mexican American community. In sum, it is the community itself and not a larger-than-life hero that, through collective action, saves the day for the people. Here are the pertinent verses:

En Tres Ríos sucedió	It happened in Three Rivers
en los tiempos de la guerra:	during the time of the war:

Félix Longoria murió	Félix Longoria died
peleando por esta tierra.	fighting for this country.
En Filipinas murió	He died in the Philippines,
este valiente soldado;	this valiant soldier;
pero nunca imaginó	but he never imagined
que iba a ser discriminado.	that he would be a victim of
	discrimination.
Cuando el cuerpo del soldado	When the soldier's body
llegó con sus familiares,	arrived with his next-of-kin,
la mortuoria de su pueblo	the city mortuary
le negó sus funerales.	denied him funeral services.
Esa es discriminación	That's discrimination
para el pobre ser humano;	against a poor human being;
ni siquiera en el panteón	not even in the cemetery
admiten al mejicano.	do they admit a Mexican.
Johnson siendo senador	Johnson, being the senator
por el estado de Texas,	for the state of Texas,
se le ablando el corazón	felt his heart soften
al escuchar nuestras quejas.	upon listening to our complaints.
Y pidió a la capital	He asked that the soldier's remains
los restos de este soldado;	be brought to the capital;
y en el panteón nacional	and in the national cemetery
Félix quedó sepultado.	Felix was buried.

The corrido "Los rinches de Texas" was composed in the aftermath of a series of strikes mounted in the summer of 1967 by melon workers in Starr County, deep in South Texas. These strikes were part of the organizing activities, including boycotts and other forms of protest, carried out by the United Farm Workers Organizing Committee (later the United Farm Workers Union—the UFW), led by César Chávez in the sixties and seventies. As happened in numerous other locales where the UFW was active, local authorities collaborated with growers to squelch the melon strikes. In Starr County even the Texas Rangers were involved, called by Starr County Attorney Randall Nye because, as he said, "The situation became electric in early

May, 1967" (Steiner 1970:372). Justifying his actions, Nye continued, "The harvest was about to begin. Evidence indicated to me that something was about to happen. I felt the situation needed the attention of the Rangers" (ibid.).

Nye was right. The workers went on strike that summer, and, in a display of naked Ranger force reminiscent of the early twentieth century (see Paredes 1958), the Rangers succeeded in breaking the strike. People were beaten and jailed, and some of the more militant organizers were targeted for special retribution. One of these was Magdaleno Dimas, about whom a Ranger reportedly said, "I'd like to hold my foot on Dimas' neck until his eyes bulge out like a toad" (Steiner 1970:368–69). Dimas was hunted down and apprehended, allegedly for threatening a deputy sheriff with his hunting rifle and "yelling *'Viva la huelga!'* to his face" (ibid.). When apprehended, Dimas was severely beaten.

While the Rangers broke the strike, the event had far-reaching consequences, some of which worked to the benefit of the local Texas-Mexican community, if not the strikers. The following year (1968) the Independent Party of Starr County, made up of office seekers sympathetic to the farm workers, swept into office, throwing out the hated Randall Nye. According to Steiner, "La Raza activists had for the first time upset a reigning dynasty in Texas politics" (1970:374). The *Valley Evening Monitor* of nearby McAllen called the election a "quiet revolution" (ibid.).

The activists' upset victory may or may not have been influenced by the corrido "Los rinches de Texas," but in any event, this ballad was composed and released for commercial distribution during or shortly after the labor turmoil. Like other postwar corridos, it depicts helpless victims, in this case striking farm workers beaten by Texas Rangers during a confrontation. The corrido concentrates on the cruelty of the Anglos, with Gov. John Connally singled out for special condemnation. Like most victim corridos, it appeals to the listener to join in collective action ("join the union") to win the struggle for justice (note the construction, "Decía . . . ; it purposely recalls the older hero corridos):

Voy a cantarles, señores	Gentlemen, I'm going to sing for you
de dos pobres infortunios,	about two unfortunate souls,
y de algo que sucedió	and something that happened
el día primero de junio.	on the first day of June.

En el condado de Estrella,	In the county of Starr
en merito Río Grande	right in Río Grande City,
junio del '67	June of '67
sucedió un hecho de sangre.	a bloody event took place.
Es una triste verdad	It is the sad truth
de unos pobres campesinos	about some poor farm workers
que brutalmente golpearon	who were brutally beaten
esos rinches asesinos.	by those murderous Rangers.
Decía Magdaleno Dimas	Then said Magdaleno Dimas,
—Yo no puse resistencia	"I didn't offer any resistance;
rendido y bien asustado	subdued and very frightened;
me golpearon sin conciencia.	still they beat me without mercy."
Decía Benjamín Rodríguez	Then said Benjamín Rodríguez
sin hacer ningún estremo:	without making a move,
—Ya no me peguen cobardes,	"Don't hit me anymore, you cowards,
en nombre del ser supremo.	in the name of the Almighty."
Esos rinches maldecidos	Those cursed Rangers
los mandó el gobernador	were sent by the governor
a proteger los melones	to protect the melons
de un rico conservador.	of a rich conservative.
Mr. Connally, señores,	Mr. Connally, gentlemen,
es el mal gobernador,	is the evil governor,
que aborrece al mexicano	who hates the Mexican
y se burla del dolor.	and is contemptuous of our pain.
Me despido, mis hermanos,	I take my leave, my brothers,
con dolor del corazón.	with an aching heart.
Como buenos mexicanos	Like good Mexicans
pertenezcan a la unión.	join the union.

Concluding Remarks

The canción, canción-corrido, and the corrido historically have played key symbolic roles in articulating the Texas-Mexican experience, in all its complexity. Although the canción is far more encumbered by conventional themes, such as that of unrequited love, which seemingly take us away from the realm of the political, such themes as the treacherous woman nonetheless can be read as coded messages for deeper processes entangling class and gender relations and their ideological negotiation. On the other hand, both the corrido and canción-corrido address politico-materialist issues much more directly. Especially with respect to the long-running conflict between Anglos and Mexicans, the two narrative genres participate in the dialectical unfolding of that conflict. The hero and victim corridos, for example, clearly correspond to distinct historical moments in the dialectical struggle. As the relations between the two groups evolve dialectically—that is, as one form of consciousness leads to another, more adequate one, in terms of the leveling of inequality—the corrido evolves accordingly. The hero corrido, based on the marked powerlessness of the Texas-Mexicans, leads to the victim corrido, predicated upon the growing empowerment of this historically subordinate minority.

By the waning years of the twentieth century, Texas-Mexican society had experienced further differentiation, now not so much along class lines as along differences between native-born and immigrant. This had at least an indirect impact on the canción, corrido, and canción-corrido, inasmuch as the tejanos and the ever-mushrooming population of Mexican immigrants subscribed to substantially different types of musical ensembles, and these in turn cultivated vocal genres with different emphases. Of course, the love song, in its endless variations and repetitions, continued to be the mainstay of all commercial ensembles and songsters, regardless of regional or stylistic differences. Interestingly, missing for the most part from the repertories of all contemporary groups was the treacherous-woman song. It is difficult to interpret this salutary development, but it may have been due, at least in part, to the growing empowerment of women and their increasing intolerance of abuse—symbolic or actual. In any case, tejano singers tended to stay away from the theme altogether, while it appeared only sporadically in the canciones of groups based in Mexico but popular among immigrants (Los Tigres del Norte and Los Temerarios, for example).

In the meantime, the presence of the corrido and canción-corrido had become quite attenuated in Texas-Mexican music, although they maintained a more identifiable presence among the groups based in Mexico. Among the latter, what we might call "neo-smuggler" *(narco-traficante)* ballads regularly gained popularity, perhaps because, to the immigrants, Mexican smugglers of cocaine and heroine still functioned as heroes, much as local tequila smugglers once had elicited the admiration of Texas-Mexicans.

The heavy commercialization of Tejano music since the 1980s by the major labels, once again active, surely exerted a substantial influence on both the stylistic and the thematic direction of Texas-Mexican vocal music, in terms of setting standards for what type of canción (or, less frequently, corrido) might or might not make the popularity charts. These standards blurred the distinction between canción romántica and canción ranchera even further: too many songs straddled the imaginary boundary, just as too many other cultural practices blurred the original point of distinction—class.

Lastly, as found in the repertoires of the most popular singers of the late twentieth century—Emilio Navaira, the late Selena, Joe López of Mazz, and others—an inane, saccharine type of love song seemed to dominate musical sensibilities at the *fin de siècle,* to the almost total exclusion of songs with more ideologically charged messages. The predominance of songs with politically neutral messages may be attributable at least in part to the general depoliticization of the masses in the United States and elsewhere at the end of the twentieth century. I defer an examination of this issue to chapter 6, when I shall discuss contemporary Tejano groups at greater length.

Notes

1. See also Burns (1980) for a trenchant analysis of the way country and city, as ideological concepts, intertwined with populist forms of nationalism and elitist notions of "modernization," respectively, to perpetuate a state of "cultural war" in Latin America.

2. For Jameson, the political unconscious is the force of class conflict "driven underground" by the power of capitalist ideology and its utopian ideas (e.g., that every individual is "free" to pursue his or her "dreams"), which constantly banish the reality of class exploitation and inequality from the social consciousness (1981: 280 ff.).

3. Such was not the case in California, however, where female duets, as well as male-female duets, were more in evidence.

4. Compare Malone's remarks on honky-tonk songs: "Songs seldom commented on work, but they spoke often of family fragility, the insecurities of love, marriage dissolution, drinking, and having a good time" (1985:154).

5. However, see Hurston (1935) and Meisenhelder (1996) for accounts of how African American women used folktales "to fight against a subservient role and to

assert their power" (Meisenhelder 1996:267). My own fieldwork on Mexican immigrant folklore suggests that women cultivate a "folklore of feminism" in opposition to men's "folklore of machismo" (see Peña 1991; n.d.).

6. In the late forties and the fifties, my family was part of the migrant stream of cotton pickers who followed the harvest around the state of Texas from about August until November.

7. According to LaCappra, "'Heterodoxia' refers to the objective condition of language marked by a plurality of perspectives and value-laden, ideological practices that are in challenging contact with each other" (1983:312).

8. Much of the study of folklore—indeed, social science generally—in the nineteenth and early twentieth centuries was predicated upon this evolutionary model (see Harris 1968, chs. 6 and 7).

9. *Mole poblano* is a Mexican dish made with chili sauce and other ingredients, such as chocolate or peanut butter.

10. *Tepache* is an alcoholic beverage made from *pulque* (alcohol derived from the maguey plant), pineapple, and cloves.

3 ✤ The Texas-Mexican Conjunto

One of the most culturally powerful regional styles to emerge among Mexicans anywhere is the Texas-Mexican conjunto. My earlier discussion of use-value reaches its full application with the development of this (originally) folk ensemble, which rose to become an eloquent voice for a tejano working-class aesthetic and its ideological underpinnings. From its introduction into Texas-Mexican music sometime in the second half of the nineteenth century, the conjunto's anchor, the accordion, gravitated toward the rural workers, who immediately embraced the instrument and initiated the slow process of stamping a unique working-class tejano identity upon it. The union with the bajo sexto was a stylistic breakthrough, providing the core for a new regional ensemble. When tejano workers migrated to the cities in the twentieth century, they took the embryonic ensemble with them, and in its urban setting the conjunto eventually blossomed into an epochal style.

The history of the Texas-Mexican conjunto can be divided into four distinct stages, or eras, themselves divisible into two broad historical periods. The first period extends roughly from 1870 to World War II and subsumes the first two stages of the conjunto; the second period begins immediately after World War II and persists until the end of the century. Of the stages, or eras, the first begins about 1870 and lasts until the 1920s. We may call this *the diffuse stage,* when the accordion had not yet been subjected to any significant degree of regional stylization, and when no fixed or organized ensemble yet existed. The second era I shall call *the formative stage;* it begins about the time the accordion was swept into the commercial market in the late 1920s, and extends to the end of World War II. This era is dominated by known historical figures, collectively referred to by Narciso Martínez—himself a pivotal accordion stylist—as *la generación vieja,* or the older generation (personal interview, August 3, 1978).

The next stage—what we may call *the "classic" era* of the conjunto—ushers in the second broad historical period of development. It too is dominated by known historical figures, whom Narciso Martínez, again, referred to as *la nueva generación* (the new generation). Its historical boundaries are the late 1940s to about 1970. Lastly, we witness an era of stylistic drift, with both consolidation and decline in evidence. This lasted from about 1970 to the end of the century.

The first part of this chapter will summarize developments during each era. The second part, based on major social differences that emerge between the first and second broad periods, delves into the ethnomusicological aspects of conjunto music—that is, it explores the specific conditions present in the emergence and maturation of the conjunto and seeks an interpretation that will make "intelligible for us why a certain style may have emerged in the social and cultural structure of a given period" (Serauky, quoted in Etzkorn 1973:9). The first part, then, is mostly descriptive, the second interpretive.

The Diffuse Stage

Developments in the nascent accordion ensemble during the nineteenth century have been summarized in chapter 1. Here I need add only that stylistic progress continued at a slow rate during the early part of the twentieth century. It is worth noting, too, that at this early juncture a common performance practice prevailed among accordionists on both sides of the Texas-Mexico border. And, while little documentation exists on the actual musical practices involved in the evolution of the ensemble during the first two decades of the new century, the oldest consultants to this study did recall the course of conjunto music in the late 1910s and subsequent years. Accordionists Narciso Martínez and Pedro Ayala, for example, both born in 1911, had clear recollections of the ensemble and its social context on both sides of the border at the end of the decade of the 1910s.

According to Martínez, Ayala, and other senior consultants, the accordion was first and foremost an instrument employed for dancing, both public and private (as also reported by the *San Antonio Express* and others for the previous century; see chapter 1). As Martínez put it, "Sometimes the accordion was played solo, sometimes with tambora de rancho. By the time I started to play the accordion [in 1927], we were using the bajo sexto more, and sometimes the guitar" (personal interview, August 3, 1978).[1] It is interesting to note that Martínez's first instrument was a two-row button accordion; only later did he graduate to the three-row model. Besides ready availability, Martínez said his initial preference for the smaller model was related to the duration of the dance prior to World War II. As Martínez described it, "You played from dusk to dawn. . . . So, to carry a three-row accordion—they were just too heavy. Now everybody uses the three-row model, but we only play for short periods, with plenty of intermissions, and the microphone helps, too."

Until the 1930s, the accordion and its variable ensemble were still instruments associated with rural life and its celebrations, although by then the music's popularity was growing among a recently urbanized population of workers in towns and cities, such as San Antonio and Corpus Christi. Martínez remembered the accordion as "popular only on the ranches—maybe in the towns, but only in little dances." Besides weddings, (which could last two days, with the dance an all-night affair), the accordion was also popular at *bailes de regalos,* dances at which customs harking back to an earlier era and its principle of use-value mixed with new practices heralding the arrival of social relations based on exchange-value. For example, in a gesture reminiscent of the relations of reciprocity governing earlier modes of production, a man would proffer a woman who agreed to dance with him a gift of candy, sweet bread, or some other edible (N. Martínez interview, August 3, 1978; Dinger 1972). Alternatively, the men purchased gifts with hard currency at rude stalls set up around the dance area by enterprising vendors.

Both Narciso Martínez and Pedro Ayala played for *bailes de regalos* in the 1920s. Interestingly, a contemporary of theirs, Santiago Jiménez (the original "Flaco Jiménez"), who was active musically in San Antonio, was unfamiliar with these "gift dances." Evidently they were not a part of the celebrations of the urbanized Mexicans of the Alamo City. Martínez and Ayala's reports of the *baile de regalos* coincide with that of Adeline Dinger, who called them "sack dances" (1972:36–37): "As was customary for such affairs, the whole family group attended, and for this particular dance the mothers came equipped with roomy sacks, one for each daughter. . . . By the time the pockets of the males were empty, the sacks of the mothers of popular daughters were bulging with several days' supply of sweets, *pasteles,* or pastries, bread and fruits. . . ." (Ibid.).

Another of the early venues for the nascent conjunto was the notorious *baile de negocio,* or "business (taxi) dance," usually held on a dance-platform built of planks adjacent to a cantina—although an area of hard-beaten earth could serve just as well. It appears that the *baile de negocio* was the twentieth-century equivalent of the "fandango house" of the previous era (see chapter 1). Again, this form of "taxi dance" seems to have been most popular in less urbanized areas of South Texas; however, compared with the *baile de regalos,* it was a purer form of capitalistic enterprise, driven as it was by the profit motive. My father, Francisco Peña, born in 1895 in rural South Texas (in the village of Salineño, on the border), attended his share of *bailes de negocio* in the Rio Grande Valley in the years 1910–40. In a taped conversation with me in the summer of 1980, he recalled a cantina in the town of Santa Rosa, run by an enterprising woman named doña Isabel, where "the same Chicho [Narciso] Martínez, *el huracán del valle* [the 'Hurricane from the Valley'], played. And then a bunch of floozies that doña Isabel brought over from the Brownsville area would show up, and things would start to liven up."

The capitalistic nature of the *baile de negocio* is worth exploring further. First, the dance itself seems to have originated in South Texas. At least according to Narciso Martínez, the *baile de negocio* evolved out of the *baile de regalos*—although it seems to have shared some of the ambiance of the nineteenth-century fandango house. Owners of cantinas began building platforms to hold their own dances, which at first followed the custom of the *baile de regalos,* with the owners making their profit by selling food "gifts" to men who in turn offered them to the women in attendance. That practice soon was abandoned, however, in favor of a token *(ficha)* that became the mode of exchange between the male and female dancers. As reported by both Narciso Martínez and Pedro Ayala, the men purchased these tokens at the "gate" for fifteen cents apiece. Each tune they danced cost them a token ("very short" tunes, according to Martínez), which they exchanged with their female partner. At the end of the dance, the women cashed in their tokens, receiving a nickel for each, with the remaining ten cents pocketed by the owner as his or her profit.

The role of women in the *baile de negocio*—the manner in which they earned wages while being exploited for their sexuality—merits discussion. Perhaps mindful of the disrepute in which such dances were held, Martínez tried to put a positive "spin" on their function, claiming they were a perfectly legitimate way for women to work: "This was a way for women to buy their

shoes and other clothes, because in those times women did no other work."
He recalled that, especially during the Depression, poor rural families brought
their daughters to the *bailes de negocio* to earn extra cash to supplement the
families' meager earnings.

That may have been the case, but Pedro Ayala disputed Martínez's observation. Ayala remembered one occasion in particular, when his father (like
don Pedro an accordionist) took his two daughters to a dance that turned out
to be "de negocio." "They started charging the men and giving a nickel to the
women," Ayala recalled. "And my father saw that, and he said, 'Get out of here,
my daughters, and go home to your mother. This dance is not for respectable
people.'" On the other hand, Ayala recognized the economic hardships that
may have forced women to patronize the *baile de negocio:* "The women who
came to these bailes were single women who had no man, who had nothing.
They went to the baile and earned their living there. But, sometimes, after the
dance was over—you know—[they engaged in prostitution]" (personal interview, August 4, 1978).

Throughout this early, diffuse stage, the conjunto was slowly evolving. As
working-class celebrations came to depend more and more on the accordion
ensemble and its affordable music, the musicians themselves experimented
and began to settle on what they perceived to be the best instrumental combinations. As Martínez himself pointed out, "In those times [the 1920s], we
played mostly the accordion by itself, or accordion and tambora de rancho.
But then I began to use the bajo sexto more and more, and then later [the 1930s
and 1940s] the *tololoche* [contrabass] and drums. But in the beginning it was
just the accordion and, sometimes, the tambora."

The repertoire of the conjunto during this stage of development consisted
principally of the salon-music dance genres popular in Mexico and the Southwest during the latter half of the nineteenth century. These included the
most favored genre, the polka, as well as the waltz, redowa, schottishe, and ma-
zurka. A regional dance from northeastern Mexico, the *huapango tamaulipeco,*
rounded out the repertoire. Symbolically the huapango was a key addition, in
that it contributed to the incipient conjunto's strengthening ethnic identity;
but it is important to note, too, that other dance genres were being subjected
to regional stylization. For example, the redowa was being transformed into
a Mexicanized category, having acquired a norteño label by the 1920s—*vals
bajito.* Conjuntos normally did not include vocal music in their dance-music

Figure 5
Narciso Martínez and
Santiago Almeida, 1936.
*Courtesy Arhoolie Records,
El Cerito, Calif., 94530.*

repertoires. By social convention, canciones and corridos were considered inappropriate for dancing—especially at *bailes decentes* ("respectable dances"). This practice did not change until the late 1940s.

The Formative Stage: La Generación Vieja

Narciso Martínez, nicknamed "el huracán del valle" by furniture dealer and talent broker Enrique Valentín, is a pivotal figure in the history of the conjunto (fig. 5). Indeed, more than one conjunto musician referred to him as *el primero*—a sort of "father" to the modern conjunto. Among Texas-Mexicans in the 1930s and a good part of the 1940s, he was indisputably the most popular commercially recording accordionist. Yet, like all the major contributors to the style, Martínez was born and raised at the very bottom of the Texas-

Mexican class structure. Even during the best days of his fifty-year career as an accordionist, he remained a proletarian worker. Except for intermittent periods, such as prolonged tours, he never earned enough to turn professional permanently.

The inability of Martínez and his contemporaries to earn their living from performance had much to do with the regional music market before World War II, and with the manner in which musicians were remunerated. For example, the major labels for which Martínez recorded were nothing short of penurious in their financial dealings with him: he was paid a flat fifteen-dollar "royalty" for each recording he made. This, incidentally, was true of all of Martínez's contemporaries. Yet, even by the 1930s, the old 78-rpm records sold for as much as thirty-five cents, a rather steep price that nonetheless did not deter the Mexicans of the Southwest from buying their share of records, ensuring good profits for the major labels. Here the observations of Mexican anthropologist Manuel Gamio are germane; he spent two years (1926–27) researching the adaptation of Mexican immigrants to the United States. According to Gamio, immigrants returning to Mexico carried with them an average of 1.18 records per person (118 per 100 immigrants), while nearly 22 out of 100 returned to Mexico with phonographs purchased in the United States (Gamio 1971 [1930]:70). We may assume that permanent immigrants and native Mexican Americans purchased these items at the same rate, if not higher.

Born in Matamoros, Tamaulipas, across the river from Brownsville, Martínez crossed the border early, although he never attended American schools. "I know the schools," he said ironically, "because I've played in them. In those years there wasn't the opportunity there is now." In fact, as Santiago Jiménez caustically observed, "the Americans always looked down on the Mexican. . . . They allowed him only a limited time in school" (personal interview, April 30, 1979). Thus, apart from his weekend occupation as accordionist, most of Martínez's adult life was spent toiling in agriculture, although his last working years were spent feeding the animals at the Gladys Porter Zoo in Brownsville.

The path-breaking contribution of "El huracán del valle" to the conjunto style consists of a new technique of accordion playing he introduced, although, in a strict sense, the technique was discovered by default. When he first learned the accordion, Martínez followed the practice of other norteño musicians: he played in what was known as the "German style," which utilized both the melody buttons on the right-hand, treble end and the bass-chord buttons on the left side. This technique made the accordion an ideal solo instrument, because performers could play both melody and accompaniment, eliminating the need for additional instruments.

By the time furniture store dealer Enrique Valentín discovered him in 1936 and introduced him to Bluebird (Victor) Records, Martínez pretty much had settled on the bajo sexto for accompaniment, a role capably filled by his friend, Santiago Almeida. Thanks to the presence of the bajo sexto, by this time Martínez also had switched techniques: he no longer bothered much with the left-hand basses and chords, concentrating instead on the melody end of the accordion. He was leaving the accompaniment almost totally to the bajo sexto. As he reasoned, Almeida provided a solid accompaniment, and the accordion's bass-chord elements seemed to provide nothing more than interference, so he began to do without the left hand.

The resulting sound was markedly different from that of the old "German" accordion. The dense timbre associated with the left-hand basses and chords was replaced by the crisp, treble notes on the opposite side, enhanced by the short, staccato style that Martínez quickly developed, especially evident in his fast-paced polkas, which became a stylistic signature for him (see Arhoolie/Folkyric Records' *Texas-Mexican Border Music* series, volume 10, for representative samples). Of equal importance was the impact Martínez had on other Tejano accordionists (but not on norteños across the border, who preserved the older Germanic style). In time, as Pedro Ayala said, "we all began to copy Narciso. . . . He started to record first, and I used to play the tunes he recorded, just like he had recorded them."[2]

Ayala's deference toward Martínez is important, because it points to an important effect of commercial recording technology on style formation. Before the appearance of the wax disc, stylistic development within the conjunto and other tejano traditions was slow and uneven. This was the result, first, of the slow diffusion of artistic innovation in a community lacking the technology for rapid communication. Second, without formal conservatories, any innovation introduced was subject to unavoidable alteration and distortion as it was transmitted orally from musician to musician, each with his own preconceptions, limitations, and, of course, memory lapses. Thus, while incipiently tejano-norteño styles did exist, these remained diffuse and localized, with no particular technical or instrumental configuration standing as *the* norm for a universal tejano aesthetic.

Recording technology changed all that. Once an identifiable style, such as Martínez's, was recorded for perpetuity and, most important, once it was accepted socially, it became the "master" imprint for others to emulate. Indeed, styles introduced commercially by Martínez and his successors became the germinal material from which música tejana derived its symbolic power. Thus, after the 1920s, most stylistic innovation was disseminated commercially, with headliners like Martínez and Beto Villa leading the way in the conjunto and orquesta traditions, respectively. Local musicians may not have lacked individual creativity, but they were strongly persuaded to follow the stylistic lead of these headliners. We must reiterate, however, that commercialization did not strip the music of its organic character. While innovation originated at the commercial level, community dances remained the sites for the cultural performance of conjunto, where its symbolic charge was continually regenerated. In most instances, local performers were responsible for this regeneration.

Besides Martínez, another notable accordionist from *la generación vieja* was Pedro Ayala, although he never recorded commercially until 1947. As we might expect, his style was reminiscent of Martínez's; however, by 1947 his technique was closer to that of the accordionists of the *nueva generación*. Santiago Jiménez is notable for his introduction of the contrabass to the fledgling conjunto, a stylistic feat he accomplished on his first recording, in 1936. Somewhat removed from the musical scene then unfolding in the Rio Grande Valley, Jiménez never followed Narciso Martínez's lead toward the emphasis on the right hand. His technique consequently remained rooted in the pre-Martínez era. Of lesser importance were such figures as Lolo Cavazos, who displayed considerable virtuosity on some of his best recordings; and José Rodríguez and Jesús Casiano, both popular accordionists who played in the old Germanic style. Rodríguez may be credited for making a bit of history: evidently he was the only accordionist to record commercially with a *tambora de rancho* (see Arhoolie / Folklyric Records, *Texas-Mexican Border Music series,* volume 4).

The Classic Era: La Nueva Generación

The years following World War II, from about 1947 to 1970, mark the classic, or golden, age of conjunto music in Texas, when all the musical elements that lend a powerful identity to the Texas-Mexican ensemble were forged to create a highly recognizable and durable style. It was at this time, also, that the conjunto emancipated itself completely from the norteño ensemble across the border. This was an important development, because in the future the two distinct though related styles would stand as tokens for two different socio-cultural realities—the Texas-Mexican and the norteño. I shall have more to say about this later.

As mentioned previously, World War II ushered in a host of changes in Mexican American society. These changes profoundly affected musical activity, encouraging innovation across the musical spectrum. An important development was the spread of commercialized public dancing, which became far more common than the *baile de regalos* or the *baile de negocio* had been. The latter survived into the early 1950s, but, according to Pedro Ayala, Narciso Martínez, and Armando Marroquín, by 1948 most cantinas had abandoned the practice of paying token-wages to women. Cantina owners apparently discovered that some women were attracted to the cantina anyway and began simply giving women free admission (but not free alcohol—women became consumers like men). The men sometimes were admitted free as well, but sometimes they had to pay an admission charge.

Meanwhile, beginning in 1948, commercial "ballroom" dances became popular, although many actually were held in armories, in Knights of Columbus halls, and even on old-fashioned platforms. This development would have at least one profound consequence for conjunto music (as it did for the orquesta; see chapter 4). After 1948, the most popular commercial conjuntos, especially those associated with the *nueva generación,* were able to rely exclusively on musical performance for their financial support. Ballroom dances sprang up simultaneously in many parts of the Hispanic Southwest in the late forties, and by the end of the fifties a solid network existed, one that extended from South Texas to Sacramento, California, and even included the less hispanicized states of Nebraska, Kansas, and Illinois. Even older performers like Narciso Martínez and Pedro Ayala benefited from the "taco circuit," as one waggish orquesta musician called the chain of ballrooms catering to conjunto dancers. In the 1950s, both accordionists toured extensively enough to stay out of the agricultural fields for prolonged periods.

Besides the ballroom, other types of dance kept conjunto music in general—not simply the headliner groups—financially healthy and dynamic during the forties, fifties, and sixties. I refer to events organized by civic clubs such as *sociedades mutualistas* (fraternal organizations) and, of course, weddings and other domestic celebrations. In sum, a strong demand from both commercial and domestic sources helped to spur the conjunto to experiment boldly during its golden age, thus ensuring its rapid evolution toward maturity. (Sociocultural pressures also contributed, as will be discussed below.)

The recording industry continued to play a key role in providing exposure for the most popular conjuntos. However, a fundamental shift occurred after World War II; the major labels were replaced by local firms such as Falcon, of McAllen, Texas, and Taxco, of Los Angeles, California. No actual documentation exists to explain the big labels' decision to end their operations in the Hispanic Southwest. The war itself had a dampening effect on recording activity, with production coming to a virtual standstill due to petroleum shortages. But when activity picked up at the end of the war, neither RCA Victor, Decca, nor any of the other major companies resumed operations in the Southwest. The various strands of American popular music exploded in the postwar years, and the big labels were, of course, in the vanguard of this development. The enormous profits they reaped from popular music may have discouraged them from pursuing more marginal markets, such the Hispanic Southwest. At the same time, RCA Victor and Columbia, in particular, concentrated their capital on the greater Mexican market, based in Mexico City, and soon began reaping massive profits there. By the end of the 1940s, Mexico City had become the center of commercially recorded music throughout Latin America, and that music was distributed heavily throughout the Hispanic Southwest as well.

Whatever the motive for the major labels' exodus, a vacuum resulted in the regional market of the Hispanic Southwest, a vacuum soon filled by enterprising Mexican Americans like Armando Marroquín, of Alice, Texas. Of his entry into the commercial recording market, Marroquín recalled:

> During the war there were no records—especially records of this [tejano] music from here. I thought, "What can I do?" I went around inquiring, and finally [I bought]—it didn't cost me more than $200—that type of machine that records on the acetate disc. . . . And I worked up the ability [to do my own recordings]. And I discovered that it was better if I could find someone to produce in volume. I found someone in California— Allen Recording, from Los Angeles. The first record that I did was Carmen y Laura, my wife, and then Narciso Martínez. Allen produced 300 records for me. . . . And Paco Betancourt found out about it; he

knew how to distribute, I didn't. He owned Rio Grande Music Company. And, since there was no competition, whatever you came out with was in demand. (Personal interview, January 31, 1980)

As Marroquín accurately observed, since "there was no competition," Ideal quickly rose to undisputed prominence in Texas and other states in the Southwest. We should note, however, in line with the argument set forth in the introduction, that neither Ideal nor any of the other regional companies sprouting throughout the Southwest in the 1940s, 1950s, and later ever monopolized the market or acted as absolute arbiters in matters of musical taste. Neither Armando Marroquín nor any of the other record-company owners in the Southwest ever could have wielded such power. They simply did not have the massive capital needed to control the direction of the market. Even so, they were no strangers to the musical traditions they were promoting commercially.

Consider the cases of Armando Marroquín of Ideal and Manuel S. Acuña of Imperial Records in Los Angeles. Marroquín's initial venture into the recording market can only be described as amateurish; and, although Ideal's position strengthened considerably, it always remained a small-scale operation, compared with giants such as RCA Victor and Columbia. Acuña and Imperial were not much different; like Ideal, Imperial remained a regional company whose capital and profits were constrained by its market. On the other hand, both Marroquín and Acuña were deeply steeped in the musical traditions they were so instrumental in popularizing. The former had been nurtured culturally on the corridos, canciones, and other musical forms embedded in tejano musical culture; and the latter was an accomplished musician and arranger, a man thoroughly familiar with the traditions thriving in the Southwest in the 1940s. Moreover, as artist-and-repertory (A&R) man for Imperial, Acuña wrote arrangements and maintained a "house band" that provided accompaniment for many of Imperial's performers.

In sum, as I argued in the introduction, the Mexican American recording market in the postwar period, and more specifically the Texas-Mexican market, remained in the hands of small-time entrepreneurs intimately involved with local traditions, as these were continually being reworked or invented. More important, innovation was substantially under the control of native artists like Narciso Martínez and (from the new generation of conjunto musi-

Figure 6   Valerio Longoria and conjunto, 1992. *Photo © by Chris Strachwitz c/o Arhoolie Records.*

cians) Valerio Longoria—artists, moreover, who were organically connected to a public eager to embrace the music these homegrown innovators were creating. In short, even within the context of a commercial market, Texas-Mexican music remained a strong cultural symbol. It remained rooted in an ethnic context circumscribed by regional boundaries and by the subordinate position of Texas-Mexicans within American capitalism.

Most responsible initially for launching the golden era of conjunto music was Valerio Longoria, whose innovations in the period immediately following World War II ushered in the most productive stage of the Texas-Mexican conjunto (fig. 6). Longoria was born in 1924, in Kenedy, Texas, not far from San Antonio. Like his predecessors, Longoria began his life mired in the poverty of the Texas-Mexican agricultural worker. His father was a migrant who spent much of his life on the harvest trail, so young Valerio was deprived of a formal education. "I had little school," he once said. "It was too hard on my father [to send me to school]; he would rather take me to work with him."

Despite his poverty, Longoria exhibited musical talent early, learning a few guitar basics by the time he was six. When he was seven, his father bought him his first accordion, a two-row model of the sort popular at the time, and he was launched on his musical odyssey. After a tour with the U.S. Army in Germany at the end of World War II, Longoria returned to Texas and began concentrating his energies on a musical career. He recorded his first cuts in 1948 for the tiny Corona label, but his first real break came when Armando Marroquín lured him to Ideal, where his fee per recording rose from fifteen to twenty dollars. Around 1949, Longoria began to turn out the hits that would establish him as the leader of *la nueva generación*.

Longoria made several key contributions to the rapidly evolving conjunto style of the 1940s. First, he appears to have been the first to introduce the canción to the conjunto repertoire. In the previous era, performers had conformed to an older norm that discouraged vocal music at dances. However, after the war, many of the old norms began to yield to new cultural practices, and in the field of music the inclusion of vocals within the dance context was one such practice. Sensing a new cultural climate, Longoria was the first to adopt sung lyrics, which he (and later others) simply grafted onto the *sine qua non* of conjunto music, the polka, to create a new genre, the *polca-ranchera*. Logically, he simply adapted the old and highly popular duet style to the conjunto, a move that guaranteed its quick acceptance among a receptive younger public.

In addition to adding the canción, Longoria also became the first to incorporate the important Cuban-Mexican bolero into the conjunto repertoire. This was a socially historic accomplishment, since the bolero had remained inaccessible to previous conjunto performers. Its music was simply too complex for the folk performers of an earlier age, and, in any case, as a form of música romántica, it had remained beyond the pale of the música ranchera favored by working-class partisans of conjunto music. As a more sophisticated musician—thanks to his exposure to other musical scenes while in the army—Longoria was familiar with a wider range of musical expression than Martínez and his contemporaries had been, and he was talented enough to assimilate the relatively complex harmony and stylistic nuances of the bolero (see "Lo dudo," on the LP *The Texas-Mexican Conjunto,* volume 24 of *Texas-Mexican Border Music,* Arhoolie/Folklyric Records). In the process, he raised conjunto music to a new level of sophistication, a move important for the ensemble in its ongoing rivalry with its sibling style in Texas, the orquesta. Lastly, Longoria reportedly was the first to integrate the modern drums into the conjunto, an addition that propelled the ensemble toward its final stylistic stage.

Figure 7   Tony de la Rosa with enlarged conjunto, early 1960s. *Courtesy Arhoolie Records, El Cerrito, Calif., 94530.*

Several other conjunto performers contributed in various ways to the stylistic maturation of the ensemble during the 1950s and 1960s. Among these was Tony de la Rosa, from Sarita, Texas, outside Corpus Christi, whose clean staccato articulation in the performance of the polka became the hallmark of the tejano style (see, for example, "Atotonilco," on the LP *The Texas Mexican Conjunto*) (fig. 7). De la Rosa also popularized a much slower polka tempo, dropping the pace from a brisk 130–35 bpm (beats per minute) range of the Martínez style to a relaxed 110–15 bpm. This shift was not entirely accidental; rather, it was de la Rosa's response to a new style of dancing introduced in the San Antonio dance halls around 1948: the uniquely Texas-Mexican *el tacuachito* ("the possum").

El tacuachito was a dance style of cultural importance. Popularized by working-class "social rebels" known as *pachucos* (see Mazón 1984), *el tacua-*

chito diverged radically from earlier tejano dance styles, all of which were variants of the European fashions introduced in the nineteenth century. Unlike the latter's vertical motions—the *pespunteado* (heel-and-toe) steps, as Narciso Martínez described them—*el tacuachito* consisted of the slow and deliberate shuffle of couples gliding counterclockwise around the dance floor. Reminiscent of a possum sauntering across an open field, *el tacuachito* represented an emphatic statement by tejano workers of their aesthetic sense—a sense captured nicely by the possum metaphor, with its evocation of an agrarian life. The slowed-down tempo of the polka and the motions of *el tacuachito* were two symbolic elements critical in stamping a strong ethnic, working-class identity on the whole music-and-dance style of the conjunto. It was, as Paulino Bernal perceptively put it, "a form of class rebellion"—the *pachuco's* "cool" *tacuachito* challenging the "square" dance styles of "high society." After de la Rosa, most conjuntos adopted the slower *tacuachito*-style polka speed.

Another of the performers of note during the classic age of the conjunto was accordionist Rubén Vela, whose group in the late fifties and early sixties epitomized the *tacuachito*-style ensemble, consisting of three-row accordion, bajo sexto (now electrified), electric bass-guitar (which replaced the *tololoche* around 1955), and drums. By Vela's day, singing had become standard practice, usually in the form of the duet. Like other conjuntos of the early 1960s, Vela increasingly depended on the canción ranchera, in *tempo di polka*—the polca-ranchera—as the mainstay of the conjunto, with a few *canciones-huapangos, canciones-boleros,* and *canciones-valseadas* (songs in waltz tempo) included for variety. Except by special request, the genres popular in the days of the preceding generation—the schottishe and redowa—were becoming extinct.

Of all the conjuntos active during the golden era, none contributed as much to its designation as the "classic" stage as El Conjunto Bernal, led by accordionist Paulino Bernal. More than any other group, El Conjunto Bernal took all the elements coalescing around the accordion ensemble in the late 1950s and raised them to a level of technical virtuosity (as defined by conjunto connoisseurs) that remained unsurpassed at the end of the twentieth century. Formed in 1954 by Paulino and his brother, bajo sexto player Eloy, El Conjunto Bernal by 1960 had risen to the pinnacle of the conjunto market. The group remained a potent force in the tradition until the early 1970s, when first Paulino and then Eloy forsook secular for Christian music.

El Conjunto Bernal's distinction as the premier group in the tradition lay above all in the technical mastery that each player achieved. A dance promoter early on advised Paulino: "Distínguete, aunque sea como idiota" ("Distinguish yourself, even if it has to be as an idiot"). He took this advice to heart and practiced long and hard on the three-row button accordion, until, by 1960, he had become the most technically accomplished accordionist in the business. His brother Eloy was equally dedicated to his instrument, and eventually he, too, became the premier bajo sexto player within the tradition. Anchored by these two virtuosos, El Conjunto Bernal was poised to blaze new stylistic trails in the still unfolding tradition. Drawn by the brothers' talent, a steady stream of equally proficient sidemen and singers reinforced the group's prodigious output at the height of its career, the 1960s. Among the drummers, the gifted Armando Peña, who also played with some of the best orquestas in Texas, stands out as a formidable addition. The brothers Solís—bassist Joe and, especially, tenor Manuel—are legendary among conjunto initiates. Also in the 1960s, the capable tenor, Juan Sifuentes, left his mark, as did a young man destined to become known among connoisseurs as an accordionist's accordionist—Oscar Hernández (fig. 8).

El Conjunto Bernal began its rise to fame slowly, when Armando Marroquín signed the Bernal brothers to a "contract" with Ideal in 1954. But it was not until 1958 that the Bernals stunned the conjunto market with their phenomenal hit, the *canción-vals,* "Mi único camino" (heard on the soundtrack of the 1996 film, *Lone Star*). In its three-part harmonies, the song was a trailblazing effort, an obvious attempt on the part of the Bernals to emulate the popular Mexican trios then sweeping the Latin American market: Los Panchos, Los Tres Ases, and others. Three-part harmonies were completely foreign to conjunto music, duets long having been the norm. But three-part singing was only the beginning in a string of innovations tried successfully by El Conjunto Bernal, although the group returned repeatedly to this highly successful experiment.

In the mid-sixties, Paulino switched to the chromatic (five-row) accordion, vastly increasing the melodic flexibility and harmonic range of his group. In 1965, the young Oscar Hernández (also a chromatic accordionist) was enlisted, and in the next year or so El Conjunto Bernal reached the apex of its career, as the group regularly featured accordion duets of considerable sophistication (as in the polka "Idalia"; see the group's LP, *Una noche en la Villita*), as well as three-part canciones sung in polka and vals tempo. Finally, the Bernals expanded the repertoire to include the newly popularized Colom-

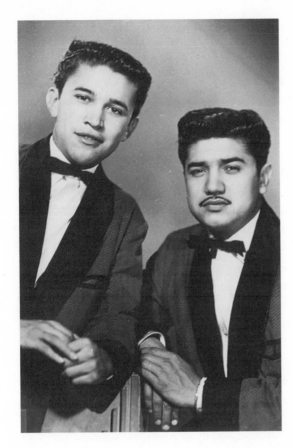

Figure 8
Paulino and Eloy Bernal,
late 1950s. *Courtesy
Arhoolie Records, El
Cerrito, Calif., 94530.*

bian *cumbia,* sophisticated boleros, and, finally, even a few rock-and-roll songs—all indicative of Bernal's desire to break with old traditions and incorporate ever more contemporary styles.

Without question, El Conjunto Bernal was the most commercially successful of the Texas-Mexican conjuntos of the late 1950s and the 1960s. The group drew packed houses of dancers wherever it performed, even in Arizona and California; and its recordings, first with Ideal and later with Paulino's own labels, Bego and Bernal, consistently sold very well by regional standards (twenty thousand units or more).

Yet the Bernals, like most of their predecessors, started out under the harshest of economic conditions. Their parents were divorced when Paulino and Eloy were youngsters; as Paulino recalled, "We lived a life of extreme poverty."

Paulino dropped out of school in the seventh grade, to play and "try and earn some money and get out of the poverty in which we lived." But perseverance and talent eventually propelled the Bernals to the pinnacle of conjunto music, and after 1958 they never returned to the cotton and cucumber fields to earn their living. More than that, as orquesta leader Tony "Ham" Guerrero stated, "El Conjunto Bernal was the greatest conjunto of all time" (personal interview, March 28, 1993).

Meanwhile, the 1960s witnessed significant changes in the norteño ensemble across the border. Beginning with a group organized by bajo sexto player Cornelio Reyna and accordionist Ramón Ayala in 1965, Los Relámpagos del Norte, norteño ensembles began to assimilate many of the technical innovations of their Texas-Mexican counterparts, including drumming techniques and formulas and, most important, the basic conjunto accordion style. Ramón Ayala, who developed into a formidable accordionist, was particularly influenced by Paulino Bernal. Many of his "licks" are reminiscent of the latter's own stylistic innovations. Indeed, Bernal discovered Los Relámpagos in 1964, in a cantina in the border city of Reynosa, while he was on a talent search for a record company he and a partner had just launched, Bego Records (Bernal interviews, May 8 and 9, 1980). Los Relámpagos skyrocketed toward unparalleled fame in a few short years, its popularity eclipsing even that of El Conjunto Bernal, especially since they did what no Texas-Mexican conjunto ever was able to do—garner followings on both sides of the border.

Toward the mid-seventies, Reyna and Ayala went their separate ways, and the latter then organized Los Bravos del Norte, a group that went on to dominate the norteño/conjunto market for over ten years. An advantage Los Bravos, Los Relámpagos, and other norteño groups held over tejano conjuntos was their freedom to play on both sides of the border. American laws were lax enough to allow them to tour the Southwest "taco circuit," while the Texas-Mexican groups were strictly prohibited by Mexican customs agents from entering Mexico with their instruments. This inequity bred strong resentment among tejano groups, but until the North America Free Trade Agreement (NAFTA) was signed in 1994, the Mexican market remained almost inaccessible to the conjuntos and other groups based in Texas and elsewhere in the Southwest.

Restrictions on Texas-Mexican conjuntos notwithstanding, norteño groups after Los Relámpagos were undeniably indebted to their tejano counterparts, even if indirectly, by way of the enormous influence Los Relámpagos exerted over all other norteño groups that followed in its path. However, in the Monterrey area, a style combining accordion and alto saxophone, popular since the 1950s, continued to enjoy enormous popularity on both sides of the border. (The accordion-saxophone combination was tried in Texas in the 1940s by both Pedro Ayala and Narciso Martínez, but it never took hold.)

In the 1970s a new norteño group, Los Tigres del Norte, began seriously to challenge Ayala's Los Bravos del Norte, eventually supplanting the latter as the premier group in the norteño market. Los Tigres and another renowned norteño ensemble, Los Humildes (Humble Ones), owed a great deal, stylistically, to Los Bravos, but in time they developed a unique norteño style that became the norm for all similar groups. While maintaining certain affinities with the Texas-Mexican conjunto—most notably the traditional four-instrument combination—the new norteño style was quite distinct, particularly evident in the much more nasalized style of singing that was strongly reminiscent of older norteño groups, such as Los Alegres de Terán. In short, Los Tigres came to epitomize a working-class Mexican aesthetic. Highly visible on both sides of the border, the norteño style eventually dwarfed the Texas-Mexican conjunto in popularity, especially outside Texas and among the tide of immigrants that flooded the Southwest after 1980.

The Era of Consolidation and Decline

Within the Texas-Mexican conjunto tradition, the seventies, eighties, and nineties marked a period of consolidation and decline, as many of the stylistic elements of the classic era—now considered "the tradition"—were worked and reworked into a less and less dynamic style. As Pedro Ayala understood it, the conjunto had been perfected ("Se perfeccionó el estilo"), and people demanded a pause after the feverish activity in the final years of its development, especially the 1960s. Paulino Bernal admitted as much when he recalled what happened when El Conjunto Bernal tried to go beyond the "traditional style": "It got to the point that many people didn't accept what we were doing; they didn't accept us because the music was too advanced" (Bernal interview, May 8, 1980).

In sum, like all major styles (that is, those considered solutions to the problems of an age), the conjunto reached its cultural limits in the three-part harmonies and in the less complicated efforts of El Conjunto Bernal's dual chromatic accordions. Beyond that, further experimentation, such as rock and roll, jazzed-up polkas, and complex polyphonic dual-accordion melodies, was rejected. Such experimentation lacked the ranchero flavor—*la alegría,* as people would say—that was so essential in defining the limits of the style, and it was soon abandoned. As Bernal observed, in order to survive, El Conjunto Bernal "was forced to play more polkas, more huapangos, and fewer boleros." After the 1960s, every conjunto was subjected to those culturally imposed limits.

It was in this conservative climate that conjuntos competed after 1970. Bucking the trend could be disastrous, as the brilliant maverick, Esteban Jordán, discovered. The most experimental of the accordionists after Paulino Bernal (and perhaps ever), Jordán was a master of synthesis, fusing a wide range of disparate musical styles, from jazz and rock to ranchero, to create arresting hybrids (see his LP *Steve Jordan,* Freddie Records) (fig. 9). Throughout the 1980s and 1990s, however, he remained a marginal performer, a sort of cult figure revered by sophisticated initiates but ignored by the masses of working-class conjunto lovers. Frustrated by the lack of appreciation accorded his music, he complained to me in the summer of 1980 that conjunto music had reached a dead end. "No le cambian, bro," he said in exasperation, "el

Figure 9   Steve Jordan, early 1990s. *Photo © by Chris Strachwitz c/o Arhoolie Records.*

mismo sonsonete—nta, nta, nta ("They don't change, bro, the same sing-song—nta, nta, nta"), referring to the standardized polka accompaniment of the bass and drums.

Meanwhile, a less musically adventurous but nonetheless innovative accordionist of the 1970s and 1980s was Santiago Jiménez's son, Leonardo Jiménez—the new "El Flaco" Jiménez. In his own modest way, El Flaco Jiménez moved the conjunto in a new direction—if not stylistically, at least commercially. He is the one conjunto performer most responsible for what some music market observers call "crossing over"—introducing marginal music such as conjunto to a wider audience and thereby increasing their own and the music's exposure.[3] Teaming up with country performer Ry Cooder, El Flaco became a musical ambassador of sorts; his name is well known in certain pop music circles as the man who brought conjunto music to the attention of Anglo-Americans and even Europeans. Although he was not the first to attempt it, he is known for having popularized the fusion of conjunto and country-western styles. In the 1980s, El Flaco was further involved in the union of country and conjunto, this time through his collaboration with Freddie Fender, Doug Sahm, and Augie Meyers in a modestly successful group, the Texas Tornados.

In the 1980s, tejano music once again came under the influence of the big labels (WEA, Sony, Capitol-EMI, Arista), and many conjuntos were signed to contracts. I shall defer a discussion of the major labels' impact on tejano music until chapter 6. Here I want to emphasize only that Sony and the other major recording companies undoubtedly introduced a global-market mentality to the hitherto regional strategies of the tejano circuit. Under the prodding of major-label executives, the marketing of conjunto music took on more of the trappings of large-scale commodity production. In brief, for commercial purposes—that is, improved audience targeting—conjunto was split into two branches, the "traditional" and the "progressive."

The traditional branch consisted of groups that continued to till the well-cultivated ground of Bernal, de la Rosa, and others dating from the golden era. This branch seems to have been targeted at older buyers, who might identify most strongly with the older style. Conjuntos included in this group were Rubén Naranjo, popular in the late 1970s and 1980s, and La Tropa F and Los Chamacos, popular in the 1990s. A long-time performer left his special stamp on the traditional conjunto of the 1990s—Mingo Saldívar, who, with his group Las Cuatro Espadas, launched a virtual revival of the old-time style. But he did it with a difference. First, unlike latter-day conjuntos, he remained a self-promoter, a performer who never fully caught the attention of the big labels. Second, as folklorist Pat Jasper observed in the documentary film, *Songs of the Homeland,* in his playing style and gyroscopic movements on stage, Saldívar represented the most expressive approach to conjunto performance ever attempted. His style, traditional yet vibrant, transformed him into a folk-music icon in the tejano community and even beyond, as his performances at the Clinton inauguration and Carnegie Hall attested—not to mention his enormous popularity in the area around Monterrey, Mexico.

The progressive conjuntos were considered a modified version of the conjunto, although, like the modern Tejano groups, they relied more extensively on the synthesizer, a latter-day substitute for the accordion. The first of the "progressive conjuntos" (albeit never recognized as such) undoubtedly was Cha Cha Jiménez's Los Chachos, a group from the seventies whose members at one time or another had played with El Conjunto Bernal. Those most active in the eighties and nineties include David Lee Garza y los Musicales, and Emilio Navaira and the Rio Band. Since Navaira became a true commercial icon, and since his music transcended the conjunto tradition, merging with the modern Tejano sound and even country-western, his impact on and contributions to Texas-Mexican musical culture will be examined more closely in chapter 6.

Regardless of their designation and perhaps because of the commodity mentality introduced by the big labels, all of the latter-day conjuntos relied on the time-tested polca-ranchera, still performed very much in the manner of El Conjunto Bernal, which had forged its basic style. Moreover, despite the endless possibilities offered by synthesized accordion sound, the progressive conjuntos stuck to certain melodic and rhythmic formulas established by groups of the golden era. This conservatism may have been a response to the same aesthetic limitations faced by El Conjunto Bernal—the need, as Cha Cha Jiménez put it, to "play everyday music" (personal interview, May 28, 1980).

In their eagerness to "stay with the people"—or perhaps because of the "play-it-safe" strategy preferred by major producers—the conjuntos of the eighties and nineties simplified harmonies greatly, in comparison to the rather bold efforts of El Conjunto Bernal; solo or simple duet singing, in parallel thirds, remained the norm. In the 1990s, the basic polka beat was slowed further, to as few as 100 beats per minute. The one component of the conjunto that became more prominent was the drums. A stronger presence was pre-ferred by most conjuntos, and drummers of the nineties engaged in more heavily emphasized rolls and flourishes than those of the sixties and seventies, with the exception of Armando Peña, whose drumming technique remained unexcelled.

In sum, the best assessment of the conjuntos of the late twentieth century, as compared with those of the golden era, is that advanced recording tech-nologies, such as digital audio technology (DAT), made for a clearer and per-haps cleaner sound. But in musicological terms—with regard to harmonic, melodic, and rhythmic complexity—none approached the trail-blazing ex-periments of El Conjunto Bernal or even Los Bravos del Norte, when that group reached its zenith in the late 1970s.

Social and Commercial Aspects of Conjunto: Organic Symbol or Superorganic Commodity?

It is symptomatic of the total penetration of the capitalist system into the heart of Texas-Mexican culture that conjunto music should reach final matu-rity only after it had been converted into a marketable commodity. Like all commodities, in its commercialized form the conjunto was susceptible to the reifying effects of exchange-value—that is, the tendency of commodities to become fetishized objects of individualized consumption limited in their capacity to transmit vital cultural communication. Yet it would be a mis-take to think of conjunto as simply another commodity being hawked by commercial peddlers for the sake of profit. That it partook of the life of com-modities is undeniable, especially in the 1990s, but commercialization never succeeded in dislodging it from its position as an organic symbol of working-class tejano life.

Clearly, Armando Marroquín, Arnaldo Ramírez (Falcon Records), and other small-time capitalists were highly conscious of the profit potential of conjunto and other musical genres of the Southwest, and much of their en-ergy was spent in maximizing return on their investments. Indeed, as an old acquaintance and neighbor of Marroquín, piano-accordionist Reymundo Treviño, once observed about Ideal's financial practices vis-à-vis its artists, "Marroquín didn't want to pay anybody anything" (personal interview, March 14, 1980). Yet like Ramírez, Marroquín had as much an ideological as an economic stake in the survival of tejano music. One suspects Ramírez—cosmopolitan that he was—even shared the views of those who, as he remarked once, considered conjunto music *una porquería* (a pig's mess; personal interview, March 27, 1980). However, he also had an intimate understanding, as did Marroquín, of the powerful ideological currents that underpinned the music and steered its stylistic direction. As tejanos deeply involved in the ethnic traditions of their people, Ramírez and Marroquín could not help identifying with those traditions.

However much petty bourgeois entrepreneurs like Marroquín and Ramírez might disdain the "low-class" origins of the conjunto, as members of the subordinate Mexican minority they were wholly sympathetic to the voice of ethnic-class reaffirmation encoded in the conjunto. Like the middle-class jest tellers in Américo Paredes's famous article, "Folk Medicine and the Intercultural Jest" (1993c), who could be quite condescending in their criticism of working-class Mexican folk beliefs, these entrepreneurs shared an enduring resentment against Anglos, whose enterprise they might admire but who they knew harbored a sense of cultural superiority toward them and their people—regardless of class status. Their interest in promoting the music, then, no matter how driven by economic self-interest, was heavily encumbered by their ideologically motivated allegiance to an art form deeply rooted in their ethnic culture.

We can well understand, then, Marroquín's own ambivalence toward the cultural value of the conjunto. On the one hand, he could dismiss the conjunto of yesteryear *("de más antes")* as "cantina music." He recalled: "Well, really, when the conjunto started, what supported that music was the cantinas. All the groups at that time hung out in 'rat traps'—the lowliest cantinas." And, he added, "Heaven forbid that they would be hired for a society dance." Yet, in a moment of reflection, Marroquín waxed lyrical about his own love for the music of his youth—music no different, really, from the early conjunto: "Ever since I was a kid I liked the music, to listen to the records of the 1920s—corridos like 'Benjamín Argumedo,' 'Gregorio Cortez,' 'Jacinto Treviño'" (Marroquín interview). His favorites were the vocal duets, Gaytán y Cantú, and Rocha y Martínez. These groups were, of course, most strongly supported by the same people who patronized the "lowliest cantinas" and the conjunto—namely, the tejano working class.

Historically, then, conjunto music may have been assimilated into the network of commodities that increasingly mediate social relations in capitalist society, but that assimilation never was complete, in the sense that conjunto never became part of the large-scale, transnational "flow" of musical commodities (Robinson et al. 1991) and thus never lost its status as an organic symbol of working-class, tejano life. It was at once a commodity *and* an expression driven by the principle of use-value. As such it could be commercialized and transacted by people wholly immersed in all the exploitive practices of capitalism—practices for which Marroquín certainly was notorious. But on the flip side of exchange-value was use-value—the dogged refusal of conjunto's clientele to relinquish its organic function—its power to speak to the core elements of a tejano working class struggling to preserve its cultural identity. Marroquín and other entrepreneurs were acutely aware of this power, because they were no strangers to its cultural dynamics.

Thus there can be no doubt that, as an emblem of a working-class, tejano cultural identity, the conjunto was intensely subjected to culturally communicative work—especially as an adjunct to the dance. In separate interviews, orquesta leader Carlos González (July 7, 1980) and Arnaldo Ramírez (March 27, 1980) of Falcon Records used identical language to describe the accordion—*"un instrumento del pueblo,"* an instrument of the working-class folk. Moreover, as perhaps *the* central icon of a tejano working-class aesthetic, the conjunto inevitably was caught up in the ideological warfare between Anglos and Texas-Mexicans, as it had been since the nineteenth century. But in the second half of the twentieth century, a new element appeared to augment the conjunto's cultural firepower—internecine class antagonism and its resultant rivalries. In short, the conjunto became a wedge between working-class and middle-class tejano ideologies.

Armando Marroquín's comments on the "rat traps" that were the conjunto's original social base and on its exclusion from "society" dances have been cited above. These comments alert us, at the very least, to those status differences within Texas-Mexican society that are symbolized by the conjunto. We have only to recall the socioeconomic position of the leading conjunto performers, each of them, from Narciso Martínez to Mingo Saldívar, at one time or another victims of the poverty endemic to the tejano working class. To this evidence of the conjunto's strong association with that class, we may add the comments of several individuals intimately familiar with the music and its social context.

We may begin with a figure central to the evolution of the conjunto and its aesthetic shape—Paulino Bernal. Keenly aware of the political underpinnings of the style, as it defined an "esoteric" group strongly attached to the conjunto, versus an "exoteric" group that favored the rival style of the orquesta (Jansen 1965), Bernal clearly recalled the class antagonism inscribed in the music during the years of its pinnacle. "Mira," emphasized Bernal, "había una división, que el que le gustaba la orquesta, odiaba al conjunto" ("Look, there was a division, in that whoever liked the orquesta hated the conjunto") (personal interview, May 8, 1980). In a subsequent interview (May 9, 1980), Bernal and I explored this critical observation further:

MP: My impression is that the people [Texas-Mexicans] who aspired to be more "Americanized," or more "Anglicized," looked upon the conjunto with disapproval. Would you agree with this? Can you tell me your own feelings?

PB: Well, there was always among *la raza*—among Chicanos—what we used to call, "No, man, you think you're really 'high society.'" That is, there was a class of people among the Chicanos who were higher up and who wanted to live like the Americans, and to live better. Of course, they had already reached a particular position— higher economically. And then there was still a lot of *raza* that was still arriving [from Mexico] and with much—struggling all the way. So there *was* a division, and that's where not only the social or economic position was divided, but the musical position was divided as well—that of the orquesta and that of the conjunto.

Mindful, however, of the basic contradiction facing the upwardly mobile tejanos—their view of themselves as "high society" in the face of the Anglos' view of them as plain "Mexicans"—Bernal offered a rather sophisticated assessment of the complex relationship between the Texas-Mexican classes, as played out in the relationship between the conjunto and orquesta. The following dialogue emerged as we explored some of the contradictions involved in the emergence of the orquesta, especially those related to its reluctance to emancipate itself completely from the ranchero aesthetic epitomized by the conjunto:

MP: We were agreeing that, when the orquesta emerged, it did so as a result of certain aspirations held by a particular group of tejanos; but isn't it true that in the course of time the orquesta drew closer in style to the conjunto? Isn't it true that many times orquestas play a lot of the same kind of music that conjuntos do?

PB: Yes.

MP: How can you explain that?

PB: Well, eventually a new trend came in [within the orquesta] that succeeded tremendously—at the time of Sunny and the Sunliners, and all that. They had an orquesta style, with the instruments of the orquesta, but at the same time they gave their music the flavor of the conjunto. Not so Balde González [a "high-society" orquesta]; there was a lot of difference between him and the Sunglows [Sunliners]. Today the orquesta style is very close to that of the conjunto. But that's because another generation came in. But the division was always there [in earlier times]. There have always been those two classes among *la raza,* the Chicanos—the class that aspires to live more Americanized, and the other that is always poorer, more working—like migrant workers, or—and then there's so many people who are arriving from Mexico. . . . And the former, since their social class is higher, they seem to dislike conjunto music. They looked for something else; they wanted something else. And instead of going over to American music completely—well, Sunny and the Sunliners and Little Joe arrived, giving them some American and some Chicano, including the accordion.

I shall have more to say about Bernal's brilliant assessment of orquesta music in chapters 4 and 5. Here it is sufficient to note that, while the conjunto represented an artistic expression solidly grounded in a working-class aesthetic with strong ideological overtones (tejano *"raza"* against a pretentious "high society"), the orquesta was much more ambivalent in its politico-aesthetic position. This ambivalence was a result of its constituents' own contradictory position in the tripartite opposition between Anglos and Texas-Mexicans and, among the latter, between upwardly mobile and working-class sectors. The conjunto's constituency, meanwhile, remained much more resistive toward the constant pressure Anglos applied on tejanos and other subordinate minorities to Americanize and to conform to Anglo "mainstream" norms. The culturally resistive stance of the conjunto and its exponents is related strongly to their class position, which was marked by oppression, an (at least incipient) sense of class, and an explicit sense of ethnic solidarity.

Roberto Pulido, long-time leader of a hybrid tejano group that successfully synthesized the orquesta and conjunto styles, understood perfectly the connection between class and musical preference and its articulation through the conjunto and the orquesta: "The orchestra has always catered to a little bit more educated crowd, *más—se creían más chingones* [more—they thought of themselves as more big-shot], money-wise and every-wise. *Y el conjunto no, el conjunto siempre* [but not the conjunto, the conjunto always] it caters to *la gente más chingoteada, la gente más olvidada* [the most ass-busted people, the most forgotten people]" (personal interview, April 2, 1980).

Pulido's statements were echoed by Martín Rosález, Jr., a disk jockey with a long and distinguished career in tejano radio. "The accordion's public is the worker, the most humble people." And, in an afterthought that accommodated the Marroquíns and Ramírezes of Texas-Mexican society, he added, "But, curiously, there are doctors, lawyers and other people of position who remember their roots, and who love the scandal [that conjunto is]" (personal interview, March 20, 1980). However, reminding us once more of the gulf historically separating "people of position" from the mass of the workers and their music is the blunt statement offered by Arnaldo Ramírez: "In earlier times, to mention the accordion to people of position was like calling their mother a name" (Ramirez interview, March 27, 1980).

In the rivalry played out between the conjunto and the orquesta tejana, then, an incipient class conflict was mediated. Naturally, the conjunto aligned itself with the working class in its ideological squabble with the middle class. At issue was the latter's perceived willingness to embrace the whole process of Americanization. Of course, the labyrinthine workings of the hegemonic capitalist system, as peculiarly wrought by Anglo-American ideology, was seeping into every corner of tejano society in the postwar period, undermining in subtle ways even the most resistive of tejano traditions, including the conjunto. But, as is perhaps true of all hegemonic systems, American capitalism was not capable of eradicating all native forms of cultural resistance. Thus, as writers as varied as Antonio Gramsci (1971), Raymond Williams (1977), Dominick LaCappra (1983), and M. M. Bakhtin (1986) have proposed in their respective contexts, Anglos and tejanos coexisted in a "dialogic," or "heteroglossic," state of cultural communication, wherein the marginalized discourse of the tejanos could and did contest the legitimacy of the hegemonic discourse of the Anglos. And the conjunto was a key voice within the crosscurrents of that dialogic, intercultural discourse; refusing to yield to commodification and exchange-value, it played its own use-value role in the "war of position" waged by the Texas-Mexicans.

Conjunto and the Chicano Movement: From Cantina Trash to Cultural Treasure

Among Mexican Americans of the Southwest, the late 1960s witnessed the emergence of a more or less coherent ideology of ethnic revivalism known as the Chicano movement. The nature and impact of this movement are explored more extensively in chapter 5, but there is no doubt the movement had a profound effect on the class and cultural status of the conjunto (and norteño music generally). As a local manifestation of an ideology known as romantic, or cultural, nationalism (Wilson 1973, Cabral 1979), the Chicano movement was defined by the intense search for "roots," in the form of an essentialized reaffirmation and exaltation of selected cultural elements seen as constituting the core of Mexican Americans' history and identity. Not surprisingly, all the "core" elements identified by movement activists turned out to have a rural, folk character, although many of these elements had been transformed in the twentieth century into urbanized working-class expressions.

To accommodate the working-class base of Chicanos' "roots," the movement adopted a powerfully homogenizing ideology that basically negated class differences. Under the influence of this nationalist ideology, class differences among Mexican Americans were temporarily repressed, while ethnic brotherhood—Chicanismo—was celebrated. (Sisterhood generally was ignored in the machistic ideology of Chicanismo.) In this climate of ethnic reaffirmation and reawakened pride in cultural "roots," the conjunto was transformed dramatically from cantina trash to cultural treasure. After about 1970, this music was viewed as the legitimate expression of a working class never alienated from its "roots"—a music that all self-respecting Chicanos should learn to value. Class snobbery no longer constituted a legitimate reason for spurning the conjunto, since ethnic pride must override all other considerations. In any case, snobbery was a function of the Anglo status system and, like all things Anglo, must give way to the solidarity of Chicanismo.

By the mid-seventies, then, the conjunto and norteño music generally had become an enduring symbol of "Chicano" culture, although its typical context remained, as always, the working-class celebration, whether in the cantina, the wedding, or the public dance. Except for its prominent inclusion in nationalistic events, such as *"Raza* days" on college campuses (especially as a component of *folklórico* dance groups), the conjunto never made much headway in the celebrations of Chicanos not of the working class, especially outside Texas.

It is somewhat ironic that, at the very moment when the conjunto was attaining legitimacy outside its working-class base, its capacity for further innovation reached a seemingly insurmountable barrier. Whether the conjunto's legitimation outside its traditional context contributed to its stylistic "freeze" (and consequent decline) is an open question. Clearly, once the ensemble's aesthetic function became blurred—once it lost its class-based identity—its ideological edge was diffused, as the conjunto came to symbolize the romantic politics of Chicanismo. On the other hand, the intense creativity and innovation that marked the conjunto's ascent, from the late forties to about 1970, could not continue indefinitely. As Pedro Ayala suggested, the four-person ensemble, as personified by El Conjunto Bernal, Tony de la Rosa, and others, was considered by tejanos as the ideal vehicle for the ranchero, *alegre* sound they held so dear. "Así es como le gustaba a la gente y aún les gusta" ("that was how people liked it and how they still like it") was don Pedro's final assessment.

In short, one may argue that by 1970 the conjunto sound had been "perfected." As far as its constituents were concerned, any further alterations, especially drastic ones incorporating foreign elements like jazz, were suspect and likely to be rejected. After all, the conjunto was the creation of a culturally conservative people—a working-class tejano community in no headlong rush to embrace the process of Americanization and its modernizing influences. On the contrary, this community was highly selective in its acculturation and did not hesitate to resist cultural or political forms that went against the grain of its deeply held sense of ethnic and class identity.

As a rapidly evolving style, the conjunto thus was a mediative artistic form. In a world of dramatic social transformation, this form itself was an agent of change—but change controlled by working-class performers and their public. Even as it evolved, it never was in any danger of losing the ethnic, working-class identity assigned to it by its creators. By 1970, however, both musical and social transformation had run their course—at least for the moment. When the Chicano movement appropriated the music for its own ideological purposes, it did so after innovation had been exhausted and the style's identity had been fixed. In sum, both as a class-based expression and as an icon of romantic nationalism, the conjunto had attained a timeless quality.

Events in the 1990s contributed to the preservation of the status quo reached in the 1970s. Despite spectacular visual changes—what orquesta veteran René Sandoval called "the MTV effect" (personal interview, May 3, 1993)—the style itself remained rather static, with only the slower tempo and more aggressive drumming distinguishing it from its predecessor. No doubt the intense commercialization of performers like Emilio Navaira heightened what Robinson, Buck, and Cuthbert call "the inherent contradiction between a global economy and local cultural autonomy" (1991:3)—that is, the old tension between use-value and exchange-value inherent in a cultural form that is both a commodity and an organic symbol. Despite intensified commercialization, however, the music remained rooted in what was still a working-class tejano aesthetic sensibility. As a legacy of the Chicano movement, it continued to be perceived romantically as music of the "roots." Chapter 6 has more to say about conjunto and its commercialization in the 1990s. Here I propose that, at the end of the twentieth century, the conjunto had become, at least in the minds of its adherents, a timeless music—seemingly without beginning and without end.

Notes

1. Quotations from Narciso Martínez also come from two other interviews, held on November 4, 1978, and February 2, 1979. The translations are mine; he spoke little English.

2. Actually, the honor of the first accordion recording belongs to Bruno Villarreal—"el azote del valle" ("the Scourge of the Valley")—who recorded for Okeh (Columbia) in 1928.

3. See chapter 6 for another version of the term "crossover."

4 ❧ The Orquesta Tejana

If the conjunto speaks historically to the politico-aesthetic interests of the Texas-Mexican working class, the orquesta from early on represented the musical aesthetics of an upwardly mobile group espousing an ideology of acculturation or, more precisely, biculturation. This group—what we justifiably may call a middle class, no matter how minuscule initially—originated in the late nineteenth century and consisted of a small group of merchants, ranchers, professionals, and the few white-collar workers to be found in business and government at the time. This middle-class sector seems to have aspired toward an accommodation with its Anglo-Texan antagonists, who were not altogether averse to such an accommodation, as scattered comments by Anglo chroniclers indicate (see Montejano 1987). It was in connection with the celebrations of this class that we find the first mention of the orquesta (see chapter 1 of this book).

In a rough parallel to the conjunto, the orquesta in Texas (and in the Hispanic Southwest generally) went through several evolutionary stages, each stage marked by certain instrumental combinations and their respective stylistic characteristics. However, unlike the conjunto, which tejanos constructed from the ground up, so to speak, the orquesta always had ready-made models to imitate, in both the United States and Mexico. In both countries, orchestral ensembles, ranging from full symphonic units to brass bands and minimal string groups, were common in the latter half of the nineteenth century, and the tejanos inevitably were influenced by these ensembles. Thus the unique characteristics of the orquesta, particularly as these acquired a strong tejano identity after World War II, never were tied to any indigenous instrumental configuration, as the conjunto was. Rather, the uniqueness of the orquesta lies in its stylistic inventions—inventions that stamped a powerful *bimusical* identity on the ensemble. As we shall see, this identity mirrored, at the level of musical expression, the ideological structures underpinning the *bicultural* identity of the middle-class Texas-Mexicans who forged the orquesta tejana.

The next two chapters approximate the organizational pattern of the chapter on the conjunto. The first reviews the stylistic evolution of the orquesta from the late nineteenth century to the 1960s. We begin with groups active from the 1880s through the 1920s, when the first orquestas were captured on wax disc. The most prominent of these were string (violin) ensembles, or *orquestas de cuerda;* consequently almost all of the first recordings were of these orquestas. The orquesta entered a second stage of development around 1930, when the first of the modern urban groups, patterned after the big American swing bands and comprised purely of wind instruments, were organized. At this time the string ensembles began to fade, and they had virtually disappeared by the onset of World War II.

The year 1947 marks an important turning point in the evolution of the orquesta in Texas. It was then that Beto Villa, the "father" of a properly native orquesta tejana, recorded his first tunes. The style Villa inaugurated—what we might call the "Tex-Mex ranchero" variant of the polca-ranchera—became the signature for the third and, to that point, by far the most important stage in the evolution of a Texas-Mexican orquesta. More important, Villa exerted enormous influence over countless epigones, not only in Texas but throughout the Hispanic Southwest.

The final stage in the evolution of an orquesta tejana style and its political aesthetic was launched in the late 1960s by Little Joe and the Latinaires. This final and most important stage came to be known as *La Onda Chicana,* and it constitutes the pinnacle of the orquesta tradition in Texas. During this period, which lasted for about ten years, a truly synthesizing bimusical style was forged. Like Beto Villa, Little Joe and the Latinaires (renamed Little Joe y la Familia in 1970) blazed a trail that was followed by lesser imitators all across the Southwest. Despite the popularity of la Onda Chicana, however, by 1985 the orquesta was in sharp decline. Except for localized groups, it had disappeared from the commercial market by the mid-nineties. The development of the orquesta during the Onda Chicana phase is rich in ideologically symbolic significance; therefore the whole of chapter 6 is devoted to examining its development and, especially, its role in promulgating the ideology of Chicanismo.

As was the case with the conjunto, chapters 5 and 6 methodically explore two key ethnomusicological questions: What is the cultural significance of the orquesta tradition in Texas? What led to its ascent and then to its precipitous decline so soon after reaching its pinnacle under the banner of la Onda Chicana? As I indicated above, the rise of the orquesta is inextricably linked to the emergence of a middle, or at least an upwardly aspiring, class and its sometimes conflictive relationship with the working class (see Paulino Bernal's statements in chapter 3 of this book). The orquesta's decline is a bit more difficult to explain, but it can be attributed to three factors: a transforming cultural economy and its consumption patterns; the decline in influence of the two "generations" (the Mexican American and the Chicano; see M. García 1989) that nurtured the orquesta; and a general drift in the politics of musical aesthetics in Texas and the rest of the Southwest.

Of foremost importance for the rise of the Texas-Mexican orquesta and the bimusical style that certified its originality was the continuing conflict between Anglos and Texas-Mexicans, regardless of the latter's class status. In a nutshell: What I earlier labeled the dialectic of conflict between Anglos and Texas-Mexicans was in the slow and tortuous process of mediation in the 1930s, 1940s, and 1950s, and upwardly mobile Texas-Mexicans found themselves caught on the horns of a dilemma. On the one hand, they desired to acculturate, to become more American; but, facing continuing discrimination by Anglos, they had no choice but to defend their Mexican culture and in the process to retreat closer to the position of the tejano working class. Yet, middle-class tejanos did not particularly want to be identified with their working-class peers, and a seemingly endless struggle ensued, in which these Texas-Mexicans vacillated between acculturation and resistance—between a Mexican and an American identity. They ended up advocating a dual identity and its attendant ideology of biculturalism. More than any other form of expressive culture, the orquesta eloquently voiced this ambivalent, dual identity.

The Early Orquestas

The early orquestas were treated briefly in chapter 1. Since the historical record relating to orchestral ensembles among Texas-Mexicans of the nineteenth century is sketchy at best, any further elaboration on the early ensembles necessarily must be incomplete and conjectural. Nonetheless, based on the available information, we can glimpse the salient musical features and sociocultural attributes of early groups. It is worth reiterating that fully equipped orquestas were uncommon among Texas-Mexicans until the 1920s. This had to do with the socioeconomic makeup of the society; as noted in chapter 1, training opportunities were severely limited. There were exceptions, however, especially as trained musicians from Mexican cities such as Monterrey and Chihuahua migrated northward to Texas. One of these exceptions was the city of El Paso.

Early on—certainly no later than the 1890s—El Paso's economy had diversified enough to enable the local Mexicans to engage in reasonably well-organized musical activity. According to the historian Mario García, Mexican orquestas (or "bands," as they often were called) were active in El Paso by 1893, at the very latest, when one Santiago Olguín Loredo advertised a coming concert by his orquesta (M. García 1981:206). In 1916, Rito Medina's Band presented an outdoor summer concert, and during the following year Raymundo S. González emerged as "the most popular band" (ibid.) in the El Paso area. But the best organized orquesta in the early period was that of Trinidad Concha, erstwhile assistant director of Porfirio Díaz's "touring band." According to García, "by 1907 Concha's Band had 40 members and performed at numerous gatherings" (ibid.:207). While García does not mention the specific instrumentation of Concha's or other orquestas, it is likely that most of these were string-based groups of the type that began to record for the major labels in the 1920s. But most important for a developing schism between orquesta advocates and those who subscribed to "folksong" groups was the genteel style of music advocated by groups like Concha's: "More sophisticated in their selection of classical tunes, which were apparently intended to appeal to Mexican as well as American bourgeois tastes, these local bands and their music stood in sharp contrast to the folksongs composed by Mexican workers themselves and indicated cultural and class segmentation within El Paso's Mexican population" (Ibid.).

We do not have the extensive historical information for other Texas cities that García amassed for El Paso, but it is plausible to assume that in cities such as San Antonio and Brownsville, local orquestas like Pablo Persio's (San Antonio) and the "Mexican Brass Band" (Brownsville) were similar sociomusically to that of Trinidad Concha. Persio, a regular at the balls organized by the Mexican Social Club in the 1880s and 1890s, was praised on one occasion by the *San Antonio Express* for his "excellent music" (July 13, 1891); in Brownsville, the Mexican Brass Band was described by the *Evening Ranchero* as "simply splendid" (July 5, 1876). The 1891 version of the latter band consisted of twenty-two instruments—four clarinets, one alto saxophone, one tenor, one baritone saxophone, three cornets, three euphoniums, three valve trombones, two tubas, one bass drum, and one snare (Chatfield 1893:13).

In contrast to disparaging reports by the *Express* and other newspapers of fandangos and their accordion music, the enthusiastic accounts of orquestas like Pablo Persio's and the Mexican Brass Band seem to indicate that, to the newspapers at least, the latter were considered more polished and hence closer to the Anglo ideal of "good" music. We may recall, too, that the audiences for whom orquestas like Pablo Persio's played invariably were identified by contemporary Anglo observers as "high-type" Mexicans. The performance context usually was the baile, or ball, organized by the "elite of Mexican society" (*San Antonio Express,* September 22, 1883), who presumably subscribed to the middle-class aesthetics espoused by Anglo newspapers. Jovita González, an early native ethnographer, seems to confirm this assessment when she states unequivocally that the dances of the elite in South Texas "marked the social feature of the year"; on such occasions, only the music of "an orchestra from town" was appropriate (1930:62).

We may assume that the town orchestras referred to by González were local equivalents of Concha's Band in El Paso, Pablo Persio's in San Antonio, and Gloria's Band in Laredo. These orchestras must have been reasonably well outfitted, and they definitely tilted toward a genteel mode of performance and a repertory commensurate with the social standing of Texas-Mexican elites. Gloria's Band, incidentally, enthralled "an extraordinarily large crowd"—both Mexican and Anglo—with its "sweet strains of music" when it played on the evening of Thursday, May 24, 1883, at Herdic Park in Corpus Christi (*Corpus Christi Caller,* May 27, 1883). The band was composed of Timoteo Gloria on lead violin; C. Batesta, flute; D. Salas, cornet; B. Bernal, guitar; F. Martínez and E. Jiménez on French horn; and M. Almaguer on contrabass (ibid.).

In sum, by the end of the nineteenth century, a number of organized orchestral ensembles were to be found in the larger cities of Texas. They provided the music for a small but growing class of upwardly mobile people who considered themselves *gente de razón* (R. García 1991)—that is, people with an outlook increasingly shaped by the positivistic ideology of capitalism, with its emphasis on progress, scientism, and a bourgeois sense of order based on a balance between "work" and "play." The latter was given full and satisfying expression in the baile, where orquestas catering to the genteel tastes of the new middle class—the *gente de razón*—were in some demand by the end of the nineteenth century.

This was the type of orquesta the major recording companies discovered when they made their first forays into the Southwest, beginning in the mid-1920s. Richard Spottswood's impressive discography (1990) of ethnic recordings made in the United States during the years from 1893 to 1942 includes many contributions by orquestas from the Hispanic Southwest. Most of these recordings were produced by the major labels, which in the 1920s began to record the myriad styles of ethnic music extant in the United States. The Texas-Mexican string orquestas were well represented.

It is perhaps fitting that the first Texas-Mexican orquesta to record for the major labels was the one directed by Eduardo Martínez, "the king of San Antonio's musicians, whose Mexican and American melodies never fail[ed] to charm," according to local historian Albert Curtis (1955:5). A figure who made the transition from the early type of string orquestas to modern brass-and-reed bands, Martínez, "el charro del violín," and his orquesta recorded two sides for the Vocalion label in March 1928: "Noche azul," a *vals;* and "Perjura," a *danza* (Spottswood 1990:2068). According to Paul Elizondo, another of San Antonio's illustrious orquesta leaders, Martínez changed with the times, and in the 1940s and 1950s "he took a whole show on the road" (personal interview, March 12, 1993). His modernized band, known by then as Eduardo Martínez and the International Orchestra (in Spanish, Eduardo Martínez y la Orquesta Internacional), toured Texas with a package that included singers and variety acts. In 1928, however, Martínez's group was still of the string variety long popular in Texas and elsewhere.

The year 1928 witnessed the debut of several other orquestas tejanas in the new commercial market. Among these was La Orquesta Mexicana Calvillo, which recorded four selections for Vocalion in March 1928, including "Monterrey alegre," a *pasodoble;* and "México bello," a *vals.*[1] La Orquesta del Norte, from El Paso, began its recording career with Victor on April 16, 1928, and followed up with sessions on April 18, 20, 23, 25, 26, and 30. Well organized and polished, the group recorded an astonishing number of tunes—thirty in all, during the various dates—ranging from waltzes and polkas to tangos and foxtrots. Directed by Fernando L. Cabello, La Orquesta del Norte originally consisted of two violins, flute, clarinet, cello, piano, guitar, contrabass, and drums. The group returned to the studio in July 1929, this time armed with two trumpets, four violins, two clarinets, flute, cello, trombone, piano, contrabass, and trap-set drums. The orquesta's final recording date was on September 2, 1934, under a new director, Armando Reyes.[2]

At least a half-dozen other orquestas recorded for the various labels between 1928 and 1938. Among these was La Orquesta Royal, which visited the studios set up by Vocalion in hotel rooms in San Antonio on two separate dates, November 19, 1936, and October 22, 1937. The group recorded polkas, fox-trots, and a one-step. On June 17, 1929, and again in November, La Orquesta de Cuerda de Alfredo Garza recorded several waltzes and polkas for Vocalion. Fred Gutiérrez and his Club Aguila Orchestra recorded a long list of tunes, both Mexican and American, for Bluebird—again, in San Antonio. La Banda Mexicana de Texas, a brass band with five trumpets, five saxophones, clarinet, three trombones, two euphoniums, three tubas, and "battery," recorded four selections for Bluebird, including the famous waltz, "Sobre las olas," by the Mexican composer Juventino Rosas.

Other orquestas recording for the major labels included Orquesta Guadalupe Acosta (Decca, San Antonio, June 1930), Orquesta Los Charros (Vocalion, San Antonio, December 1936), Orquesta Mexicana Los Compadres (Okeh, San Antonio, June 1929), Orquesta Las Fichas (Bluebird, San Antonio, August 1935), Orquesta Mexicana Francisco Mouré (Vocalion, El Paso, March 1928), Tomás Núñez y su Orquesta (Columbia/Vocalion, El Paso, October 1934), and Orquesta de Cuerda de Villalobos (Brunswick, San Antonio, October 1929). Finally, Bluebird and Vocalion maintained "house bands" in San Antonio and El Paso, respectively, in the 1930s. Apparently these bands were made up of Mexican musicians (the Vocalion band was directed by a don Ramón), and they recorded music similar to that of the other orquestas I have mentioned.

Among the orquestas recorded by the major labels, one stands out for its virtuosity. I refer to Emilio Cáceres y su Orquesta del Club Aguila. A brilliant violinist with an enduring reputation as one of the finest jazz musicians to come out of the orquesta tradition in the Southwest, Cáceres and his orquesta recorded seven selections for Victor at the Texas Hotel in San Antonio, on April 4, 1934. Unlike other orquestas of the time—and indicative of his musical assimilation—Cáceres shunned the traditional polka but did include several Americanized numbers. Noteworthy among these was "Jig in G," a highly sophisticated, jazz-oriented tune that represents the most ambitious foray by a tejano orquesta of the thirties (and perhaps even the forties) into the world of swing-jazz (see Arhoolie Records, *Orquestas Típicas: The First Recordings, 1926–1938* [CD 7017]). The instrumentation, incidentally, heralded the shape of things to come: except for Cáceres's violin, the group consisted of big-band components that by then were standard—two trumpets, three saxophones, a trombone, piano, guitar, contrabass, and trap-drums.

One final orquesta deserves mention in this summary of recording activity during the twenties and thirties. I refer to La Orquesta Típica Fronteriza, from El Paso—one of the best organized and most genteel of the early orquestas, to judge by the quality of its recordings. It debuted with RCA Victor on April 15, 1928. During the next two weeks, the group recorded numerous selections for Victor, including waltzes, polkas, *pasodobles,* and even a fox-trot. Directed by Armando Reyes, La Orquesta Típica Fronteriza consisted of two violins, four mandolins, three bandolones, two cellos, two guitars, two bajos sextos, two contrabasses, a tympani, and drums. On October 23, 1934, the Orquesta Típica Fronteriza returned to the studio once more, this time with Decca, and recorded a dozen tunes. The group had augmented its personnel with the addition of a flute and a clarinet (Spottswood 1990:1890–91).[3] Clearly, through its musical sophistication, La Orquesta Típica Fronteriza "indicated [the] cultural and class segmentation" that was present in Mexican American society by the 1930s.

The label *típica* in Orquesta Típica Fronteriza merits a word on the sociomusical nature of the early orquestas. So-called *típicas* had been common in Mexico since at least the mid-nineteenth century (Mayer-Serra 1941). They often consisted of ad hoc instruments, pieced together in bricolage fashion, and they were associated with peasant and working-class sectors. In the late nineteenth century, when Mexico was experiencing a mild form of romantic nationalism (a much stronger form flourished immediately after the Mexican Revolution of 1910–17; see Franco 1970), the bourgeois flirted for a time with folk forms, including musical ones. In the spirit of nationalism, Carlos Curti at the Mexico City Conservatory in Mexico City organized an *orquesta típica* in 1884, even adopting charro outfits as a token of its folk-nationalist orientation.[4] Curti's novelty worked: folkloristic *típicas* began to crop up all over Mexico among urban petit bourgeois groups, and soon Curti faced competition from such renowned *típicas* as that of Miguel Lerdo de Tejada and Juan Torre Blanca, two groups that also recorded and toured extensively in the United States.

Texas-Mexicans eventually climbed on the *típica* bandwagon. In the 1920s, *orquestas típicas* proliferated all over the state of Texas, as tejanos embraced the nationalistic spirit embodied in the Mexican *típica*. Several of these recorded for the major labels, including the most famous of them all, the aforementioned Orquesta Típica Fronteriza. La Orquesta Típica Laredo apparently was very popular in the 1930s. In a gesture redolent of the transnational solidarity the *típica* engendered, the formation of a new Texas *típica* in 1930 elicited a photograph and a brief report in one of Mexico City's principal papers, *Excelsior*. Titled "Nueva Típica Mexicana en Houston," the report complimented Mexican Houstonians on their musical efforts, lauding el maestro Torres and the Orquesta Típica Mexicana de Houston as "enthusiastic Mexican musicians who have gained notable triumphs with their *orquesta típica*, to such an extent that the large recording companies have offered them lucrative contracts in the manufacture of movie musicals" (March 6, 1930) (see fig. 10).

Figure 10   Orquesta Típica Torres, Houston, 1930. *Courtesy Houston Metropolitan Research Center, Houston Public Library.*

The emergence and subsequent role of the Mexican *orquesta típica* ultimately is tied to musical nationalism. As Gerónimo Baqueiro Foster observed, "We must speak, of course, of the founding of the Orquesta Típica Mexicana [the first bourgeois *típica*] as a monument in honor of musical nationalism in Mexico" (1964:533). The Mexican Revolution strengthened that nationalism, a role shared by the *típicas* of the Hispanic Southwest. At a time when American cultural citizenship was not an option to the vast majority of Texas-Mexicans, cultural affirmation continued to flow from south of the border. The revolution and the nationalist cultural ferment that followed resonated strongly in the consciousness of all Mexican Americans, and the Texas-Mexicans quite naturally turned to the *orquesta típica* to express their own sense of Mexicanness *(mexicanidad)*. The *orquesta típica* enjoyed great success throughout the twenties and thirties; but by the forties, when a changing relationship with Anglo-Texans and a new sense of cultural citizenship solidified, the *típica* had begun to lose much of its previous appeal. It disappeared soon after World War II.

The Emergence of the Modern Orquesta

The next stage in the evolution of an orquesta tradition in Texas began around 1930, when a new type of ensemble appeared, this one modeled stylistically and repertorially after the big swing bands then sweeping the American musical scene. However, even by the 1920s, groups with a new look had begun to appear. But the earliest modern-style orquesta to come to my attention is Los Rancheros, organized in Houston about 1930 (see fig. 11). Los Rancheros is the prototypical urbanized orquesta tejana. Paradoxically, the group chose a pastoral name—Los Rancheros—despite its urban dress and Americanized repertoire. How can this apparent inconsistency be explained? Here a bit of social history may be enlisted, one that draws on my previous discussion of the contradictory relationship between the country and the city.

Until the 1930s, Texas-Mexicans remained relatively unassimilated, spatially and culturally, by American capitalism: they were overwhelmingly rural, and their culture was still in the painful process of transformation from an agrarian to a more urbanized and modernist orientation (Foley 1988; Taylor 1971 [1934]). Mexican immigration heightened the disparity between the two lifestyles—agrarianist and urbanist—since most immigrants came from rural areas. As Mexican anthropologist Manuel Gamio (1971 [1930]) so ably demon-

Figure 11   Orquesta los Rancheros, Houston, 1930. *Courtesy Houston Metropolitan Research Center, Houston Public Library.*

strated, by their sheer presence the immigrants helped to perpetuate older forms of Mexican culture in the Southwest. As Gamio observed, theirs was a "folk culture, plainly distinguishable in type from modern civilization" (ibid.:74). While Gamio at times was unduly critical of what he saw as the immigrants' backwardness, he intuitively understood what he was witnessing: a clash not only of races but also of cultural economies.

The Mexican Americans, meanwhile, were, as Gamio understood, "reflections" of the capitalist, American "environment" (ibid.:76). He described their celebrations as consisting of mixed elements, in particular musical elements: "Suppers of Mexican food, enchiladas, tamales, are served. The music is a combination of American fox-trots alternating with the singing of Mexican ballads to the accompaniment of guitars" (ibid.).

In sum, the Mexican Americans were experiencing the transition from a Mexican to an American cultural orientation, with all the complications involved in that process. Caught on the cusp of the transformation from a folk, agrarian mentality to a modernistic one, the Texas-Mexicans displayed contradictory forms of cultural action. They cherished—sometimes in a romanticized fashion—the lifestyle they were leaving behind, even as they were captivated by the modern technology of capitalism. But, like the Europeans of an earlier era (Williams 1973), they also cultivated a certain disdain for *lo ranchero* and its presumed backwardness and lack of *savoir faire*. Lastly, they feared the American city's worldliness, its economic rapacity, and, especially, its haughty intolerance toward traditional Mexican ways of life. The latter attitude was encoded in one word: jaitón.

One solution to the Texas-Mexicans' contradictions was to take, early on, tentative steps toward biculturalism. But this biculturalism, tending always toward the hybrid in its cultural expression, was, like all hybrid forms, rife with tensions of its own. For the Texas-Mexicans, the uneasy relationship between ranchero and jaitón was emblematic of their transitional position between two cultural economies, subsistence and capitalism, each with specific attributes—Mexican and American, rural and urban, traditional and modern. The first historical bloc to practice biculturalism was the group both Mario García (1989) and Rodolfo Álvarez (1973) called "the Mexican American Generation." Staking its fortunes on an American future but reluctant to forsake its "roots," this bloc mounted a prodigious effort to overcome the contradictions it faced. It began by attempting to reconcile the antinomies present in its everyday life.

We can understand, now, why an orquesta that was urban through and through could choose a name like Los Rancheros. The oxymoronic name was not only emblematic of Texas-Mexicans' dilemma; its juxtaposition of country (Los Rancheros) with city (dress and repertoire) set the tone for Texas-Mexican musical culture for the next forty years. The inherent instability of this juxtaposition (ranchero [country] versus jaitón [city]) was not resolved until a synthesis of the two antinomies finally was achieved—not by the Mexican American Generation but by its successor, "the Chicano Generation." Meanwhile, enhanced by racial and cultural complications, the ghost of el rancho would continue to bedevil the Mexican American Generation during its entire historical tenure. A product of the massive contradictions facing these cultural pioneers, Los Rancheros thus vacillated—agrarian in name, they wore the vestments of urban middle-class businessmen (see fig. 11); Mexican in ethnicity, they performed mostly American music.

Figure 12   Alonzo y sus Rancheros, ca. 1939. *Courtesy Houston Metropolitan Research Center, Houston Public Library.*

Here another bit of localized musical history may help in elucidating the complexities of the ranchero/jaitón polarity. In the spring of 1993, I interviewed Frank Alonzo, then eighty-five years old, and his wife, Ventura, aged eighty-eight, in their home in Houston, regarding an orquesta they once had led as a husband-and-wife team. The orquesta initially was known as Alonzo y sus Rancheros. When they organized their orquesta in 1938, the Alonzos led a ragtag collection of musicians which only by a stretch of the term could actually be called an "orquesta" (see fig. 12). According to the Alonzos, at this time the group played what they labeled música ranchera—traditional polkas, schottishes, redowas, and the like—all genres by then assimilated into a Mexican folk-music repertoire. The Alonzos operated at the fringes of the urban sphere—in little towns surrounding Houston, where the traditions of an earlier, pastoral era had not yet disappeared.

But in time, seeing all around them the changes overtaking orquesta music and sensing that they were being marginalized, the Alonzos took action. Their group began a metamorphosis—from a motley group of folk musicians into a true orquesta with a more sophisticated, urban approach to performance

Figure 13 Alonzo y su Orquesta, early 1950s. *Courtesy Houston Metropolitan Research Center, Houston Public Library.*

(see figs. 12 and 13 for the visual transformation of Alonzo y sus Rancheros). According to Mrs. Alonzo:

> [Dance establishments] didn't want us [after the advent of World War II] because we were "rancheros." We played all música ranchera, and there were clubs around here that just didn't want that music. So I said, "I'm gonna get a saxophone." And I put in two saxophones. And then I put in two trumpets, and three saxophones, accordion, bajo sexto and contrabass. And then everything was fine. (Personal interview, April 25, 1993)

As a final gesture signifying their emancipation from the stigma of *lo ranchero,* the Alonzos dropped the words "y sus Rancheros" from the band's name. By the end of the war, they were known simply as Alonzo y su Orquesta. The experience of Frank and Ventura Alonzo demonstrates that, from its inception, the modern orquesta claimed to represent the aesthetic sensibilities of an urban, upwardly mobile class. Mr. Alonzo, a man of humble origins (he had almost no education), originally misread the class and urban character inscribed on the orquesta as a symbolic form. His inclination was to perform the music of his rural, working-class roots. However, Mrs. Alonzo, a better educated, proud, and assertive woman of petite bourgeois background (her father was a small merchant, first in Mexico and later in the United States), recognized soon enough that the future of their orquesta lay in embracing a more cosmopolitan and urban character and repertoire. She therefore became the driving force in the band's effort to raise its status.

In a profession long dominated by men, Ventura Alonzo stands as a shining beacon for other female performers in and out of the orquesta tradition. A woman with more education than was typical for a Mexican American of her time (she attended school in Matamoros, first, and then the eighth grade in American schools), Mrs. Alonzo took command of her life early. When she married Frank Alonzo following a divorce from her first husband, she did so with a tacit understanding that she would not accept a subordinate role in the marriage. Thus, when Alonzo y sus Rancheros was organized, she played a leadership role from the beginning. As we were discussing Frank's early life and his poverty, lack of schooling, and inability to read, his wife intervened. "But I was there," she said. "I was the one who arranged everything. And I'm still here. At Ripley House [where they serve "seniors" a daily meal], we go there to play. I sing and act as master of ceremonies. I dedicate songs and introduce everyone and I talk to everyone. They all know me."

Beto Villa: "Father" of the Orquesta Tejana

Notwithstanding the Alonzos' desire to upgrade their orquesta from ranchero to jaitón, neither the orquesta tejana nor its core constituency, the upwardly mobile Texas-Mexicans, was in a position to emancipate itself completely from the contradictions enmeshed in the ranchero/jaitón dichotomy. Particularly during the reign of the Mexican American Generation—from the thirties to the mid-sixties—these contradictions dogged the Texas-Mexican middle class, pulling it in diverse ideological directions that ultimately could not be reconciled. As noted earlier, the only available solution to this predicament was a bicultural strategy in which the antinomies of class, race, and economic systems could be juxtaposed dialectically and eventually mediated. Through this biculturalist strategy, the Texas-Mexicans could accommodate the country *(lo ranchero)* and the city *(lo jaitón),* their working-class roots and their middle-class aspirations, and, especially, the essential conflict between their pastoral Mexican identity and a growing sense of urban American cultural citizenship.

In the field of the symbolically important orquesta, one man stands out as the consummate mediator—saxophonist Beto Villa, whom we justifiably could call the "father" of the modern orquesta tejana. More than anyone before him, Beto Villa grasped the aesthetic possibilities open to the Texas-Mexicans as they struggled to reconcile the contradictions surrounding them. In forging a bimusical repertoire for the orquesta—one that tapped both Mexican-latino and American musical cultures—and, especially, in inventing a uniquely "Tex-Mex" ranchero style, Villa opened a musico-symbolic berth in which the Texas-Mexicans could anchor the slippery ship of their hybrid identity. In subscribing to Villa's bimusical style, they could be both Mexican and American, ranchero and cosmopolitan. While their newfound prosperity might distance them from their working-class brothers and sisters, the ranchero strains of Villa's new orquesta tejana reconnected them in complex and subtle ways to a working-class culture that still held powerful associations to a nurturant ancestral "heritage." [5]

It is with Beto Villa, then, that an orquesta tejana style properly emerges. However, before discovering the artistic treasures hidden in Texas-Mexican biculturalism and the musical benefits they could yield, Villa himself had to traverse the assimilationist path laid out by his peers in the Mexican American Generation. Thus, in his early musical career in his hometown of Falfurrias, Texas, he had embraced an American repertoire, although he never was able to forsake his Mexican musical roots altogether. When he organized his first musical group as a high school teenager, Villa immediately sought an American identity: he called the group "The Sonny Boys." This was in 1932. One of the few Mexican Americans of his generation to attend high school, Villa was influenced by his music teachers in high school, who themselves were products of the '"big band" era of the Dorsey Brothers, Benny Goodman, and others.

But Villa's father, a tailor by profession, also had a successful career as a musician, and he too influenced the younger Villa, at least to the extent that he encouraged his son to earn extra money by performing with local Mexican bands. These, like Alonzo y sus Rancheros, still subscribed to the salon music long identified with a norteño repertory and style. Thus, notwithstanding his Americanization, Beto Villa did assimilate the style associated with *orquestas típicas,* a style at once urban and at least quasi-pastoral. This experience with the old orquesta repertoire and style left a profound impression on Villa's musical sensibilities. These sensibilities not only would contribute to the saxophonist–band leader's impact on the bimusicality of the Texas-Mexican orquesta, but they would also leave his mark on the biculturalist ideology emerging in the 1940s—an ideology Villa transformed into a musical aesthetic.

After several years imitating the big American swing bands (in the late 1930s, Villa played regularly in the Anglo dance halls of the oil boomtown of Freer), in 1946 he finally hit upon the idea of wedding the hitherto urbanized orquesta (the big-band version born in 1930, not the traditional *típica*) with a ranchero style. At this time, Villa led what can only be termed a minimal orquesta—himself on alto saxophone; his brother El Tordo on trumpet; another brother, Oscar Villa, on drums; Fidel García on contrabass; Reynaldo Barrera on electric guitar; and an old sidekick, Reymundo Treviño, on piano-accordion (fig. 14). Eager to translate his ideas for a new sound into a com-

Figure 14   Beto Villa y su Orquesta, ca. 1949. *Author's collection.*

mercial venture, the future father of the modern orquesta tejana approached his friend, Armando Marroquín, of the newly founded Ideal Records, with a suggestion. According to Marroquín, "He came to me and said, 'Say, listen, I'd like for you to cut a record for me. I want to hear what it sounds like.' The group was not very good, shall we say, professionally speaking. So I said, 'Yeah, why don't we record?' At that time música ranchera was heard only on the accordion or on the violin. I said, 'Let's see if my partner [Paco Betancourt] likes it'" (personal interview, January 31, 1980).

This historic first recording—a 78-rpm acetate disc mastered directly on a primitive phonograph—consisted of a polka, "Las delicias," on one side; and a vals, "Porqué te ríes," on the other. Marroquín sent the record to Betancourt, who was unimpressed. "No," Marroquín remembered his partner saying, "not this mess."

"So I told Beto," recalled Marroquín, "'Say, I'm sorry, but he says no.'"

"Okay," replied an unfazed Beto Villa, "tell him I'll pay for the recording." Sensing the potential for success, Marroquín finally prevailed on Betancourt. Here is the way events turned out, according to Marroquín: "So we finally came out with the record. Oh, man! About a month after he [Betancourt] started to distribute it, he said, 'Say, tell Villa to record some more.' They were asking for it in bunches. It was more like a conjunto; it wasn't even an orquesta yet. . . . He had only about five or six [musicians]—real small—ranchero-like *[arrancherado]*. . . . This was around 1946, around that time" (Marroquín interview).

For the next three years, Villa exploited to the utmost the new *arrancherado* orquesta sound he had invented, conveyed mostly through the genre that quickly became the hallmark of the new style, the polca-ranchera (as it had become earlier for the conjunto). Yet Villa was not happy with the group he led. He longed for the music he had come to embrace—the more sophisticated sound of the swing bands, as well as an increasingly popular Latin American music, of urban middle-class origin, that orquestas south of the border were exploiting successfully (e.g., Xavier Cugat). This Latin American style was dominated by Afro-Caribbean rhythms and genres, including the Cuban-Mexican bolero, in the form of a reincarnated canción romántica, the *danzón*, and other "hot" rhythms that eventually came to be known as *salsa* (e.g., the *guaracha;* see Manuel 1995).

Prodded by Marroquín, whose own aesthetic and ideological interests leaned toward a bimusical sound that would include both American swing and the music of the new Latin orquestas, Villa took action. Marroquín recalled his advice to Villa:

> "Say," I told Beto, "Why don't you fix your [band]? I've heard of some very good musicians—the brothers Pepe and Chuy Compeán." Chuy was an arranger of the first line. So he got them and he organized his orquesta real nice—now with arrangements and everything. And it was no longer the [little ranchero group]—no, no, what can I say. He would go on tours—he toured for ten years, and he played everything, he mixed it up. Because la raza from here, our people, like everything, we take a bit from everywhere. We like Western, we like the Cuban, we like music from Mexico, we like all kinds of music—or at least certain kinds. (Marroquín interview)

Wishing to pursue further these important sociomusical developments, I engaged Marroquín in an extensive review of Villa's efforts to push tejano music in new directions. The following is an excerpt from the interview. (Except for the key phrases, "high class" and "a lot of firsts," this segment and most of the interview were conducted in Spanish; the translations are mine).

MP: Would you say that when Beto Villa first entered the commercial market, the orquesta was like an answer to the accordion, shall we say, except that it was a bit more "high class"?

AM: More high class, yes—

MP: —that the people who had rejected the accordion felt that the orquesta gave them a bit more?

AM: Yes, and especially since he played *polcas*, música ranchera. And the other orquestas [before Villa] did not play that in those times. . . . At that time the tango was big. . . . But Villa had everything. . . . In other words, what helped Villa was that he could play both ranchero and high class—or jaitón, as people used to say. He had very competent musicians. I have many of his recordings. . . . By this time [1949] we had tape recorders, but only one-track. I used about five microphones, and you could hear the big band *[el orquestón]:* Compeán's arrangements—lots of American pieces: "Boquita de cielo,"

"I'll Remember"—lots of American tunes. Bilingual tunes—and
now they think this is new. We did it in 194[9]—a lot of "firsts."
(Marroquín interview)

Another perspective on Villa's musical maneuvers comes from his old
friend and colleague, Reymundo Treviño, who in an interview recalled Villa's
efforts to "modernize":

Several of us were bounced—myself; Ferro, because he was not a very
good pianist; and the trumpet player [El Tordo]. See, Beto made a new
arrangement, with modern musicians, and the Compeanes came in, and
they also bounced Fidel, because the Compeanes' father was a bass player.
And the orquesta became pretty large and modern—like Luis Arcaraz
[a large Mexican orquesta], like that. I think that was Beto's downfall,
because the people no longer got the old flavor—the rancherito style.
(Personal interview, March 14, 1980; translation by Peña)

Perhaps still bitter about the way Beto Villa had "bounced" him out, don
Reymundo failed to appreciate Villa's domination of the orquesta market of
the Southwest for the better part of the 1950s—all because, as Armando Marroquín correctly observed, he could "mix it up," he could play both ranchero
and jaitón. Indeed, throughout the 1950s and even into the sixties, weekend
orquestas all across the Southwest—those active in local club and wedding
dances—took their cue from Beto Villa. Lalo Guerrero, the legendary singer-
composer from Los Angeles, who at one time led his own band, put it
succinctly: "Beto started it all. He had such an impact, you know, and he influenced a lot of people after him" (personal interview, May 28, 1993).
Meanwhile, in discussing the difference between the orquesta's clientele
and that of the conjunto, Treviño pointed out that Beto Villa's crowds, and
those of orquestas generally, were "more educated":

[The orquesta fan] was another crowd. I'm sure that the people who
went to the dances to hear this music [orquesta] were not going to listen
to Chicho's [Narciso Martínez's] music.

MP: What distinguished one crowd from the other?
RT: It was a different group of people—a bit more educated, I believe.

Because this was a well-dressed crowd, the ones that came to our dances—well behaved. And, you know, in the times of Narciso it was old boots, and kicking and kicking at the air, heh, heh.[6]

(Treviño interview)

Altogether, Villa recorded over a hundred singles for Ideal in 78 rpm, as well as a dozen or so long-playing (LP) albums. The Beto Villa orquesta also recorded a few singles and a couple of LPs for Ideal's most important rival in the tejano market, Arnaldo Ramírez's Falcon Records, from nearby Mission, Texas. Marroquín admitted to "doing well" off Villa's recordings (don Reymundo Treviño claimed that Marroquín "enriched" himself at the expense of Villa and other artists), but Villa himself enjoyed a long period of prosperity. In a telephone interview, his widow remembered one public dance where so much cash was collected that they had to bring in a wheelbarrow to cart it off.

Marroquín recalled one performance at the Riverside Ballroom in Phoenix, Arizona, where a typically overflowing crowd prompted the promoters to call for security reinforcements: "I remember in Phoenix, the first time we went there, we had a packed crowd at the Riverside Ballroom, and the promoter—he was a gringo—called police headquarters. "Send me more policemen," he said, "I've got every Mexican in the state of Arizona here tonight" (Marroquín interview).

Fracturing Villa's Ranchero/Jaitón Compromise: Balde González versus Isidro López

Villa's solution to the jaitón/ranchero opposition and its contradictions was a compromise: by juxtaposing the two styles—performing one against the other—he astutely tapped the emerging aesthetic sensibilities of the dualistic Mexican American Generation. The mixed repertoire of American foxtrots and sophisticated Latin American styles, on the one hand, and Tex-Mex polkas, on the other, took Mexican Americans by storm; and they rewarded Villa with unparalleled fame. Every orquesta after Villa's was to be influenced by this bicultural compromise. As we shall see, the orquesta leaders of the next generation—the Chicano Generation—were to carry Villa's efforts even further, forging a powerful bimusical synthesis that remained beyond the range of the musico-cultural possibilities available to Villa and his contemporaries.

The limitations of stylistic juxtaposition—as opposed to a true synthesis—are exemplified by two important orquestas, that of Balde González and that of Isidro López. Neither was yet capable of melding Mexican and American, ranchero and jaitón, into one seamless musical fabric. Both tended instead to gravitate toward one or the other style—ranchero in the case of López, jaitón in the case of González—thus undermining the delicate balance that Villa had achieved.

In examining, first, the music of Balde González, we are struck immediately by his steadfast avoidance of the more blatantly ranchero style fashioned by Villa, particularly in the performance of the Tex-Mex polca-ranchera. Indeed, we note in González's repertoire an almost deliberate neglect of that genre, despite the fact that, as Marroquín emphasized, "everybody had to play polkas."

Born blind in 1928, in Beeville, Texas, González attended the state school for the blind in Austin, which he left in 1948, "ya para acabar la escuela" (just as he was about to finish school), according to his mother, María Delgado (personal interview, April 8, 1993). While in Austin, González learned to play the piano, saxophone, and clarinet, performing at parties with "a little band the students had going," according to his daughter, Sylvia Wilton (personal interview, April 8, 1993).

Shortly after he returned to Beeville from Austin, González formed his own orquesta, beginning at the same time to sing professionally. Like many orquestas of its time, González's was a rudimentary ensemble, consisting of trumpet, alto and tenor saxophones, contrabass, trap-drums, and piano (fig. 15). But González's newfound singing talent attracted the attention of Melco, a small label from Corpus Christi, and his commercial career was launched. This took place around 1949. Having been strongly influenced by his experiences playing American music in Austin, González early on chose to emphasize cosmopolitan styles, especially the bolero, although he also recorded a number of fox-trots. Wary, perhaps, of "crossing over," he always sang the latter in Spanish. His polkas were few, and they always had a polished, well-arranged gloss to them.

By 1951, González had enlarged his band, which now featured three saxophones, two trumpets, piano, bass, and drums. Now on the Ideal roster, he recorded a number of songs—boleros and fox-trots—that earned him considerable fame as a crooner. His suave style, delivered in a deep baritone voice, is reminiscent of such American singers as Bing Crosby and Perry Como. As

Figure 15   Balde Gonzales y su Orquesta, ca. 1950. *Courtesy Sylvia Winton.*

Isidro López characterized it, González's style "was more Americanized" (personal interview, May 31, 1979). Some of his memorable hits, all confined to the southwestern market, included "Oye corazón," "Qué me puede ya importar," "Cuéntame tu vida"—all songs composed by the blind band leader. González's choice of musical style—quite sophisticated, by Texas-Mexican standards—ensured him a place at the jaitón pole of the orquesta tejana, but his avoidance of the more rustic ranchero style associated with Villa tended to limit his popularity.

By the late 1950s, González's star was on the wane, and in the 1960s he "went solo," playing piano and singing at such places as the Ramada Inn in Houston. His daughter, Sylvia Wilton, recalled:

When he stopped the orchestra, he went more Americanized. I remember he used to have a—well, back in the early sixties, he had a big, big book that he called the Bible. And it was all the old songs in English. . . . So back in the early sixties, he was more into Americanized music. Pero [but], while he had his orchestra, all the time that he had his orchestra, he was Spanish. Once that orchestra stopped, he did not play Mexican music. He went more to clubs and played American. (Wilton interview)

Balde González died in 1974, in Houston, at the age of forty-six. He was inducted posthumously into the "Texano Music Hall of Fame" on February 20, 1985, in recognition of his "excellence in the tejano music industry." Among his surviving peers, he became known as the man who "brought a little class" to the orquesta tejana tradition (Moy Pineda, personal interview, May 4, 1993).

Isidro López, a late contemporary of Balde González, began his life in relative poverty, in the hamlet of Bishop, near the city of Corpus Christi, Texas, in 1933.[7] Unlike most orquesta musicians, he experienced the sweat of the cotton fields, and he remembered living in a two-room house, although his father was an automobile mechanic. He did manage to graduate from high school and even attended Texas A&I College in nearby Kingsville for a year, before dropping out to dedicate himself to professional musical performance. López learned to play clarinet and saxophone in high school; he played the latter with various orquestas, including his own—but, like Balde González, he is remembered mostly as a singer. Unlike González, López opted early for the canción ranchera as his ticket to fame.

López recalled his initiation into the ranchero mode of performance: "I latched onto Narciso Martínez, around 1951–52. He played the accordion, I played the saxophone." Playing polkas with the "father" of the Texas-Mexican conjunto, as well as the popularity of Beto Villa's polkas, convinced López to make that genre the staple of his repertoire and style, although, as a singer, he naturally grafted the ranchera lyrics onto the polka. "We played polka," he said, "because the people from here dance to the polka." More than that—perhaps because of his own working-class history and persistent allegiance to that class—López initially denied any difference between the orquesta and the conjunto, or between ranchero and jaitón. "It is true," he finally acknowledged, "that among some of our orquesta colleagues, some of them say, 'Accordion? That's trash.' But they are people who have something wrong with their heads, because for me an accordion or a saxophone—to me they're equal."

Yet, when I shared with López the statements of other informants regarding the differential identities of the conjunto and the orquesta—the former ranchero, the latter "high class"—he did acknowledge some differences. Here is an extended portion of his commentary:

> Well, I saw that myself. It's just that among classes of people—to me the *pachuco* [Mexican American zoot-suiter], or the poorest or the richest— to me they're all equal. Because the richest will not do more than I have done in my life. I have picked cotton, I have been everywhere. But the reason those people [the upwardly mobile] think that way [i.e., think that the orquesta is better than the conjunto] is that those same people like to dress in style, and to cut themselves off from the other [poorer] people. . . . And that's what I have seen always among us—that there are other people who, because we have better means, think that we are better than them, but not for me. But there are people who—I don't know how to put this—but within the conjunto there are people who are more ignorant, who go more to the conjunto dances than to orquesta dances.
> (Personal interview, November 29, 1979)

For Isidro López, then, some differences did exist between the conjunto and the orquesta, particularly social differences: the more "ignorant" tended to patronize conjunto dances, rather than those of the orquesta. But his strategy was to bridge those differences—to forge a distinct ranchero style for the or-questa that would transcend class and appeal to the ethnic sensibilities of all tejanos. Thus he became famous for his polcas-rancheras (for example, his hits "Ando sufriendo y penando" and "Emoción pasajera"); but, as he himself admitted, he tried to add sophistication to his music—and thus cover the middle-class flank—by including well-arranged boleros, *danzones,* and the like. "I knew that my records were going to sell," he said. "We would record one of my rancheras—a vocal—and on the other side I would stick in a filler, like a bolero. And people would listen to it because it was Isidro López." In the late fifties and early sixties, this strategy kept López atop the popularity charts in tejano music.

Consolidation and Impact of the Orquesta Tejana: The Aesthetics of Class and Ethnic Conflict

Beto Villa initiated a new tradition of orquesta tejana music built around the "rancheroized" polka. Armando Marroquín was essentially correct when he observed that Villa had "invented" *música Chicana*—at least insofar as the orquesta is concerned. In the forties, fifties, and sixties, countless localized orquestas, not only in Texas but elsewhere in the Hispanic Southwest, contributed to the spread and popularity of the orquesta tejana style. For example, in the early 1960s, while residing in Fresno, California, I played with the band of Manuel Contreras. This group, like many similar orquestas, kept busy throughout the year playing for ballroom dances, civic club functions, and domestic celebrations such as weddings and anniversaries. I recall Contreras directing us to play certain polkas "Texas style"—that is, in the style of Beto Villa. By this time, the style had become fixed in the musical traditions of Mexican Americans, and, no matter how varied an orquesta's repertoire might be, by popular demand Beto Villa polkas were indispensable.

Quite naturally, however, the most important orquestas in the new tradition hailed from Texas. Sustained by the activities of Ideal, Falcon, and other tejano recording labels, a number of professional orquestas operated from their Texas bases, many of these touring the ballroom circuit then flourishing in the Southwest and beyond (in the Midwest, for example). Among the better-known tejano orquestas in the 1940s, 1950s, and 1960s were Mike Ornelas from Laredo, Eloy Pérez from Houston ("The Glenn Miller of the Latin American hipsters," according to a poster put out by the League of United Latin American Citizens [LULAC]), Darío Pérez from Victoria, Eugenio Gutiérrez from Weslaco, Chris Sandoval from San Antonio, and La Orquesta Falcón from Mission. In addition to these, however, dozens of orquestas thrived in more localized areas, some of them known well beyond their own locales. Among these, at least two or three stand out—the previously mentioned Eduardo Martínez from San Antonio and the various orquestas led by the Galván brothers from Corpus Christi—Ralph, Bobby, and Eddie. The Galváns owned and operated the Galván Ballroom, where many groups appeared, including outstanding artists from Mexico (see fig. 16).

The consolidation of the orquesta tejana style—or styles, actually—can be understood only as a response to social forces long at work in tejano society. In addition to long-standing intercultural conflict with the Anglos, newer processes emerged during and after World War II, including urbanization, socioeconomic diversification, and acculturation leading to biculturalism. Steady immigration from Mexico contributed its share to the social and economic diversity of tejano society, as newly arrived immigrants were incorporated into

Figure 16 Ralph Galván Orchestra with Mexican star Toña la Negra, late 1950s.
Courtesy Bobby Galván.

the lower levels of the working class. Since most of these immigrants were from the northeastern tier of Mexican states (Tamaulipas, Chihuahua, Nuevo León, Coahuila; see Taylor 1968:42), the working-class, norteño stream of Mexican culture (León-Portilla 1972) was constantly replenished, adding a measure of cultural continuity (and resistance) to an already sturdy tejano, working-class culture. It was among both tejano and norteño workers that conjunto and música norteña generally flourished.

Among upwardly mobile people, meanwhile, a mainstream, middle-class American culture and its ideological pillars—patriotism, individualism, consumerism, a particular sense of aesthetics, and even nativism—was seeping inexorably into the social consciousness. In short, middle-class Texas-Mexicans were becoming Americanized. For these tejanos, as anthropologist Arthur Rubel correctly observed of the Texas-Mexicans of Weslaco (my hometown), Americanization brought with it a desire to emulate the "life goals" of their

Anglo counterparts (1966:12). In their sometimes frustrated effort to gain a sense of American cultural citizenship, the upwardly mobile engaged in a host of contradictory cultural practices, as ably demonstrated by Américo Paredes (1993c [1968]) and others (Jordan 1972, 1981; Rubel 1966; O. Simmons 1974 [1952]). One of these practices was the conscious rejection by tejanos of certain aspects of their Mexican ancestral culture, especially those aspects that seemed to conflict with American capitalism's notion of the "modern," such as folk healing and other Mexican folk practices (Madsen 1964; Paredes 1993c [1968]; Rubel 1966).

"Stoop labor" and cultural practices associated with it also were rejected by the upwardly mobile. Among these practices was conjunto music—perhaps the quintessential emblem of both the agricultural worker and the urban, proletarian *pachuco*. As described in chapter 3, the whole musical culture of the conjunto acquired strongly negative associations among tejanos with middle-class ideas. These associations had to do with the less desirable elements of life on the rancho and their presumed incompatibility with urban American life. Like the lowly tortilla taco—another symbol of the poverty associated with Mexican agrarian life—the conjunto was something to be avoided. As one former conjunto musician put it, "To play in a conjunto was just like trying to eat tortillas in public. . . . A lot of people didn't know that I played in a conjunto when I was fifteen, sixteen, and still in high school, you know. 'Cause it would degrade them, you know, for me to say that I played in a conjunto" (Richard Herrera, in Héctor Galán's video documentary, *Songs of the Homeland*).

But the road to assimilation was far from smooth for the Texas-Mexicans. Neither *el rancho* nor *curanderismo* (folk healing), conjunto nor tortilla, the working-class nor *lo mexicano,* could be discarded easily. The long-standing prejudice of the "host" society—the Anglos—guaranteed a slow and torturous journey toward the ultimate but elusive goal: an untrammeled sense of American cultural citizenship. Thus, as Moy Pineda, a veteran of the orqusta circuit, put it, "You can take the raza out of the country, but—how does that [you can't take the country out of the raza] go?" Indeed, the segment of the interview from which this statement is taken can serve as a testimonial to the dilemmas facing Texas-Mexicans as they made the transition from Mexican to American identity and from working-class to middle-class status.

Speaking of the Alhambra Club, an "elite" group of Texas-Mexicans in the

Rio Grande Valley, for whom Moy Pineda, his wife Delia Pineda, and their band played every year, Pineda commented,

> And now look, I'm talking—these guys are all professional people: doctors, lawyers. We're talking about the elite crop. . . . I change my whole book for them. We try to keep up with the times. We do a little disco, salsa, los boleros, ballads, some of the new fox-trots.

MP: Now these people want a good band; they wouldn't hire a conjunto— or would they?

DP: No, they wouldn't.

MoyP: No—unless they could get ten guys up there on the bandstand. See, this is for show—I mean, I'm talking about guys that make $100,000 or better a year.

DP: But it is true; the reason they hire a big band is they want something that according to them is the best. So they want to show off by getting a big orchestra, and they have their daughters presented to society. It's supposed to be very, very exclusive. . . . And, of course, they want the very best. And the band—it has to be something real nice. I don't think they will get a conjunto up there.

MoyP: They want that big band, and we got those fancy tuxedos. . . . But the music—if I started playing some of the stuff that we do right now, they'd run me off.

MP: But they eventually revert to form, no?

MoyP: Right, they go back—*n'hombre, cállate* [no, man, listen]—I already have it timed real good. The first hour we do, man, special arrangements. And nobody's dancing. But about an hour [later] I take off *con* [with] "Los laureles," "El abandonado" [ranchero tunes]. As soon as we start that, man—ching! Everybody gets on the dance floor. . . . When they start drinking, they go back to their roots.

The interview with the Pinedas took place in 1979. Many of the dancers in their story probably were cultural throwbacks to the Mexican American Generation. To those individuals, the aesthetic separation of class and ethnicity was still a vivid reminder of their dual cultural identity. In other words, the orquesta and its dual stylistic face—its vacillation between jaitón and ranchero—still served for them as a token for the reconciliation of vastly disparate cultural modalities, of which ranchero and jaitón are but one symbolic manifestation. At a historical juncture during the dialectic of conflict (the 1930s to the 1960s), when Mexican Americans faced change and difficult adjustments on diverse fronts, symbolic activity addressing that change flourished. And this activity was caught inescapably between the poles of cultural assimilation and resistance, between a Mexican and an American identity, and between middle-class gentility and working-class "scandal." The cultural result was a state of continuing contradiction—a yearning for the niceties of modern urban life, coupled with nostalgia for a romanticized ethnic heritage. Orquestas captured those contradictions perfectly.

Economist Paul Taylor captured a sense of the massive contradictions facing upwardly mobile Texas-Mexicans, especially in their attitudes toward cultural citizenship. The comments of one individual (out of many dotting Taylor's book) will suffice to illustrate the dilemma facing these Texas-Mexicans: "The world war taught us a lesson. We had thought we were Mexicans. The war opened our eyes. . . . We have American ways and think like Americans. We have not been able to convince some [American] people that there is a difference between us [and the Old Mexicans]. To the average American we are just Mexicans" (1971 [1934]:245; brackets in original).

Taylor's informant was correct on two critical points. First, the cultural identities of Texas-Mexicans of the Mexican American Generation indeed were ambivalent, as discussed above. The dialectic of conflict driving Anglo-Mexican relations made cultural ambivalence inevitable. It was out of this dialectic that such contradictory forms of symbolic expression as the orquesta emerged. Second, while the conflict was beginning to unfold toward a substantial realignment in the relationship between Anglos and Mexicans, at this early stage the attitudes of the former were still dominated by their sense of racial and cultural superiority. Taylor fathomed the creeping acceptance on the part of the Anglos, just as he documented their entrenched racism. The following statements may serve as examples of the two contradictory forms of thinking; note how the notion of class inflects the Anglo attitude toward Mexicans:

If a Mexican is high class, they [Anglos] admit him, and if of the lower class, they don't; they draw the line on the laboring class. (1971 [1934]:251)

We [Anglos] feel like we are a superior race. You know they [Mexicans] are a lower civilization and you can't mix oil and water. (1971 [1934]:255)

Thus caught on the edge between two disparate cultural orders, Texas-Mexicans of the era after World War II, especially the upwardly mobile, vacillated between one extreme and the other as they searched collectively for a sense of self. Were they Americans, or were they Mexicans? Were they really modern middle-class citizens, or were they, as Moy Pineda claimed, still children of the rancho? Unable to resolve the contradictions, these Texas-Mexicans took the only alternative available to them: they became Mexican Americans, in the process adopting a pervasive biculturalism. Of course, this was no simple biculturalism; rather, forged in the dialectic of conflict, it was a hybrid form, or an unstable mode of communication tending toward, but never fully achieving, a synthesis of the polarities involved. This biculturalism was, in Bakhtinian terms, the dialogic interplay of two conflictive cultural voices—the dominant and authoritarian (middle-class) Anglo-American, and the subordinate and repressed (working-class) Mexican (Bakhtin 1986; Todorov 1984).

In this protean struggle between two class-cultural orders, the range of expressive culture was as expansive as it was contradictory, encompassing bilingualism and its verbal art, as well as bicultural beliefs and practices, and, of course, music. It was within this betwixt-and-between cultural space that the orquesta emerged as a potent symbolic force in its own right, its many stylistic faces responding to the Mexican American Generation's struggle to make sense of the contradictions it faced. Like its exponents, then, orquesta was equally at home playing jaitón music (swings, boleros, *danzones*) and música ranchera (or, as Moy Pineda called it, "roots" music).

It is important to emphasize, however, that in the forties, fifties, and early sixties, the orquesta was limited to a juxtaposition of disparate stylistic elements—American versus Mexican, ranchero versus jaitón, middle- versus working-class. A fuller synthesis, one that at least momentarily would "resolve" the symbolic contradictions at play, was beyond the reach of orquestas of the Mexican American Generation. As we shall see, such a synthesis did take place, but it was left to the next generation of musicians—the Chicano Generation—to achieve. The next chapter elucidates the social, political, and ideological forces at work in this process of musico-cultural synthesis.

Notes

1. For a reissue of the recordings of La Orquesta Calvillo and others mentioned in this section, see the Arhoolie/Folklyric Records series, *Mexican-American Border Music,* vol. 4: *Orquestas Típicas (1926–1938),* CD 7017.

2. Apparently Cabello was involved with the major labels during an even earlier period. La Orquesta Mexicana de Fernando L. Cabello traveled to New York City, where it recorded 32 tunes between December 1918 and October 1919 for the Pathé and Emerson labels. All of the tunes bore Spanish titles; they included several schottishes, long popular with Mexicans, a number of *danzas,* and two *danzones cubanos* (Spottswood 1990:1716).

3. A small detail about the directorship of La Orquesta del Norte and La Orquesta Típica Fronteriza suggests that the two ensembles may have shared personnel. Armando Reyes, the director of the latter, is listed as director of La Orquesta del Norte on Decca's ledger for the session of September 2, 1934 (Spottswood 1990:2155).

4. Curti must have been musically active for many years. His orquesta recorded numerous tunes for Columbia, American, and Son-O-Phone between February 1905 and June 1912. The group went by various names, including Orquesta Mexicana de Curti, Curti's Orchestra, Curti's Mexican Orchestra, and, of course, Orquesta Típica de Carlos Curti.

5. I use the word *heritage* in quotation marks in recognition of Barbara Kirshenblatt-Gimblett's cautionary note that a sense of heritage, or "peoplehood," is always contingent and often invented (1995).

6. Compare this last statement to Martín Rosales, Jr., on conjunto music as "scandal."

7. Information on Isidro López derives principally from personal interviews with him on May 31 and November 29, 1979.

5 ❧ La Onda Chicana

Pinnacle of the Orquesta Tradition

In 1964, Tony "Ham" Guerrero, a trumpeter from San Angelo, Texas, was playing with a jazz group in Oakland, California. Guerrero eventually would become the lead trumpet for Little Joe and the Latinaires, the kingpin group during the final stage of the Texas-Mexican orquesta's one-hundred-year-long history. But at the end of 1964, tejano music was the last thing on Guerrero's mind. The young trumpeter was getting "the education of my life" playing with the Ed Kelly Quartet. Then he ran into an old friend from San Angelo, who told him, "You know what, here [in the Bay Area] la onda tejana is hitting big time. There's a new band out of Texas that's called Little Joe and the Latinaires, and another that's called Sunny and the Sunglows, and these guys are kicking Isidro López's ass all over the place."

Guerrero's friend, who sponsored public dances at the Newark Pavilion, wanted Guerrero to form a "house band" to "host" groups he was bringing in from Texas. "I've got some money," he said, "and I'll back you up." Guerrero took the offer and organized the Tony Martínez Orchestra from San Angelo, and his band soon became the local union backup for all the groups brought in from Texas. Guerrero recalled his experiences:

> These were the biggest tejano dances, Chicano dances [in the Bay Area]. *Raza* gathered there from all over the area. A thousand tejanos would show up to drink, dance, and raise hell. They'd have a riot every Saturday night. Little Joe played there, and Los Gorriones del Topo Chico; Tony de la Rosa; Rubén Vela. At that time the greatest conjunto of all time played there—El Conjunto Bernal. . . . I was there playing tejano

music—the host band each weekend. Rudy and the Reno Bops would go there. . . . The only band that I got off to was Sunny's band [Sunny and the Sunliners]. Of course, I dug Little Joe's band, too [the Latinaires]. (Tony Guerrero interview, November 14, 1992)

As Guerrero attests, by the middle of the 1960s, a new generation of orquestas was eclipsing the stars of the previous era: Little Joe and Sunny Ozuna were squeezing out Isidro López as the new icons of the orquesta tejana tradition. Little Joe and Sunny's growing success and their challenge to Isidro López were attributable to one factor—the emergence of a new generation of Texas-Mexicans, children of World War II. Themselves members of this generation, Sunny and Little Joe represent a departure from the cultural position of the previous historical bloc, the Mexican American Generation. They were raised in Texas-Mexican communities already deeply immersed in the process of Americanization. The dilemmas that had plagued the Mexican American Generation—were they Mexican or American, rancheros or urbanites?—were far less pressing to the postwar bloc. Members of the latter were more "naturally" American, just as they were less competent than their predecessors in the communicative ways of traditional Mexican culture.

As well, in their relationship to the Anglos, the Texas-Mexicans had gained considerable status by the mid-1960s, as the dialectic of conflict continued to unfold. The old relationship between dominant Anglo and subordinate Mexican had given way to a more contestable struggle. Although racism and discrimination against Mexicans still prevailed across the Southwest, as a number of investigators have observed (Barrera 1979; Foley 1988, 1990; Gómez-Quiñones 1990), many Mexican Americans had achieved a reasonable degree of "structural" assimilation within the American political economy and its social networks (the "integrated sector," Barrera called it [1979:130ff.]). As Gómez-Quiñones observed, the "conscience" of Anglo-America, "aroused by the burgeoning Black civil rights movement" (1990:66), was actually making it possible for oppressed minorities to participate on a more equal basis in activities across the social spectrum. The social structure was opening up to minorities.

Mexican Americans' participation in upwardly mobile occupations made acculturation inevitable, especially with the increased schooling made available to most young people. With this schooling came increasing exposure not only to formal indoctrinating mechanisms (such as "civics" classes) designed to promote cultural citizenship, but also to informal activities such as band, football, clubs, and "cultural arts" in general (Foley 1990). Sunny, Little Joe, and countless other Texas-Mexican youths partook of these acculturative activities, and their cultural identities inevitably were affected. Like many youngsters across the Hispanic Southwest, they were influenced particularly by rock-and-roll, the key development in the American youth music market of the 1950s and 1960s. Both future giants in the orquesta tejana tradition thus began their pursuit of musical glory in the "top-forty" field. Indeed, it is remarkable that both musicians eventually abandoned more or less their pursuit of fame in that market and returned to their tejano "roots."

Little Joe and the Latinaires: From Cotton Field to Top-Forty Field

Like Isidro López, Little Joe Hernández represents an interesting socioeconomic exception to the norm among orquesta musicians. More than was true of López, Little Joe's cultural patrimony descends through a proletarian line. José María de León Hernández was born in Temple, Texas, on October 17, 1940, the seventh of thirteen children. As he recounted: "I was born in a three-wall car garage—dirt floor—that belonged to *un compadre de mi jefito* [a *compadre* of my old man]. I was the seventh, and I was the first to be born in town. Two weeks after I was born, my family had to move out of there. Because of flood, that area would flood, *y salían los animalitos, los tacuaches* [the little animals, the possums, would come out]. And I almost drowned—two weeks—and my mom, the kids, got flooded in there."

The Hernández family struggled while continuing to multiply. The family moved to the "negro section," where Little Joe was introduced to African American culture. He recalled, "My first recollection is me as a kid, and there were black kids, black neighbors all the time." Through his black neighbors' influence, he learned to appreciate blues and jazz, although he also was exposed to *música mejicana,* which played on the radio at home, and even country-western. Through it all, the one constant was poverty:

> I grew up picking cotton and *desaijando* [thinning] with the family. We didn't think we were poor; we were a big family. My dad worked in the railroad, and he would come and go with us. Do seasonal work off and on. My mom was always there, pregnant, pulling the sack with kids riding

on it and kids under the trailer *del algodón* [that hauled cotton]. In 1954 my dad got busted for possession of a couple of joints, and in 1955 they sent him up. . . . He got twenty-eight months. And I was fifteen at the time he went in. When he got out I was seventeen, and I assumed command of my family, because my older brothers were in the service. (Personal interview, November 23, 1991)

It was difficult for Little Joe to attend school. "I picked cotton till I was seventeen," he recalled. "I graduated the following year."

"From high school—you did graduate from high school?" I asked.

"No—from the fields. I dropped out in the seventh grade. Dad was in the pen."

But José María de León Hernández's fortunes were about to change. He did, indeed, graduate—from the cotton field into the field of music. Little Joe had learned the "basics" on guitar from friends and relatives, and in 1957 he joined the newly organized David Coronado and the Latinaires. The group consisted of Coronado on alto saxophone, Little Joe on guitar, Tony Matamoros on tenor saxophone, and Jacinto Moreno on trap-drums. The band quickly began to hire out for weekend dances, and interestingly, that same year the Latinaires opened for Isidro López in Victoria, Texas. "He had a big band," recalled Little Joe, "and I had a four-piece band. It wasn't even Little Joe at the time—it was David Coronado and the Latinaires—and we played on the floor for him [while he played on the stage]."

The next year the Latinaires came to the attention of Torero, a label from Corpus Christi, and the group recorded its first single (45-rpm record), a rock tune entitled "Safari," parts 1 and 2. "Safari" is an important milestone in tejano music, because it well may have been the first rock-and-roll tune recorded by a tejano group. More than that, it testifies to the intensive assimilation of popular American music taking place among Mexican American youth throughout the Southwest. Like many tejano youngsters, Little Joe and his fellow band members were grounding at least part of their identities in an American musical culture. And, like many young Mexican American musicians, the Latinaires hoped to crack the rock-and-roll market and become glamorous stars like Elvis Presley, the African American Chuck Berry, and other early idols of rock-and-roll.[1]

Thinking back to that time, Little Joe remembered the Latinaires actually performing Beto Villa's polkas and even some Balde González music. But when Torero gave them the opportunity to record,

> it was the rock-and-roll days, you know, and that was 1958. So, we put together an instrumental ["Safari"]. We were playing, you know, Beto Villa's music, and Balde González. But when we recorded, we recorded something original. And that's what we came up with.

MP: But didn't you—even after that, when you kept recording—didn't you at some point in time say, "I wish I could crack the top forty" like Sunny did?

LJ: Oh, yeah, yeah, of course. Yeah, yeah, that was everybody's dream, you know—to get on the Dick Clark Show.

Little Joe never was able to penetrate the lucrative top-forty market that rock-and-roll had become, but in 1959, when David Coronado moved out of the state, he did assume leadership of the Latinaires. Unable to compete in the top-forty field, the Latinaires turned to the traditional tejano market. However, it took time for Little Joe to make an impact in the latter. During the early sixties, Isidro López continued as the standard-bearer, while the Latinaires remained mired in obscurity. Then, in 1964, the Latinaires recorded a long-playing (LP) album, *Por un amor,* with Zarape Records, a label from Dallas. That album, and the lead song in particular ("Por un amor"), was the band's ticket to regional fame. Little Joe may have exaggerated when he claimed it was "the biggest hit that started playing outside Texas," but it did launch the Latinaires in their drive toward the pinnacle of tejano music.

In the mid-1960s, the Latinaires usually consisted of six instruments—alto and tenor saxophones, trumpet, guitar (played by Little Joe), bass, and drums, with Little Joe's brother, Johnny, included as solo vocalist or, more often, as a second voice in duets with his brother (see fig. 17). The polca-ranchera (a canción ranchera in polka tempo), relatively unadorned and unpolished, was the group's staple, often featuring Joe and Johnny singing simple duets in the traditional ranchera style, parallel thirds. Although the band's popularity clearly was on the rise, technically and stylistically the group was still immature. It was not yet on the level of Isidro López, who at this time was drawing some

Figure 17   Little Joe and the Latinaires, mid-1960s. *Courtesy Joe Hernandez.*

of the best tejano talent into his orquesta. Nonetheless, in 1965, the Latinaires recorded another LP for Zarape Records, *Amor bonito*. The new LP gained considerable popularity, enabling Little Joe to maintain his momentum for the next two or three years, when the Latinaires entered its second and most successful stage. That stage ushered in a whole new era, but I shall defer discussion of that era until the early career of Little Joe's contemporary, Sunny Ozuna, has been explored.

Sunny Ozuna: "El Monito de Chocolate" Strikes Gold

After the decline of Isidro López, Little Joe's fiercest rival remained, always, Sunny Ozuna, nicknamed (among other monikers) "El monito de chocolate" ("the chocolate figurine," after the title of a Sunny LP). Born in a barrio on San Antonio's turbulent South Side, Ildefonso Ozuna—Sunny—early on decided he wanted to play in the top-forty rock-and-roll market. He was incredibly fortunate, "squeezing through the eye of the needle," as he himself characterized his glorious, if brief, stay near the top of the charts in 1962 and early 1963. He even realized the dream of every neophyte tejano musician of his generation: he actually made a guest appearance on Dick Clark's television show, *American Bandstand.* That one-shot exposure to national fame may have been fleeting—Sunny quickly faded from the top-forty scene—but it established him as "el consentido" ("the favored one," another of his stage nicknames) in the field of tejano music.

Singer-guitarist Sunny Ozuna was born in 1943, the third of eleven children. Like Little Joe, he was no stranger to poverty. In an interview, he recalled his early life: "We had the john out in the backyard, and we used Sears and Roebuck catalogue for toilet paper" (personal interview, March 5, 1980). Sunny did finish high school, however, and his experiences in the urban San Antonio school system had a profound impact on his musical sensibilities. Early in his musical development, he acquired a predilection for American popular music—in particular, rock-and-roll. In fact, so strong was his desire to become part of the world of popular American music that he also cultivated a pronounced dislike for Mexican music—especially the tejano variety. For a time, at least, Sunny was able to keep alive his assimilationist fantasies.

Sunny Ozuna began his musical career in the late 1950s, when he and a friend, Rudy Guerra, organized the group, Sunny and the Sunglows. According to Sunny,

> I was coming out of high school, and because of Elvis Presley and all the rock-and-roll era—in the fifties—we kinda started playing more for record hops in the high schools. . . . I guess the height of that was around sixty-two, sixty-three. Then things started changing; then we went to the ballrooms. We used to play places like Patio Andaluz, Arthur Murray's, the Tourist Ballroom. . . . But we were still basically concentrating on just English [American] music during that time.
>
> The group was called Sunny and the Sunglows; [it] existed for about four and a half years. . . . Toward the time we were gonna break up, we decided to record a song, "Talk to Me". . . . It started to get concentrated air play. Then at the time that we broke up, there was this guy named

Huey P. Meaux—he came into the picture. He picked up the song, ran with it, and made it into a national hit. Through Meaux[,] the song was in the top forty for fourteen straight weeks—latter part of '62 through '63.[2]

The circumstances surrounding the breakup of the Sunglows remain unclear; Sunny did not elaborate. But Manny Guerra, a tejano drummer-turned-entrepreneur who initially mentored the Sunglows (his brother Rudy was a member of the original group), feels that Sunny was enticed by greedy "others" (perhaps Meaux) into dumping the original group and seeking fame on his own. Sunny himself now views that period as one in which a bewildered teen was talked into signing a "fifteen-page contract where they would own just about everything of the guy who recorded" (personal interview, March 5, 1980). In any case, a new Sunglows group was formed, this one managed by Meaux. According to Sunny, "It was a question of getting people to understand that it was the same guys as far as the front was concerned, but it was another group."

For a few heady months in the second half of 1962 and early 1963, Sunny and the Sunglows basked in the top-forty limelight. "Talk to Me" had struck "gold" (reaching sales variously estimated at between 100,000 and 250,000 units), and, according to Sunny, Meaux was eager to exploit the group's bicultural versatility, in hopes of reaping another bonanza:

Since we were bilingual—we were all Spanish boys—he figured, "We ought to try some new ideas." So the more we started to tinker with it, we came up with a song called "Cariño nuevo." It was the perfect thing to do with my first album. . . . Being that we were getting all this attention with "Talk to Me," was the reason la Onda [the post-Isidro tejano sound] got a chance for someone to pay attention to it. Now, Little Joe had recorded a few things by then. But he was not really getting the attention. (Personal interview, March 5, 1980)

Sunny's notoriety in the top-forty market indeed may have helped launch his career in the tejano market, just as it is quite possible that his manager, Huey Meaux, saw the potential for success in that regional arena. "Cariño nuevo" did very well, establishing Sunny as a force in tejano music. Many subsequent recordings would keep "El monito" near the top of the tejano charts for years to come. But the indisputable fact is that Sunny and the Sunglows were unable to duplicate the success of "Talk to Me," and Meaux may have made a strategic decision to test Sunny's drawing power in the less competitive tejano scene. Sunny himself recognized the transient and fickle nature of the rock-and-roll market. He contrasted the dynamics of the two markets and commented on his decision to concentrate on tejano:

> There were several things. When I got to the stage where a lot of people that are still in my—talking about Little Joe, Jimmy Edward—that would still like to know what it feels like to have a national hit. I lived in that jungle for a while, and I didn't like it. I'm not saying that I wouldn't like to have another "Talk to Me," and make the money that comes off it, but it's a jungle. You have friends and money only while you're there. The minute that song dies, "Sunny who?" Now, la Onda—what is nice is that if you're cold for awhile, they still come out to see you. The white market is not that way. Chicanos hold on to their roots, and hold on more to their stars. They back them better. (Personal interview, March 5, 1980)

"Chicano stars" did indeed enjoy long careers, as Beto Villa, Isidro López, and Narciso Martínez demonstrated, but in the early sixties, Sunny was not looking forward to such a career. He was still enthralled by the glamour of top-forty fame, and his entry into the tejano circuit was reluctant at best. Manny Guerra, by then a seasoned drummer with Isidro López, recalled: "When I started the Sunglows, I told Sunny, 'You guys should learn a few polkas.' And Sunny said, 'I hate Spanish music. I don't want nothing to do with Spanish music.' I said, 'If I'm gonna send you to the circuit where I play with Isidro, you need to play some polkas'" (personal interview, November 27, 1992).

His loathing for "Spanish" music notwithstanding, as the luster of his meteoric rise in the "white" music scene dulled, Sunny began to reconcile his dreams with the more limited possibilities that the tejano market might offer. In 1966, he recruited the three Villanueva brothers from Houston, known as the Rocking Vs, reorganized and renamed his group Sunny and the Sunliners, and began to concentrate his energies more and more on the tejano market (fig. 18). Música tejana would remain his staple for the rest of his long career.

Figure 18   Sunny and the Sunliners, mid-1960s. *Courtesy Ramón Hernandez.*

Rise of the Chicano Movement: Birth of la Onda Chicana

In 1965, in Delano, California, César Chávez led a group of farm workers out of the vineyards and began the long and bitter grape strike that would serve as a catalyst for the wholesale mobilization of a new generation of Mexican Americans—the Chicano Generation. Symbolically, the farm workers' walk-out marked the beginning of a politico-ideological explosion, known as the Chicano movement, in the Hispanic Southwest (Gómez-Quiñones 1990; Muñoz 1989; Rosen 1975). Within a few years, Chávez had organized a full-fledged union, the United Farm Workers Union (UFW). Inspired at least in part by Chávez's odyssey, a small but vocal intellectual bloc centered in various universities followed his example and launched the Chicano movement.

Propagated from universities such as the University of California at Berkeley, the University of California at Los Angeles, and the University of Texas at Austin, the fledgling Chicano movement was in a strategically advantageous position to spread its ideological agenda into the grassroots communities, thanks to a dedicated cadre of students eager to disseminate the agenda's ethnocentrist politics. The central tenet of the Chicano movement, which it shared with the black-power movement and other "decolonization" projects, was romantic (cultural) nationalism (Fanon 1965; McLemore 1980; Memmi 1965; Murgía 1975). The driving ideology of romantic nationalism, first articulated by the German philosopher Johann G. Herder, is the militantly romantic notion of "one people, one language, one glorious heritage"—all in need of reaffirmation at critical moments, when its advocates perceive threats from within or without (Wilson 1973). The Chicanos declared the 1960s their critical moment.

Perhaps because of the totalizing aims of romantic nationalism—its drive to forge a monolithic cultural voice—one of the Chicano movement's central objectives was to suppress factional opposition within the Mexican American population, particularly opposition rooted in gender and class difference. Women were subsumed under the category "Chicano," as if the masculine noun could gloss over real gender disparities, especially the subordinate position of women in and out of the movement.[3] Class, meanwhile, became a nonentity, except as a label to be used against upwardly aspiring Mexican Americans seen as assimilationist *vendidos* (sellouts) "imitating the way of the patrón" (Valdez 1972:xvi; see also Valdez's play *Los Vendidos*). To be or act "middle-class" and *agabachado,* or Americanized (the two were viewed as synonymous), was to betray the ideal of *Chicanismo:* a *carnalismo* (brotherhood) born of the mystical link to the land, the campesino (field worker), the barrio (neighborhood), and, ultimately, the cultural economy of kinship and reciprocity thought to have governed indigenous "ancestors" (see Franco 1970: chs. 3 and 4).

As noted, the defining features of the ideology of Chicanismo were the intense search for "roots" and the need to reject the "alien" culture of the Anglo. Driven by the mystical bonds of Chicanismo, those involved in the movement began to search in earnest for the Mexican Americans' cultural heritage—which often was traced all the way back to ancient pre-Columbian civilizations. According to movement doctrine, these ancestral civilizations, long "buried under the dust of conquest" (Valdez 1972:xiii), had been decimated by two waves of invaders—first, the Spaniards, who crushed the pre-Columbian peoples; and then the Anglo-Americans, who colonized their descendants, the Chicanos. For too long, the hyphenated "Mexican-Americans" had denied their "true" cultural identities, foolishly (and fruitlessly) trying to become Europeans. Only through a determined effort to resurrect the "myth of Aztlán" could the "Mexican-Americans" be transformed into "Chicanos" and thus begin the arduous road toward reconciliation with their legitimate cultural ancestry.[4]

The task of cultural revival naturally fell to the movement to accomplish. And so, through the artistic arm of the movement, "The Chicano Renaissance" (Ortego 1970), a campaign was mounted to restore the ancient patrimony and to revitalize "Chicano culture." The revivalist campaign may have been centered in key universities, but—as a result of student activism; the participation of grassroots organizations (e.g., La Raza Unida Party, the Crusade for Justice); and, to a certain extent, the mass media and its legitimation of ethnicity in the United States—some aspects of Chicanismo gradually filtered through the Mexican American communities of the Southwest. In the process, at least some of the key strategies of the Mexican American Generation were thrown into doubt. The most important was the touchstone of that generation's agenda—acculturation, or Americanization. That agenda was replaced by one of *disassimilation,* a repudiation of what Luis Valdez called "neon gabacho culture" (1972:xv). Even among the more culturally accommodationist Mexican Americans, ethnic consciousness was heightened, as well as willingness to acknowledge their Mexican origins. In short, for many Mexican Americans, it became acceptable to be "Chicano"—someone proud of his (or her) indigenous and mestizo "roots."

The drive to reaffirm "Chicano" culture took many directions. It was evident, first, in the field of literature—a logical development, since the universities were the key breeding grounds for a new ideology of nationalism, Chicanismo.[5] Poets and writers like Luis Valdez, Alurista, Inez Hernández, Rudolfo Anaya, Raúl Salinas, and many others consciously tapped the cultural wellspring of indigenous/mestizo Mexican culture to create a truly romantic-nationalist literature (see Lomelí 1993). Meanwhile, writers less overtly nationalist—Tomás Rivera and Rolando Hinojosa-Smith, for example—relied upon the lived experiences of contemporary Mexican Americans to evoke the full range of *mexicano* culture in the United States.

Among the most culturally important creations in the world of literature were those that resonated with developments taking place in everyday contemporaneous culture (as opposed to literary works reinventing the Chicanos' past). I refer to an increasing literary use of bilingualism, which paralleled the rapid evolution in everyday speech practices toward a synthesizing bilingualism known in some linguistic circles as "compound bilingualism" (Erving and Osgood 1954; Lambert 1978; Vaid 1986). "Spanglish," the Mexican American variety of compound bilingualism, consists of the practice wherein speakers alternate between English and Spanish within the same sentence.[6] As sociolinguists have demonstrated, the hallmark feature of compound bilingualism, intrasentential code-switching, is governed by certain rules related to syntax and grammar (Jacobson 1978; Vaid 1986). Within the Chicano Renaissance, notable examples of the literary use of compound bilingualism include José Montoya's "La Jefita" (1972), Alurista's "Mojologue" (1979), and Inez Hernández's *Con razón corazón* (n.d.; passim).[7]

Most strongly associated with the historical bloc Álvarez and others have called the Chicano Generation, compound bilingualism has been theoretically linked to a more global form, "compound biculturalism" (Peñalosa 1980). Both are a product of the intense process of cultural synthesis going on in the sixties and seventies, through which cultural antinomies were subjected to a powerful form of mediation, or "reconciliation of opposites" (Williams 1977:97–98). But, ultimately, Spanglish and other forms of bicultural expression were the logical outcome of the dialectic of conflict defining the Anglo-Mexican relationship in the Southwest. The decade of the 1960s was the historical moment, or conjuncture, when intercultural conflict—this time fomented by the Chicano movement—could be quite intense; paradoxically, interethnic cooperation reached unprecedented levels. As Gómez-Quiñones observed, "There was change as well as lack of change" (1990:101). The dialectic of conflict had attained full momentum.

Besides literary (and folkloric) bilingualism, the one medium of artistic expression most responsive to the cultural synthesis then being forged by tejanos was the orquesta. Indeed, as early as 1967, the label La Onda Chicana was coined by Johnny González of Zarape Records as a way of linking the new style of Little Joe and the Latinaires to the ethnocentered consciousness emerging among Mexican Americans. We may recall that, during the days of Beto Villa and Isidro López, the form of bimusicality practiced was what we may call "coordinate bimusicality," consisting of the juxtaposition—but seldom the synthesis—of American and Mexican, ranchero and jaitón, styles. Orquestas played one or the other, just as "coordinate" bilinguals speak one language or another but never mix the languages in the flow of conversation, especially at the intrasentential level (see Erving and Osgood 1954; Jacobson 1978; Lambert 1978).[8]

In the 1970s, however, orquestas tejanas launched an intensive stylistic transformation: they began to alternate Mexican-ranchero and American-jaitón styles *within* the same musical piece—that is, at the level of the phrase—to create a synthesis or hybrid: compound bimusicality, a musical homologue to compound bilingualism. The effect was nothing if not arresting, as normally incompatible musical elements were brought together to form new and hitherto unimaginable musical gestalts (see, for example, Little Joe y la Familia's LP, *Para la gente*). How this development—compound bimusicality—interacted with developments at the level of politico-ideological activity is a fascinating subject for interpretation. I explore that interaction in connection with Little Joe and Sunny's own changing musical sensibilities.

Little Joe and La Onda Chicana: Pinnacle of a Musical Ideology

In 1967, Little Joe Hernández began in earnest the reorganization of his orquesta. Up until then composed of *músicos líricos*—musically untrained musicians—the Latinaires fluctuated between overtly rock-oriented tunes and simple, relatively unpolished rancheras. All the arrangements were improvised, or learned "by ear," the band members "sit[ting] around for hours trying to figure out their parts" (Tony Guerrero interview, March 28, 1980). In 1967, however, Little Joe brought in Tony "Ham" Guerrero (a.k.a. Martínez), a skilled and experienced trumpet player. As Guerrero recalled, "None of the guys read music; [when] I suggested that we read some good charts, they all laughed at me" (ibid.). However, eventually Guerrero did get the Latinaires to "read some good charts," and in 1968 the band recorded its first album in three years, *Arriba,* now with a label Little Joe had launched, Buena Suerte Records. According to Guerrero, "The album was so different . . . the size of the band went from six or seven to ten, and—the style of music didn't change, the *sound* changed—became hipper, became a bigger sound" (ibid.).

Meanwhile, the whole aesthetic sensibility of the Latinaires was changing. Guerrero recalled "a little stagnant period" in 1969, when Little Joe finally decided that "the James Brown look," with its "$250 suits," was "dated." Ac-

Figure 19   Little Joe y la Familia, 1972. *Courtesy Ramón Hernandez.*

cording to Guerrero, here is what followed: "He [Little Joe] said, 'I've decided we're gonna drop the Latinaire bullshit, and we're gonna go to *la Familia,* and we're gonna become hippies with long hair.' So we dropped it [the name] . . . and all of a sudden the guy says, 'I'm gonna grow my hair long.' And he became the first freak *en la Onda Chicana. Andaba* [went around] Little Joe with real long hair down to his ass. He looked like a cross between a hippie and a militant Chicano" (ibid.).

By 1970, the aesthetic transformation was complete—new fashions and hairstyles (hippie/militant Chicano), a new name, a countercultural lifestyle that included drugs (principally marihuana), and, for Little Joe at least, a drift toward the ideology of Chicanismo (figs. 19 and 20). The last is critical, for it points to the connection between the Chicano politics of the sixties and seventies and the powerfully symbolic name change, from the anglicized Latinaires to the nationalist *la Familia.* Little Joe himself expounded on this connection in a couple of interviews (November 23, 1991, and May 6, 1993).

Figure 20   Little Joe and brother Johnny in performance, late 1970s. *Courtesy Ramón Hernandez.*

An extended excerpt from the 1993 interview follows; it reveals the extent to which the movement influenced Little Joe's musical ideology.

MP: What brought about the change from Latinaires to la Familia?

LJ: Uh, well, the fact that I was born and raised in Temple, Texas, where everything was pretty much—still is—black and white [i.e., in terms of racial segregation]. Uh, and then in the late sixties, uh, hanging around the Bay Area, playing all around San Francisco, around there, and becoming aware of *latinismo*. And that was during the days—late sixties, early seventies—when Santana was just taking off, when so many other groups from the Bay Area [were "taking off"]. I just became aware of, really, *latinismo*, uh, *la cultura*, and our heritage, our music. . . . And I just became aware *que* [that] speaking Spanish was hip, you know, that was the thing happening. And I knew I needed to make a change, uh, from Latinaires to something closer to home, something closer to roots.

MP: Was the fact that the Chicano movement was going strong at that time—did that have any influence on you?

LJ: Uh, the Chicano movement—La Raza Unida and all that—uh, was not really at that time part of that, but during that time, also, early seventies, uh, Luis Gazca and Jim Castle made me aware of César Chávez and the Farm Workers' movement. And I got involved in doing concerts, and I met César, and that was one part of it. Then La Raza Unida happened as well, you know.

MP: Did you become involved in that?

LJ: Very much so, *con José Angel Gutiérrez.*

MP: Didn't you go to Mexico as an ambassador once, sort of like a musical ambassador, with Gutiérrez?

LJ: Yes, I did, with a delegation of representatives *de aquí de los Estados Unidos* [from here, from the United States], and I remember reading the, uh—and hearing the news in Mexico, *"Llegaron los líderes Chicanos a México"* [the Chicano leaders have arrived in Mexico]. And we met *con el Presidente López* [López Mateos]. . . . And, uh, yeah, I was very much involved with the, you know—supporting *la causa* [the cause]. And it, again, you know—more so, I just reaffirmed my commitment to *música chicana*—that we have something of our own, you know. . . . And, uh, no matter what kinds of music I do play, I know we have our own, and that movement just made me reaffirm that.

(Personal interview, May 6, 1993)

Thus, despite Little Joe's initial denial, and as his explanations make abundantly clear, the Chicano movement did influence his changing musical ideology, and his decision to adopt a name "closer to roots." What could be more "Chicano" than "la Familia?" He was particularly affected by the Farm Workers' movement and the politics of José Angel Gutiérrez's La Raza Unida Party. In sum, the ethnic politics of *la causa* generally resonated with Little Joe's own awakening sense of cultural nationalism, hastening the transposition of his political views into a musical ideology. We pursued the connection between political ideology and music further:

MP: Do you think your music—even though most of the time it wasn't overtly political—that there was something about it that awakened in *la raza* [the Chicano people] a certain feeling of ethnic pride?

LJ: I think—yeah, that happened; even today, you know, there's a lot of Chicanos that take pride in everything that we do—how we talk, how we dress, how we eat, how we do our music. But this is something the younger generations . . . aren't really aware of, you know. . . . Uh, and we need another movement; we need to become—make this a movement, and music's always played a big part in making things happen. . . . We need to bring that awareness to *la raza,* and music is a big part of any movement.

Music was thus an integral part of Little Joe's political ideology as it evolved in the early 1970s. At the same time, however, influenced by Santana and other groups in the Bay Area, Little Joe's continuing aim was to upgrade his orquesta. According to Tony Guerrero, in 1971 Little Joe approached him and said, "Ham, I want to make my band the baddest, heaviest band that there's ever been, because we want to get into the rock market. You know a lot of good musicians. Why don't you put a band together for me?" (T. Guerrero interview, November 14, 1992). Little Joe confirmed Guerrero's statement: "So it was through him [Guerrero] that we contacted [trombonist-arranger] Joe Gallardo . . . and we got Gallardo in the band and other real good musicians" (Little Joe Hernández interview, November 23, 1991).

Now surrounded by the "baddest" band, at least in the tejano circuit, Little Joe was ready to launch la Onda Chicana to the next level of its development—although he still kept an eye out for the possibility of breaking into the rock market. In 1972, la Familia recorded an album for Little Joe's Buena Suerte Records, *Para la gente,* that was to rival anything Beto Villa ever marketed, especially beyond the state of Texas, the traditional stronghold of orquestas tejanas. Several of the numbers on the album became instant standards for "copy-cat" orquestas all across the Southwest, including the most memorable cut of all, "Las nubes," which became a virtual anthem of the Chicano Generation.[9]

Para la gente was the first LP by any tejano group to exploit what I earlier called a "compound" form of bimusicality—where styles identifiable as Mexican ranchero and those identifiable as sophisticated American swing-jazz were yoked together within the same musical piece to create, in effect, a hybrid or synthetic music in a relation homologous to compound bilingualism. Several of the tunes prominently displayed "intrasentential code-switching" between ranchero and sophisticated.

For example, the most arresting piece on the album, the polca-ranchera "Las nubes," opens with an instrumental introduction (two trumpets, trombone, two saxophones, plus rhythm section of electric guitar, electric bass, Hammond organ, and trap-drums) marked by a strong ranchero flavor. Very shortly, however, a totally unexpected string ensemble joins the horns, creating a lush orchestral effect that threatens constantly to dissolve the basic ranchero style. Later, after the duet of Little Joe and his brother Johnny finishes singing the chorus, a *legato,* almost *andante* interlude, featuring the violins in rich harmonic clusters, contrasts dramatically with the *allegro con brio* that dominates the vocal sections. At the end of the string interlude, a shrill guitar note abruptly ushers in a saxophone duet in the harmonic stereotype of the ranchero style, parallel thirds, before Little Joe and Johnny reprise the chorus. Meanwhile, the horn obbligatos inserted between the vocal phrases maintain a steady barrage of jazz-oriented licks in what amounts to a constant code-switching between a Mexican and an American musical "language" (ranchero and swing-jazz).

Little Joe understood—at least implicitly—the symbolic magnitude of his innovations. I elicited from him several statements about his state of mind at the time *Para la gente* was produced. The following comments, on the "blending" of swing-jazz and ranchero in "Las nubes," illustrate his bimusical strategy:

> I wanted to do something different, and I wanted to put some class into the music. . . . But you just can't put a round pad [jazz] in a square [ranchera]. It doesn't work that way. Things have to follow naturally, and they have to blend and to connect. They have to synchronize. . . . when you go from the jazz feel to ranchera, everything can blend if you ease it in and out. But the whole idea is in the feeling. It has to feel like that is your intention. . . . So for me to blend all these things together *es una capirotada, una ensalada de música* [it is a *capirotada,*[10] a music salad].

It's possible only because that's all in my head and in my heart—because I live it. (Personal interview, May 6, 1993)

But the full realization that he was capable of dominating a "bilingual, bicultural" music did not dawn on Little Joe until all the necessary variables were in place—a receptive public (the Chicano Generation); a chain of radio stations sympathetic to tejano music; and, above all, musicians like Joe Gallardo and Tony Guerrero, who proved to be masters of the art of bimusicality.[11] *Para la gente* was the first—yet already fully ripened—fruit to blossom from Little Joe's newfound competence in the art of bimusical performance, and it took the Mexican American community by storm, not only in Texas but throughout the Southwest. His and others' labors in the field of compound bimusicality would produce many more harvests. Among la Familia's most successful efforts should be included the LPs *Total* (1973), the overtly nationalist *La voz de Aztlán* (1976), and *Sea la paz la fuerza* (1978).

Perhaps because it was homologous to compound bilingualism, the "compound bimusicality" of *Para la gente*—the constant switching between Mexican ranchero and American swing-jazz—resonated deeply within the aesthetic sensibilities of Mexican Americans throughout the Southwest, and particularly among the younger Chicano Generation. Most important of all, however, was the symbolic erasure of old class-based distinctions encoded in the ranchero/jaitón cleavage. Just as the ideology of Chicanismo momentarily effaced class distinctions, so did la Onda Chicana obliterate its aesthetic corollary, the conflictual distinction between ranchero and jaitón. More than that, by synthesizing American and Mexican musical horizons through the fusion of swing-jazz and ranchero elements, la Onda Chicana marked a high point in the dialectic of conflict driving Anglo-Mexican relations in the Southwest. This was the moment when—thanks to the agitation of the Chicano movement—the hyperbola of conflict reached the point of saturation or infinity, only to reappear as a new set of coordinates based on accommodation and even intercultural assimilation. In their own dialectical fashion, Anglos and Mexican Americans were transforming difference into identity.

Sunny Ozuna and the Sediments of Contradiction

La Onda Chicana may represent the triumphal moment of synthesis in a long history of aesthetic opposition, but it never fully succeeded in transcending that opposition. Even at its zenith, la Onda as a synthesizing artistic movement betrayed the telltale sediments of its conflict-ridden social origins. More than Little Joe, Sunny Ozuna embodied the uneasy truce between musical synthesis and social contradiction. His characterization by a playful Tony "Ham" Guerrero as the "city mouse," in opposition to Little Joe, the "country mouse," pinpoints Sunny's ambiguous position within the romantic-nationalist ideology that made possible la Onda Chicana.

To begin with, Sunny never was involved in any active way with the Chicano movement—hence, he lacked the explicit political ideology that motivated his chief rival in la Onda. Second, Sunny and the Sunliners never committed themselves exclusively to la Onda Chicana. As Sunny recalled, "We didn't concentrate totally on la Onda Chicana. Onda Chicana was just one phase of what we were doing. The mariachi thing was another, and then the English thing was another" (Ozuna interview, March 5, 1980). Finally, and most important, despite some spectacular breakthroughs in musical synthesis by the Sunliners, Sunny never quite unscrambled—as Little Joe did— the ideological underpinnings that made possible the compound bimusicality involved in the ranchero-jaitón synthesis forged by la Onda Chicana. Instead, having basked—if only momentarily—in the national limelight of the top-forty market, Sunny always considered himself a higher-class performer. Although of humble origins, he perceived his music as more "middle-class" than that of Little Joe. His perception of la Onda Chicana and its sociomusical dimensions merits further examination.

It is worth pointing out, first, that others, too, perceived Sunny as more urbane and "citified" than Little Joe. Tony Guerrero, who dubbed him the "city mouse," remembered his early impression of Sunny as "more sophisticated." Johnny Zaragoza, Sunny's long-time agent, spoke of him as more "middle-class oriented" than Little Joe or some of the more ranchero Onda Chicana orquestas, such as Agustín Ramírez and Freddie Martínez. "Sunny tries to cater more to the middle class than Little Joe does," was his assessment. Lastly, a dance promoter described Sunny's influence on la Onda as follows: "Besides being an innovator, Sunny put 'class' into la Onda Chicana. His dances were a gala affair. He offered quality, and people dressed up to go see him. Women wore gowns, and guys would at the least wear ties" (Marcelo Tafoya, publicity bio, Manny Music [n.d.]).

In an interview, Sunny described his own sociomusical position, and in so doing, he revealed some of the contradictions confronting him. For example, he characterized the supporters of la Onda Chicana as "simple-minded" and "average" (not unusual, however, for orquesta musicians to consider themselves more sophisticated than their public). Here is a segment of that conversation:

MP: Are they working-class people?

SO: Yes, they are. And it's your everyday Joe walking on the street. He lives in the barrios. He does fix himself up and goes to discos, he does go to rock concerts, he does all this stuff. But mainly he stays within his own—the biggest percentage of the time he stays within his own particular environment, his own particular barrio.

MP: Let me interrupt you. You're saying something slightly different from what Johnny Zaragoza told me—an interesting remark he made in talking about some of the basic differences between you and Little Joe. He said, "Little Joe is more ranchero. Sunny caters more to the middle class." Do you agree with that?

SO: I feel that, and I'm gonna clear that up for you. This is what it is: The reason why Joe sounds more ranchero is because Joe records songs and flavors them more to what we call barroom songs— songs that you're gonna hear in all your cantinas. . . . Our type of thing has been more—this is gonna sound a little offensive: Joe, Freddie, Agustín cater to what we call a lower class. By lower class we classify this way: migrants, real into-the-barrio people, people that have more tendency to have problems, and to be more in the wrong place at the wrong time. What we have tried to work for— Jimmy Edward, myself, Latin Breed—have gone into what we call "middle class." . . . I'm not looking down on [Little Joe's audience], but I like my particular audience.

(Personal interview, March 5, 1980)

Yet, Sunny recognized that a rigid dichotomy between working and middle classes was no longer possible, insofar as what constituted the core audience of la Onda Chicana. Specifically, he realized that, despite Little Joe's reputation as a ranchero performer, the latter was capable of matching his own most sophisticated efforts. By way of probing the social implications in the relationship between ranchero and sophisticated within la Onda Chicana, I engaged Sunny in the following dialogue:

MP: Isn't Joe encroaching on conjunto audiences when he plays that kind of music ["barroom" rancheras]?

SO: Very much so. Where conjunto people would not follow me, those people have a 75 percent chance that they're gonna follow Joe. Where really, they shouldn't be following Joe, 'cause Joe should be classified more to the middle class. . . . Now me, I've got a direction, and whether I'm going deeper into the middle class, or whether I'm going to reach some kind of medium between the upper class and the middle class—I don't really know where it will lead to, but for the time being I've got to follow it. Now, don't get me wrong; there's a lot of people in the lower class who come to see us, and wanna understand, and wanna come up. They don't want to stay there. . . . And there's a lot of us—for example, I come from the barrio myself. I come from a family of eleven kids myself. And we had the john out in the backyard, and we used Sears and Roebuck catalogue for toilet paper, you know? I wasn't born in the middle class, but I wanted to progress, and I'm what I would consider the middle class for now.

(Personal interview, March 5, 1980)

And so, wishing to remain "middle-class," Sunny and the Sunliners projected an image of sophistication, and his clientele responded by dressing up for his dances (fig. 21). Nonetheless, Sunny intuited, at least, that ultimately la Onda Chicana transcended class tastes, if not contradictions. He understood la Onda as a musical expression that appealed as much to the ecumenical ethnic as it did to narrow class interests. He expounded on this understanding in our discussion, first, of the symbolic role of the polca-ranchera in la Onda Chicana and tejano music generally; and, second, of the influence of the Chicano movement on his music. Discussing the roles of the various genres in tejano music (cumbia, bolero, rhythm-and-blues), Sunny offered his assessment of the polka:

MP: What about the polka? It seems to me that tejanos want their polkas. They'll take the other stuff, but, don't they always wanna come back to the polka?

SO: Sure.

MP: To what do you attribute that? Why haven't Chicanos become like

Figure 21
Sunny in performance,
late 1970s. *Courtesy
Ramón Hernandez.*

other Americans? Why must they have Sunny Ozuna, Little Joe? Is
this for lack of acculturation, discrimination—what?

SO: I don't think it's any of that. I think that variety is the spice of
life. . . . That we have boleros . . . cumbias . . . cha-cha-chas . . .
polkas—we can appreciate all of it. For some reason that I don't
totally understand yet. . . . We keep coming back to the polka. I
don't know whether it's because of the barrio roots, the way they
were brought up. . . . If you get a little drunk, for some reason you
wanna hear a polka more than anything else.

(Ozuna interview)

Sunny and I had been discussing his entry into the tejano market in the
mid-sixties when he made the comment about Chicanos' "holding on to their
stars." That prompted the following exchange concerning the influence of the
movement on his music:

MP: This might be way off, but you remember the Chicano movement
of the sixties? Chicanos began to wake up, so to speak, and along

with this there was a back-to-the-roots movement. Did that affect you or la Onda Chicana in any way?

SO: It brought us a lot more customers, because in the awakening they wanted to relate back to—OK, I'm Chicano. So a lot of people that were lost into a white world, at the time—when the awakening came—it made them realize, "Hey, man, you do have black hair, and you do have brown skin, and you are Chicano." So when they turned around to look for roots, not only did they look into ancestry and all that, but they started to look into "What music is gonna represent me? Where are my roots?" If country-western represents the cowboys, we automatically became la Onda Chicana. So they related to Joe, Jimmy [Edward], and everyone else [in la Onda]. A lot of them looked to us and a lot looked to conjunto, but they considered themselves Chicano.

(Ozuna interview)

The bedrock of la Onda and conjunto was the polka—or, since the late fifties, the polca-ranchera (the canción ranchera in *tempo di polka*). But the orquestas in la Onda took the logical final step: they took this quintessentially tejano genre and interlaced it with elements from swing-jazz to create the ultimate ranchero-jaitón synthesis—compound bimusicality. Having inherited a bicultural sensibility from the Mexican American Generation, Onda Chicana musicians like Sunny and Little Joe naturally were predisposed toward some kind of fusion of the disparate elements circulating in tejano music since the 1940s. The back-to-the-roots thrust of the Chicano movement, the conjunctural alignment of Anglo-Mexican relations in the long-running dialectic of conflict, and especially the synthesizing impulses of the Chicano Renaissance—all these provided the requisite climate to bring about what Little Joe called the "synchronization" of various musical elements and to forge the compound bimusicality of la Onda Chicana. Aesthetically, this was a perfect—if temporary—resolution of the contradictions dogging Texas-Mexicans since the 1920s, when they first began to agonize over their cultural citizenship.

As a musician thoroughly familiar with both American and Mexican music—one who, moreover, had bridged the yawning contradiction symbolized by the backyard privy and the glittering set of Dick Clark's *American Bandstand*—Sunny became one of the great exponents of the hybrid I have called compound bimusicality. Beginning with an LP titled *Los enamorados,* recorded in 1974, Sunny and the Sunliners experimented with this hybrid style until 1980, when they began to retreat toward a harmonically simpler, less bimusical approach.

One particular number in *Los enamorados* stands out as perhaps *the* most ambitious fusion of swing-jazz and ranchero in the whole field of la Onda Chicana. This was a bolero entitled "Y" ("And"), transformed by the Sunliners, naturally, into a polca-ranchera. "Y" begins as a polka, but almost immediately it is overwhelmed by an insistent swing-jazz effect that shifts back and forth among the various instrumental lines, most notably the bass line. The overall result is a constant assault on the integrity of the polka rhythm. While most Onda Chicana arrangements observed the principles of "intra-sentential code-switching," in the sense that the style-switching from ranchero to swing-jazz was effected at discrete junctures (usually at the end of vocal phrases, in the form of instrumental obbligatos), in "Y" the style-switching occurs *simultaneously* at various levels. For example, at any given moment the singing and trap-drum accompaniment may be within the ranchero style, but the bass line conforms to the "walking-bass" pattern, in eighth-notes, typically associated with swing-jazz. These cross-rhythms blur the basic "feel" of the polca-ranchera, threatening to dissolve the integrity of the genre. But to the Texas-Mexicans, the ranchera-swing-jazz hybrid was eminently satisfying, aesthetically. Unconsciously they may have perceived the style-switching peculiar to la Onda as an extension of the speech they used in their most intimate circles.

Sunny's discography, like that of Little Joe, is extensive. In addition to numerous singles (45-rpms) released in the 1960s, first the Sunglows and later the Sunliners together released over fifty LPs under various labels, including Sunny's own Key-Loc Records. Among the most memorable in the rock and rhythm-and-blues venues are *Talk to Me* (1963) and *Yesterday—and Sunny Ozuna* (1976; a reissue of many of Sunny's 1960s tunes). In the more prolific tejano output, *Cariño nuevo,* Sunny's first in the tejano market, is a notable contribution. In his later, Onda Chicana phase, *Los enamorados* (1974) stands out, as we have seen, as the most ambitiously bimusical. But *Grande, grande, grande* (1978) represents the stylistic pinnacle of Sunny's career in la Onda Chicana. The arrangements are polished and sophisticated, and the bimusical synthesis of swing-jazz and ranchero is subtle yet pervasive.

Demise of la Onda Chicana: End of the Orquesta Tradition

During its brief heyday, from about 1970 to 1980, la Onda Chicana churned out innovative polcas-rancheras at a dizzying pace, as several orquestas contributed to the new style, in addition to Little Joe y la Familia and Sunny and the Sunliners. In 1973, Tony Guerrero and Joe Gallardo led a mutiny against Little Joe, convincing most of the band members to join them in forming a new group, Tortilla Factory. Tortilla Factory's first LP, *La Malagueña* (1973), for Manny Guerra's GCP Productions, continued la Familia's bold experiments in compound bimusicality. The LP *Tortilla Factory* (1974), recorded with Falcon, contains some of the most outrageous examples of musical code-switching. A polca-ranchera entitled "Tu amor y el mío," for example, self-consciously divides jazz and ranchero elements into "clauses," as ultra-ranchero vocal phrases alternate with jazzy instrumental obbligatos in what amounts to a dialogic parody of the two styles.

The Latin Breed, an orquesta from San Antonio organized in 1973 by Gibby Escobedo and Rudy Guerra (of the original Sunglows), contributed some brilliantly executed bimusical numbers. Just as Tortilla Factory was an offshoot of Little Joe y la Familia, so was the Latin Breed a reconstituted version of Sunny and the Sunliners (without Sunny, of course; he went on to re-organize his orquesta). Escobedo recalled the group's origins: "Everybody left Sunny except for the drummer. . . . So the whole horn section [from the Sunliners] came here—all of us" (personal interview, February 19, 1980). Throughout most of its existence in the 1970s, the Latin Breed consisted of two trumpets, three saxophones, trombone, and the usual rhythm-and-harmony complement of bass, guitar, keyboards, and trap-drums.

Like most Onda Chicana bands, the Latin Breed was exceptionally versatile, performing a wide spectrum of musical styles from boleros to rock to salsa, but the group's most memorable tunes were in the quintessential Onda Chicana style—the bimusical polca-ranchera. Two fine lead singers span the era of the Latin Breed—Jimmy Edward (Treviño) and Adalberto Gallegos. The most memorable LP the group recorded with the former as lead singer was *The Return of Latin Breed,* and an outstanding contribution featuring the latter was the *Power Drive* album. That LP includes a polca-ranchera (originally a bolero), "Hay que saber perder," which represents the epitome of musical code-switching in a tightly arranged, highly sophisticated—yet also ranchero—mode.

Jimmy Edward Treviño, from San Antonio, quit the Latin Breed in 1976 and organized his own group, which simply went by the name "Jimmy Edward." Thoroughly bimusical, the Jimmy Edward band contributed at least a couple of albums that represent the high point of synthesis achieved within la Onda Chicana. These were *My Special Album* and *Jimmy Edward: Romántico*. Like the other tejano orquestas of the seventies, Jimmy Edward's consisted of a more or less typical complement in the horn section—two trumpets, trombone, and two saxophones—in addition to the usual battery of accompaniment instruments.

Two more orquestas deserve mention in this survey of la Onda Chicana before its collapse—those of Agustín Ramírez and Freddie Martínez. These two represent a marked departure from the bimusicality that was the norm among Onda Chicana orquestas. Singer Agustín Ramírez is noted for his *voz apretada* ("tight," or forced, voice) style, as Tony Guerrero described it, and his rather long, if unspectacular, presence on the orquesta tejana scene. Indeed, his voice style, considered hard-core tejano ranchero, influenced several other singers in the Onda phase, including Joe Bravo, Carlos Miranda, and Freddie Martínez. The style of Ramírez's orquesta was perfectly compatible with his singing: it featured the simple two- or, at most, three-part horn harmonies common in música ranchera. *El barco chiquito,* produced by Zarape Records, is one of Ramírez's most popular albums and is representative of his style, although his best-known song undoubtedly was the polca-ranchera, "Qué chulita estás."

Freddie Martínez and his orquesta were particularly active in the early seventies, when the group issued the LP *Te traigo estas flores,* one of the best-selling records during the Onda Chicana period. But Martínez's productions were strictly mono-musical works in the polca-ranchera genre, characterized by stubbornly simple, unadorned harmonies. Martínez made no attempt to delve into the bimusical world of Little Joe, Sunny, and other Onda Chicana orquestas.

"Why the simplicity?" I asked (personal interview, March 13, 1980). "Was this by design?"

"La gente le entiende más [people understand it better]," responded Martínez. "I could've done arrangements that would knock everybody out, as far as musicianship. Pero yo sé bien que la gente quiere simple stuff [But I know well that the people want simple stuff]. . . . It's been proven over and over."

Yet, of course, Little Joe, Sunny, Latin Breed, and others proved the opposite—that the complex synthesis of ranchero and jaitón they invented could elicit a strong response from "la gente." But that response was keyed to a unique historical moment and its politico-cultural milieu—a Chicano Generation educated and Americanized enough, yet ethnically sensitized enough, to appreciate the synthesis forged by innovative Onda Chicana groups like Little Joe y la Familia. In 1980, however, on the eve of the collapse of la Onda Chicana and the whole orquesta tradition, Freddie Martínez could argue that Little Joe and Sunny had "failed." They may have been successful briefly with their bimusical and "more progressive" experiments, but, he claimed, "nobody followed Joe and Sunny. Latin Breed kinda tried, and then they broke up. So they all realized that—y se vinieron pa' atrás donde están ahora [and they came back to where they are today]" (Freddie Martínez interview).

Freddie Martínez was correct in sounding the death knell for la Onda Chicana, at least as it was constituted in the 1970s by a complex synthesis of ranchero and jaitón. But the consequences were to be much more drastic than that: the era of the orquesta itself, as a commercially viable ensemble, was about to end. What was happening? Why, in the midst of its efflorescence, was la Onda Chicana collapsing so precipitously?

To begin with, Freddie Martínez was absolutely correct when he pointed out that Sunny, Little Joe, and other Onda Chicana orquestas had retreated to "where they are today." One notices this retreat in the albums issued by both Sunny and Little Joe beginning in 1980. Sunny's LP, *Amor de mis amores,* for example, is notable for the relative simplicity of its arrangements. Although a few flourishes are heard here and there, none of the dense harmonies and complex cross-rhythms of earlier productions are present. Most important, the strong bimusicality—the bold shifts from ranchero to swing-jazz— is absent from the music in *Amor de mis amores.* Lastly, the presence of the synthesizer in several numbers foreshadowed the shape of things to come. As Sunny recalled, "We were starting to tinker with synthesizers, trying to change the trend" (personal interview, January 23, 1997). In the end, however, the changing trend was not directed by Onda Chicana orquestas. The next generation of musicians assumed that role, making the synthesizer the centerpiece of their music—which became known as Tejano (with a capital "T").

Little Joe took a similar path. In two LPs, *De colores* (1980) and *Prieta linda* (1981), a much more ranchero and unadorned sound is evident, a sound harking back to the years before *Para la gente.* Also evident in both LPs is a downsized horn section. As with Sunny, the ranchero-jaitón synthesis of the 1970s is conspicuous by its absence. Like Sunny, Little Joe was plunging into the synthesized music of the 1980s. Finally, in the case of both giants of la Onda Chicana, after 1981 their record releases began to consist more and more of "oldies-but-goodies" collections, as they capitalized on their legendary status rather than innovating. For example, in Little Joe's discography after 1980, "old hits" albums outnumber new productions by at least three to one. Clearly, the older icons of música tejana were being eclipsed by new ones—groups such as Mazz, La Mafia, and others who would define the new musical era, moving it from "la Onda Chicana" to simply "Tejano."

The demise of la Onda Chicana and, with it, the whole orquesta tejana tradition, can be attributed to several factors.[12] First, and most readily recognized by orquesta musicians themselves, are two related developments—the recession and hard economic times of the early eighties, and the affordability of downsized groups built around the synthesizer. Manny Guerra put the matter succinctly when I asked him what had brought about the demise of the orquesta:

MG: What did away with so many people working? Machines did. It's the same with music. I get in the studio and I can take any part of any kind of music and put it any way that I want, electronically. I wouldn't be able to afford that, if I had to hire the people.

MP: So it's a matter of economics, then?

MG: That's what it is. Nowadays it's all synthesizer.

(Personal interview)

Guerra praised the convenience of the synthesizer, compared to undependable or talentless musicians, while he defended the new Tejano groups as superior in innovative capacity to the older Onda Chicana orquestas: "Today we have the capability of doing things that we never dreamed we could do. . . . That's why I welcomed the electronic age. When you have someone playing [electronic] keyboards, and he can play all three, four parts, he can play them individually on different tracks, and the thing never gets out of tune."

But perhaps the ultimate blow to the orquesta tradition was administered by a new generation—what we may call the "post-Chicano" or "MTV" generation. Strongly influenced by the electronic age generally and the pervasiveness of synthesized music and visual effects in the era of MTV, younger Texas-Mexicans, now thoroughly "postmodernized,"[13] drifted inexorably toward the glitter of "smoke and bombs," as veteran orquesta musician René Sandoval characterized the music emerging among Texas-Mexicans in the 1980s. As the irrepressible Tony Guerrero put it, "You want to know what really changed la Onda Chicana? The bottom line—MTV. People today listen to music with their eyes" (Guerrero interview, November 14, 1992).

Freddie Martínez, by 1980 the owner of a successful regional label, Freddie Records, summarized the negative influence of rock music in market terms: "In the early seventies, a strong hit record [in la Onda] could easily do 50,000 units. There wasn't as much hard rock then as there is now. All the young kids would buy our stuff as well. Now, my kid listens to Ted Nugent, Kiss . . . and all his friends are the same way. Thousands of [tejano] kids go to the [rock] concerts instead of going to our dances, and that has hurt our record sales" (personal interview, March 13, 1980). In fact, as Martínez hinted, the musical fragmentation of the post-Chicano generation was draining the very life out of la Onda Chicana. It did not survive much beyond 1980.

Meanwhile, música tejana was rediscovered by the major labels—Capitol EMI, CBS, WEA, Sony—and many of the newer synthesized groups were embraced and marketed by these labels. Mazz, la Mafia, la Sombra, and later groups like Emilio Navaira and his Rio Band signed major-label contracts, having been preceded by the Onda Chicana icon himself, Little Joe Hernández, who signed with CBS in 1985. Many groups also renewed the practice, initiated by Sunny, of "crossing over"—recording for two different markets, the tejano-latino and one of the proliferating American segments—country-western, rhythm-and-blues, top-forty, etc.

Fittingly enough, perhaps, as la Onda Chicana waned, so did its most basic emblem, the polca-ranchera. The newer Tejano groups began to rely more and more on a pan-latino cumbia, which was more marketable internationally than the polca-ranchera. A genre first popularized in Latin America in the 1960s, the cumbia by the 1980s had become an international symbol of (mostly) working-class latino identity. Manny Guerra, who in 1992 had a distribution arrangement with WEA Latina, summarized the order of things when he stated, "What we're doing is, our music has been changing constantly to a more commercial sound" (Guerra interview). Then he added:

> For example, *la polca se está dejando ir poco a poco* [we're letting go of the polka little by little]. *Y al ratito ya no va a haber polcas* [and after a little while there will be no more polkas]; it's gonna turn into *baladas* and *cum-*

bias or that type of Latin music. . . . Where we're going is—instead of seeing what the tejano wants, we're catering to the Hispanic. . . . We're trying to find a central place where someone in Panama, El Salvador, Mexico, can identify with it [our music]. Then you have a potentially worldwide hit in the Latin market. (Guerra interview)

Thus ended the reign of the orquesta tradition in Texas and the Hispanic Southwest, its departure marked by the gradual disappearance of the polca-ranchera. New economic realities, electronic musical means, a new generation, and a global market strategy all conspired to undermine and then displace what once had been a powerfully symbolic music. Playing a part in all of this was the dialectic of conflict itself—that engine of culturally symbolic activity so central to the aesthetic process in Texas-Mexican life. With the decline of the ideological activism of the Chicano Generation and the retreat of American politics toward a reactionist stance, the 1980s and 1990s witnessed a retrogression in Anglo-Mexican relations. New and subtler forms of discrimination appeared—forms seemingly concealed within the deepest folds of the social structure evolving in American life.

Having lost the ideological intensity of the sixties and seventies, minorities such as the Mexican Americans were unable to present a unified political front against neo-racism. Cultural and political fragmentation now became the rule. In sum, the post-Chicano era was one of cultural and political (in)difference. The Mexican American population in the Southwest was scattered, like its music, into myriad fragments.

In Texas itself, the process of creating a new music to supplant la Onda Chicana was fraught with cultural pitfalls. When the major labels once more injected themselves into the Texas-Mexican market, they induced a climate of opportunism that undermined the commitment to "Chicano" music once evinced by Sunny and Little Joe. Old dreams of "cracking the big time" resurfaced, as the new commercial opportunities conjured visions among Tejano groups of fame, glory, and fortunes to be made. Encouraged by their big-label producers, one after another considered "crossing over" into this American market or that, or else catering to the hemispheric "Hispanic" market. The "cross-over" and "go-latino" strategies of Tejano musicians inevitably implicated the distinctions discussed earlier—organic versus superorganic; music driven by use-value versus music subject to exchange-value; and, most important, music as cultural symbol versus music as commodity.

The heightened commodification of Tejano music raises an intriguing question: Was la Onda Chicana the last of the unambiguously organic musical symbols of a tejano identity? The next chapter explores the tension between Tejano music as organic culture and as superorganic commodity.

Notes

1. I was living in the Rio Grande Valley in the 1950s. In 1958, Henry Ayala, Eddie Ramírez, Luis Sosa, and I formed a rock-and-roll group, the Rocking Kings, which eventually became the Matadors. Ours was one of several Mexican American youth bands in the Valley who concentrated on the exploding rock-and-roll music scene. However, most of us also performed in tejano orquestas. The Matadors eventually made a brief foray into the commercial rock-and-roll market, recording two singles with Backbeat Records, out of Houston, in 1959.

2. Information on Sunny derives principally from an interview, March 3, 1980. I interviewed him briefly again on January 23, 1997.

3. See Chabram-Dernersesian (1992) for a review of the dissenting views of Chicanas.

4. Cf. Padilla (1989:114): "Without heroic dreams and cultural symbols of mythic proportion, the material aims of a nationalist movement may lack the spiritual center which sustains struggle."

5. See, e.g., the two founding "charters" for the Chicano movement, "El Plan Espiritual de Aztlán," and "El Plan de Santa Barbara," both promulgated by activists in academia (Anaya and Lomelí 1989; Muñoz 1989).

6. An example of intrasentential code-switching is this statement by the orquesta musician, Delia Gutiérrez Pineda: "As time changed, ya ni podías ir a los bailes, porque se juntaba pura pachucada" (As time changed, you could not even go to the dances, because nothing but pachucos [tough, lower-class zoot-suiters] would gather). (Moy and Delia Pineda interview, July 9, 1979).

7. See Jordan (1972, 1981) on the use of compound bilingualism in folkloric verbal art.

8. According to Lambert (1978:218), "Early bilinguals seem to develop more pervasive superordinate systems which subserve both languages [compound bilinguals]. . . . Late bilinguals seem to have relatively more compartmentalized semantic systems . . . their two language systems seem to be more functionally independent [coordinate bilinguals]."

9. At that time I was playing with Beto García y sus GGs, an orquesta in Fresno, California. The GGs and the other dozen or so orquestas in Fresno all made

"Las nubes" and other tunes from *Para la gente* part of their repertoires. The music was immensely popular with the local Mexican American dance crowds.

10. A *capirotada* is a dish concocted from various ingredients—bread, cheese, raisins, cinnamon, egg—all blended in such a way as to yield a unique taste distilled from all the ingredients.

11. Radio coverage was a crucial variable. Disc jockeys often were unsympathetic to música tejana, particularly those from Mexico. As many Onda Chicana musicians complained, the Mexican disc jockeys played this music grudgingly or not at all.

12. Orquestas as such did not die out, of course. Up until the 1990s, localized orquestas continued to exist in Texas and elsewhere, but there were of the jaitón, or what Manny Guerra called the "high society," variety. Among these were Ricky Díaz's group in Houston and Paul Elizondo's in San Antonio. An orquesta tradition with the ideological charter that empowered Beto Villa and Little Joe ceased to exist in the early 1980s.

13. The term "postmodern" has many meanings. I use the term here in two related senses: the emphasis on transient surface appearances and their shifting effects and the impact on social life of the political economy of the commodity-as-sign. Both, it is claimed, have a "decentering" effect that makes permanent social formations (such as class) difficult if not impossible. See Jameson (1984b, 1994) and Balibar (1994).

6 ❊ Tejano

Music of the Post-Chicano Era

"Tejano," as the various Texas-Mexican musical groups and their styles are labeled collectively in the 1990s, labors under a formidable contradiction: it is torn between the traditional role of música tejana as an organic cultural expression and the goal of Tejano's big-label sponsors to transform it into a profitable mass-market commodity. On the surface, this tension between organic symbol and superorganic commodity manifests itself in a struggle by Tejano artists to reach larger audiences, even as they tacitly recognize that, historically, theirs is a music with strong regional and ethnic roots. There is thus a constant effort by major Tejano performers such as Emilio Navaira, the late Selena, and others to internationalize their appeal, ever aware that, as long as they are identified as "Tejano," their marketability remains handicapped by their association with what major-label producer Cameron Randle called a "regional, blue-collar" music (personal interview, May 9, 1996).

The tension between the localized identity of contemporary Tejano music and its large-scale commoditization merits closer examination, as it bespeaks of the tendency of "postmodern" culture generally to dissolve identity into (in)difference. Identity is nurtured by cultural forms that galvanize groups into self-proclaimed communities, lending them a sense of shared "peoplehood" and a common ideological purpose. Mass-commoditized music thrives in the atmosphere of "decenteredness" promoted by the commodity-mediated social relations present in many contemporary social formations, where the communicative function of artistic culture is articulated through objects consumed in atomistic patterns that weaken, rather than solidify, community bonds based upon shared ideological interests. Caught on the cusp, Tejano music—

like its core constituency, the Texas-Mexican community—wavers between the world of local, organic symbols and their use-value, and the marketplace of superorganic commodities and their exchange-value.[1]

This chapter explores the contradictions between contemporary Tejano music as an organic artistic expression and as a mass commodity, recalling the earlier discussion of use- versus exchange-value and cultural performance versus spectacle. The operative principle in this chapter is best summarized by a Mexican proverb: "El que mucho abarca, poco aprieta," which in one sense may be translated as, "The wider the coverage, the weaker the grip." In the case of Tejano music, this inverse relationship seems to obtain between its commercial expansion and its symbolic "grip."

Origins of Contemporary Tejano

Journalistic writers describe Tejano as "basically Mexican polkas and cumbias, mixed with elements of rock, pop, country, and even rap" (Burr 1993:41). This description is adequate enough in a rough sense, in that all Tejano groups rely upon three common genres for their repertoires—the well-worn polca-ranchera, the *balada* (a love song in slow tempo), and the cumbia, this last often laced with elements from various extraneous styles (reggae and rap, for example). Nonetheless, there is a vast symbolic difference between the polca-ranchera and the other two, and any snap descriptions will miss this critical difference, not to mention important variations among the groups that labor under the rubric "Tejano."

For example, despite stylistic and repertorial overlap, there is significant variation between El Grupo Mazz and Emilio Navaira and between La Mafia and Selena—all considered "Tejano." All, of course, owe a debt to the traditional conjunto and to Onda Chicana orquestas, in terms of the stylistic thread and unique emblem that historically has linked tejano music: the polca-ranchera. But some Tejano groups—La Mafia and Emilio Navaira, for example—have relied on the polca-ranchera much more than others, although in the nineties La Mafia shifted decidedly toward the internationalized cumbia and balada (see, for example, the LP *Un millón de rosas*), while Navaira turned his attention toward American country-western (as in his LP, *Life Is Good*).[2] Groups like Mazz, on the other hand, have staked their fame on the balada, which has more transnational appeal than the polca-ranchera. And the "Queen of Tejano" herself, Selena, achieved fame through the most universal of commercialized latino genres, the cumbia.[3] Other Tejano groups share the stylistic and repertorial range of the "Big Four."

It is important to keep in mind that Tejano groups, in line with their stylistic distinctions, vary with respect to their links to earlier Texas-Mexican forms such as the orquesta and the conjunto. Emilio Navaira, David Lee Garza, and other "progressive" conjuntos clearly are positioned in a long line descending from early conjuntos like Narciso Martínez and Valerio Longoria. Like other contemporary accordion-based groups, Navaira and Garza are unequivocal heirs to a persistent tradition with deep roots in tejano communities, a tradition whose trademark remains the polca-ranchera. Strengthening the ties between progressive conjuntos and their historical counterparts is the presence of conjuntos known commercially as "traditional," such as Los Chamacos, La Tropa F, Mingo Saldívar, Michael Salgado, and others, who adhere more closely to the style of the sixties and seventies.

The stylistic difference between "traditional" and "progressive" conjuntos is sometimes difficult to pinpoint. However, the former generally preserve the four-instrument ensemble, as forged by postwar pioneers—three-row accordion, bajo sexto or guitar, electric bass, and drums. Their style, particularly with respect to the polca-ranchera, is not significantly different from that of the earlier conjuntos. Progressive conjuntos, on the other hand, are more apt to include synthesized keyboards and to branch out in diverse stylistic and repertorial directions, in particular country-western. Cameron Randle, an executive with Arista Records, described the latter as "turbo-conjuntos"— "rocked up conjunto [that] has transcended what conjuntos have traditionally been able to present in concert" (Randle interview).

The other generic styles current in contemporary Tejano, the balada and cumbia, stand unequivocally outside the core Texas-Mexican traditions. This is not to say that they were foreign to the conjuntos and orquestas of the sixties and seventies; but the cumbia was performed infrequently and only after being subjected to a process of "tejanoization," whereby it was reformulated to conform to the styles peculiar to the conjunto and the orquesta. The balada almost always was transformed into a *canción-bolero* by the earlier tejano groups. Both the balada and cumbia had become enormously popular in Latin America by the late 1960s, when *grupos tropicales,* or *gruperos,* such as Rigo Tovar, Mike Laure, Los Bukis, and others, and *grupos modernos,* such as Los Angeles Negros, Los Babys, and Los Yonics, swept the latino market. Utilizing the synthesizer's predecessor, the electronic organ, as a melodic anchor, these groups made a considerable impact in the Hispanic Southwest, particularly among Mexican immigrants.

Balada and cumbia groups were not especially popular in Texas, where la Onda Chicana and the conjunto reigned supreme; but as immigration from Mexico mushroomed in the 1970s, both types of group ascended to prominence in the Lone Star State. El Grupo Mazz appeared at this historical moment (in 1977), becoming the first tejano group to make consistent use of the synthesizer *and* stray from the polca-ranchera, yet still achieve widespread popularity among Texas-Mexicans. La Mafia, from Houston, debuted shortly (in 1979); it became the first tejano group to wed permanently the polca-ranchera to the synthesizer. Between them, El Grupo Mazz and La Mafia shifted what soon would be christened "Tejano" music closer to the transnational, synthesizer-driven latino style then gaining strength in urban Latin America. Incorporating the cumbia and the balada into their repertories on a consistent basis, Mazz and La Mafia soon eclipsed the Onda Chicana bands, with their brass-heavy jazz-*polcas.*

Unlike progressive conjuntos, whose reliance on the accordion and the polca-ranchera grounds them to a tejano aesthetic, ensembles like Mazz have been inevitably tempted to go the way of the cumbia and the balada. However, by the mid-nineties, Tejano cumbias were taking on an increasingly diffuse character, in the form of a pastiche consisting of basic cumbia, glazed with elements from ska, reggae, and even hip-hop or "funk" (see, for example, "Estúpido romántico" and "Traicionera" from Mazz's LP, *Solo para ti* [1995]). It could be argued, of course, that the cumbia-plus-reggae or cumbia-plus-funk experiments represented a new synthesis rivaling that of la Onda's bimusical jazz-*polcas.* However, careful listening reveals the superficiality of the mix. In "Estúpido romántico," for example, the cumbia rhythm is dominant, with the reggae barely perceptible as a surface effect in the bass and guitar accompaniment. The deeply dialectical fusion of jazz and ranchero found in la Onda polkas is missing in the "cumbia-plus" mix. What we find in the latter is a mimicry of diverse styles "stored up in the imaginary museum of a now global culture" (Jameson 1984b: 65).

In any event, for Mazz and its epigones (La Diferenzia, for one), the accordion remained a token of their tejano origins, used only for the occasional polca-ranchera (absent the jazz-ranchero fusions, of course). The synthesized keyboard had otherwise become the workhorse for melodic development and obbligato backgrounds.

Manny Guerra and others maintain that synthesized keyboards provide a limitless range of sounds to the new *grupos*—a reasonable assertion. In practice, however, ensembles like Mazz and La Mafia tend to "play it safe." With few exceptions, they have adopted what old-time orquesta musicians Tony Guerrero and René Sandoval hear as a "bland" sound, best described as an amalgam of synthesized violin and the "Hammond organ" effect popular in the sixties and seventies.[4] As for the rest—guitars, bass, percussion, and special electronic equipment (e.g., "samplers")—a wide assortment of effects has been achieved, some quite novel; but, on the whole, the *grupos* have not strayed very far from the styles of their predecessors in the seventies, especially in the realm of harmonic progression. Cumbias, in particular, but also baladas, still tend to use many of the harmonic formulas of the sixties.

In sum, the principal advantage of contemporary Tejano groups over those from la Onda Chicana is the vastly improved recording quality provided by digital audio technology. Liberally underwritten by the big labels (and their big money), this technology has spawned lavish studios able to enhance the surface dazzle of the synthesizer. Meanwhile, the allure of the "big time" has motivated a host of young tejano composers and certain instrumentalists (bassists, guitarists, keyboardists, drummers) to strive for a more virtuoso level of competence. In short, electronically enhanced instruments, good talent, and digital audio technology consistently deliver smoother—certainly glossier—performances than were common in the heyday of la Onda Chicana.

Tejano Music and the Commercial Market

Intense commercialization of Tejano music began in the mid-eighties, coincidental with the changed state of Mexican American society after the retreat of the Chicano Generation, with its essentialist ethnic strategy (see chapter 5). Tejano music is a product of the post-Chicano generation, a generation influenced more strongly than its predecessor by the cultural economy of "late capitalism" (or "postmodernism"; see Jameson 1984a, 1994) and its trends, which have swept the industrialized world in the last quarter of the twentieth century. A heightened reliance on commodities as emblems of individuality marks the post-Chicano bloc, as does the surface adoption of multiple identities (including musical identities; "all-over-the-dial" listeners are common), a reduced awareness of the political (hence, the bloc's depoliticization), and a general sense of cultural drift ("Generation X," its larger American cohort is called).

The cultural economy of late capitalism was transforming the post-Chicano generation into a fragmented, heterogeneous mass with a "decentered" sense of ideological purpose. Out of this mass emerged Tejano, a music at once rich in history and devoid of it.

Key to the heavy commodification of Tejano music at the end of the twentieth century is the participation of the major labels since about 1985, when the epitome of Texas-Mexican music himself, Little Joe Hernández, signed a recording contract with CBS International (later bought by Sony). Why the major labels reentered the música tejana market at this juncture, after having abandoned it at the outbreak of World War II, is unclear. In 1985, the music was in a state of relative flux, with la Onda Chicana in full retreat and its successors, the various Tejano groups, active but not yet dominant. In any event, according to Freddie Martínez, Jr., who had succeeded his father, Freddie, Sr., at Freddie Records, "I think they [the major labels] just sort of saw the buzz happening at the time and they felt they could come in here and cash in on what the independents were already doing. I think they were just expecting too much too soon. It wasn't worth the time, money, and effort they were putting into it" (Patoski 1995:80).

Eventually, of course, the big companies' entrance into the tejano market paid off handsomely for them. By 1989, Capitol/EMI (EMI Latin), CBS/Sony, and WEA Latina, as well as Mexican labels like Fonovisa, apparently had become convinced that Tejano music had an as-yet-untapped potential for significant profit. Patoski described that potential in the hyperbolic language of journalism: "Tejano wasn't just a popular ethnic regional music anymore. It was an economic sleeping giant, waiting for the right people to discover it" (ibid.). Judging from the music's success by the mid-nineties, the "right people"—the major labels with their big promotional budgets—indeed had struck a vein of gold.

More important, however, the majors introduced a new mentality into the regional orientation of Texas-Mexican music. I am not arguing here that the local tejano labels, or "indies," provided an "alternative and more sincere form of musical production" than the majors (Negus 1992:18). They, too, aimed to maximize profits. Despite the profit nexus, however, the localized market complex upon which the orquesta and conjunto relied for their livelihood—the "indies" themselves, the dance-hall circuit, and the tejano social base—all had contributed fundamentally to the symbolic power of these homegrown ensembles and their styles.

It may be true that the "introduction of major labels has fortified a record business infrastructure that was disorganized, haphazard, or, in some cases, nonexistent" (Burr 1993:41). But the intervention of the majors also led to a different dynamic: the logic of large-scale commodity production and its internal regulator, exchange-value, supplanted the independent labels and their reliance on small-scale cultural performances and their internal regulator, use-value. Nickel-and-dime tactics aimed at an endogenous regional audience were replaced by global strategies designed to attract heterogeneous audiences and far greater profits than the "indies" ever imagined.[5]

We thus hear periodic assessments of a Tejano market "exploding," "mushrooming," or "burning hot and spreading fast" (Burr 1994:30), now that the majors have taken charge. Sales indeed have boomed since the early nineties, when the "Big Four"—Selena, Emilio Navaira, La Mafia, and Mazz, all by then under contract to major labels—began to reach new levels of exposure. For example, by 1994, La Mafia had sold over 400,000 units of each of its recent albums, *Ahora y siempre* and *Estás tocando fuego* (Burr 1994:32).[6] Similarly, Selena's LP, *Entre a mi mundo,* had sold 385,000 copies in the United States and 200,000 in Mexico (ibid.). And Selena's last recording, the pop-rock album, *Dreaming of You,* debuted in the summer of 1995 as the top album in the "Billboard 200" charts; it had sold 331,000 units by the end of its first week on the market (Burr 1995:39). This sales bonanza contrasted with patterns prior to 1990, when, according to Burr, "the upper sales plateau for a Tejano act was a mere 50,000 albums" (ibid.), with sales of 10,000 to 20,000 units a more common ceiling. Along with skyrocketing record sales, the phenomenal success of Tejano artists in live concerts signaled their emergence as major market attractions. At the Houston Livestock Show and Rodeo in 1995, Selena and Emilio Navaira set an attendance record for a single performance. Over 61,000 fans attended their joint concert in the Astrodome (*People Weekly,* Spring 1995:70).

Critical to the expanding success of Tejano was the nature of the mass-music industry, particularly its capacity to control the market. By inquiring into the circuits of distribution, we can glimpse the qualitative difference between the methods of the major labels and those of "indies" like Joey, Freddie, Hacienda, and other firms operated by tejanos. Record executive Cameron Randle offered a lucid account of the dynamics involved in major-market distribution. First, unlike the limited, hit-or-miss tactics of the regional tejano labels, the majors have the capacity to saturate a targeted field. As Randle explained, "The key to success is distribution. It's the capacity of the record company not just to make records, but to make sure that those records can be placed in record stores, in as broad and far-reaching a context as possible. Every major label has a distributor. And that's why the term 'major' is even in use. A major label, as distinguished from an independent, means . . . you have major distribution. You have national or international distribution" (Randle interview).

Ray Martínez, an executive with Sony Discos, amplified on the concept of major distribution: "What's happened in the market, sales-wise, is rapid expansion of mass merchandisers like Wal-Mart, Circuit City, Best Buy, K-Mart, etc. Now distribution to these accounts is very much improved to where we can get the product in the stores at the right time, at the right locations, and make it available to the public. Before, it was kind of a hit-and-miss situation" (Burr 1995:39). And, as a veteran local distributor added, "When the majority of the labels were independent [i.e., tejano], they didn't have entrée into those accounts [Wal-Mart, K-Mart, etc.]. . . . But the majors already have their distribution outlets established" (ibid.).

Equally important for distribution is the air play given new artists, especially. Interested in learning how the majors cope with competition and the need to expose their artists, I brought up the old practice of payola during the interview with Randle. I asked how contemporary labels ensure air play for their records. Randle responded:

> What's happened, really, in essence payola has shifted. The concept has remained the same [but] the translation into reality has changed. And instead of money and drugs and women, which was prevalent, you know, for a couple of decades out there, payola now is in the form of gratuities like tickets to athletic games, airline tickets to showcases in, uh, places that make for fine vacation spots. Flying radio programmers in and out, uh, to showcases and special events. Merchandising—those sorts of things.

MP: That happens, it seems, in all—even outside the music. I mean, it happens in any kind of market—

CR: Sure, sure. It's the same as washing-machine vendors, you know, working their account, you know—giving their account reps tickets to the World Series. That's the sort of thing that we're talking about, that greases the wheel.

MP: In that context, Little Joe was telling me that a big company—I think we were talking about Capitol / EMI—if they want to, he says, if they want to really push a record, they're in a position where they can make it go. And, uh, I guess he was talking about the influence they have. So do big labels have influence like that?

CR: Yes, and I'll tell you part of the reason for that influence—is that a label like EMI Latin, which happens to be the largest in the Tejano world, uh, they'll go in and, let's say they want to get a new single by Bobby Pulido, uh, added to the radio. Their interest is in breaking this new artist, Bobby Pulido. Well, if radio likes Bobby Pulido and wants to respond immediately and play that, EMI Latin's in good shape. If there's some hesitancy, however, EMI can respond, and that response can be subtle or it can be less than subtle. They have, by virtue of their size, a roster that includes Selena, Mazz, Emilio. And their conversation with the station about Bobby Pulido can take the course that says, "If you play Bobby Pulido for us, and push this record and help us break this artist, then you'll be included in the promotion that we're putting on, giving tickets away to see Mazz on New Year's Eve"—you know—"in Houston. If, however, you choose not to help us with Bobby Pulido, your competitor may be the one that ends up with tickets to Mazz." So it's that sort of influence; it's using, you know, the prestige and the allure of one artist to promote the career of another. That's the benefit that a major label has.

(Randle interview)

Such, then, is the power of a major label—massive ability to flex its economic muscle to promote its artist-commodities. But the majors promote their artists for their exchange-value (their capacity to generate profits), not for their use-value, or the potential for galvanizing particular ideologies, especially those that may contest the social arrangements basic to the capitalist order.[7] In the ruthless, competitive climate of the mass record market, the use-value inherent in Emilio Navaira's organic links to his ethnic, working-class constituents or in the ethnically generated power of a Mexican *banda* is completely irrelevant to the logic of capital accumulation. The motive is profit, not the promotion of cultural or ideological solidarity; and the means to secure that profit is to apply pressure on those in the broadcast media, especially radio—hence the updated version of "payola."

Nonetheless, even in the calculated maneuvers of the global market, a small opening is left for local, autonomous voices to be heard. Paradoxically, even as they push for expanded markets for their productions, the majors keep their ears to the ground, so to speak (see Negus 1992: ch. 1). The perceptive Cameron Randle, again, explained the relationship between what Robinson, Buck, and Cuthbert refer to as the "global economy and local cultural autonomy" (1991:3). I asked Randle about the intricate diversification of giant conglomerates like WEA and its implications for music making "at the ground level":

MP: Is that [diversification] a more efficient way to conduct business?
CR: Absolutely. . . . As an example, again, I'm using BMG [Bertelsmann Music Group, Arista's parent conglomerate], just because that's our company, but it's true across the board for all the majors. If you look at the Arista world, BMG, which owns us and distributes us—beneath that umbrella is Arista Records, okay? Now, beneath Arista New York [and] Arista Nashville we have LaFace Records, which is a combination of producers L. A. Reed and Baby Face. It's two African American producers who have come together and merged their names and created LaFace Records, which is owned and distributed by Arista. But by the time the African American rap and R&B audience goes to their record stores in the 'hood to buy their albums, they have no clue that that's coming from Arista, which is coming from Bertelsmann. . . . that's distilled, you know, as it were, all the way down. The same thing happens in the rock and alternative market, in that corporations will have "imprints," as we call these record [labels], which are four or five levels removed from the parent corporation. And that is because there is at street level, at grassroots level, a stigma against buying what is perceived as a commercial and, therefore, less substantive product, lyrically and musically, if it's coming from the mother ship.
MP: They wanna stay as close to the ground as possible, as a marketing strategy.
CR: Absolutely.

And so, in the homogenizing world of exchange-value and the cutthroat tactics common in the mass market, the recognition exists among top executives that, at the "street level," real cultural and ideological differences do exist—differences that have led to the "decentralization" of the multinationals (Negus 1992:14 ff.). These differences are manifested in resistance on the part of certain populations to buy music perceived as alien to their esoteric tastes. Punk rock, African American rap, and even salsa are highly profitable commodities—no doubt *the* reason the major labels invest in them—but they are esoteric enough that, despite their commercial profitability, they retain an "alternative," organic quality. This quality resists the logic of the market—which is constantly to widen the circles of consumption, thereby flattening the curve of social difference and increasing profitability.[8] Tejano—especially conjunto—would seem to fit the esoteric category. Despite ambitious and increasingly successful efforts to transform and expand it from a regional to a more global market, conjunto music, like rap and salsa, remains rooted in its indigenous and esoteric base, albeit in increasingly tenuous fashion.

Meanwhile, in the transformation of Tejano from a small-scale music still rooted in community-defining use-value to a mass-produced commodity driven by exchange-value, the status of the artists inevitably was affected. Stars such as Little Joe and Sunny justifiably may be labeled "organic intellectuals" (Gramsci 1971; see Peña 1985a) who spoke, however inchoately, for the politico-aesthetic aspirations of their followers (see their comments, ch. 5). It is difficult to evaluate Emilio Navaira or Selena in the same terms—especially since their fan base no longer is confined to a geographic locale, but rather encompasses Hispanics from Anchorage, Alaska, to Monterrey, Nuevo León. And, while stars like Emilio indeed may have a vague sense of the central role of música tejana in defining the culture of their core audience, these latecomers inevitably are caught up in the commercial frenzy overtaking Tejano and in the new strategy aimed at loosening its identification with blue-collar tejano workers. International stardom, glamour, and big money beckon just beyond the Texas borders.[9] In this context, the historical significance of Texas-Mexican music—its status as an organic cultural emblem—could only recede in the social memory of the new Tejano stars.

We should note, however, that, in line with their stylistic and cultural differences, not all Tejano groups have been affected equally by the logic of commodity production for exchange-value. Despite their inclusion under the "Tejano" rubric, conjuntos—whether "progressive" or "traditional"—have achieved only limited success in the international Hispanic market, except in northern Mexico (particularly the large Monterrey market), where many recently have enjoyed a surge in popularity. On the other hand, conjuntos continue to thrive within the confines of the Texas-Mexican market. The irony, of course, is that, in the "mainstream" industry, Tejano music generally is considered "a regional blue-collar music," as Cameron Randle put it, "a secondary genre of music that is confined to a geographical area [Texas]" (Randle interview).

Yet, it is precisely its regional identity and secondary status in the commercial market that ensures conjunto's organic connection to Texas-Mexican culture. To the extent that the style remains rooted within its tejano base, it resists the reification that mass commodification and large-scale distribution promote. The question may arise, perhaps, whether a "tejano base" exists at all, given the "postmodernization" of Mexican American society generally. The answer must be, at least tentatively, in the affirmative. The very name, "Tejano," as a generic label, attests to a locus of identity for the music. Moreover, the continued concentration of Tejano—especially conjunto—within a Texas-Mexican market, and the undeniable identification of tejanos themselves with the music, are strong indicators of Tejano's persistent ties to its original, and to date still its strongest, social base.

Despite these ties, progressive conjuntos continue to strive for expanded markets, perceiving the polca-ranchera as a limitation to be "transcended" in order to facilitate mass appeal (see Manny Guerra's comments in chapter 5 of this book). Cameron Randle and I discussed that very contradiction—in particular, conjunto's symbolic (and commercial) strength within the tejano communities, juxtaposed with its efforts to break out of its regional mold. In speaking of the phenomenon known as "crossing over" or "crossover," and Tejano musicians' constant efforts to achieve it, Randle touched on various points related to music, identity, and the mass market. According to Randle, "'Crossover' is pretty much one concept . . . which is to cross over from a more obscure genre, a more confined genre of music, into a mainstream awareness or consciousness." Furthermore, for Randle, crossing over involves "filling in the blank—where you wish to cross over, as long as it is mainstream music."

MP: But even there [in the "mainstream"], there's gonna be many different styles.

CR: Many different styles.

MP: So, crossover would imply—

CR: That any of those styles comprise markets that are huge, compared to the size of Tejano.

MP: So, then, a crossover involves a move from a smaller to a larger market, but does it also involve a stylistic crossover as well?

CR: Absolutely.

At this point Randle broached the key question of the relationship among music, identity, and the mass market:

CR: So the question becomes, ultimately, in my mind, in the Tejano world, how much do we view Tejano music as a means to an end? You know, are we in danger—when you are Selena, and you're successful in Tejano, but your dream and your goal is to be a pop crossover, and you're Emilio, and you're successful in Tejano, but your dream and your goal is to be a country star—are you by that very process reinforcing the secondary nature of Tejano music? In other words, are you saying—are you sending a subliminal message which says—

MP: "Tejano's not good enough."

CR: "—this music is fine—for us Mexicans—but it's not the real deal." We just came back from the *Billboard Magazine* Latin conference in Miami. And you go down and get a very sobering reminder of Tejano's place within the latino family, musically. It's still treated, essentially, as a blue-collar, secondary genre of music that is confined to a geographical area. Now, that's within the context of latino music in general, let alone getting beyond that language border, you know, into the English-speaking market.

Thus burdened with a regional, ethnic identity of long standing and dismissed by the international music industry, Tejano music wavers in its commitment to its traditional Texas-Mexican constituency. Tejano musicians perceive the polca-ranchera as the link between their music and a strong tradition dating back into the mists of time, but they also see it as an impediment to "crossing over" into "mainstream" markets. For a promoter like Randle, one solution is to strive for "a mix of some traditional accordion-based [polkas], but also some cumbia and international pop flavors." Another option is to cross over into American mainstream markets, such as country. At this point in our interview, I asked:

MP: So is the cumbia the entry into the latino market; you've gotta do cumbia in order to—?

CR: The cumbia is an entry. I don't think—it's not necessarily required for the Tejano world. It *is* required to get beyond Texas.

MP: That's what I meant. The latino world.

CR: Exactly. Absolutely. Cumbia's what opened the door for Selena. Same thing for Emilio. Emilio's doors into life beyond Texas were initially opened by his duet with Selena. Now that was not a cumbia, that was a balada duet, but her success in cumbia enabled people to pay attention to her doing a ballad, and she did a ballad with Emilio, who was then brought to the attention of audiences in Mexico and California.

MP: I just can't picture Emilio doing cumbias.

CR: Well, it's in—Emilio has for several years focused on breaking into Mexico. And I assure you, you know, that he's worked his share of cumbias. And, it's considered the musical passport to Latin America, you know—the cumbia.

(Randle interview)

A passport, indeed, but one that in significant ways departs from a tejano musical identity and moves the artist in the direction of a diluted transnational latino "flavor"—a flavor, moreover, largely divested of the power to galvanize the politico-aesthetic interests of self-defined communities, such as the historically identifiable Texas-Mexican. Thus, Selena and Emilio, both of whom started as tejano-based acts (though Selena always was more eclectic), in the 1990s began to drift away from the polca-ranchera, the style most iconically connected to their fan base. It is true, of course, as Patoski maintains, that the "new [tejano] fan was a more modern animal who wanted to hear covers of the latest pop tunes as well the reformulated versions of rancheras, polkas, cumbias" (1995:106). But, beyond that, a real identity crisis was occurring in the 1990s, a crisis precipitated by the grinding shift of tejano society from a "centered" cluster of communities held together by cultural forms grounded in use-value to a "decentered" and increasingly fragmented population immersed in the amorphous flow of transnational commodities and their exchange-value.

Symbolic of the shift taking place at the infrastructural level of the society was the change in musical strategies—Tejano's new emphasis on the international genres, the cumbia and balada. As Patoski observed, for a surging Selena in the early nineties, "Polkas were out. Cumbias were coming on strong" (1995:107). But Selena plunged into the international fray rather late. The shift from the "centering" polca-ranchera to the "decentering" cumbia and balada actually started earlier. A group remarkable for its prescient sense for the future of Tejano had preceded the diva from Corpus Christi by at least fifteen years. I refer to El Grupo Mazz, which appeared in the mid-seventies.

El Grupo Mazz: Breaking with Texas-Mexican Tradition

Although it predated the "smoke-and-bombs" era of Selena and Emilio Navaira, El Grupo Mazz nonetheless emerged within a transforming market dynamic (as did La Mafia). While its predecessor, Los Chachos (a seventies prototype of contemporary Tejano), made tentative forays into the international style of the cumbia, Mazz early on yielded to its influence and, especially, to that of the balada. In this way the group anticipated the direction in which the major labels would move Tejano—toward styles and repertoires with a universal appeal among latinos in a transnational setting. Here it is worth recalling Manny Guerra's comments about Tejano's "catering to the Hispanic . . . where someone in Panama, El Salvador, Mexico, can identify with [our music]." This seems to have been El Grupo Mazz's objective from early in its career. Thus, while conscious of its tejano flank (and thus bound to the polca-ranchera), Mazz nonetheless projected a non-tejano aesthetic. This aesthetic was pegged to the synthesizer-driven cumbia and balada, both genres now extensively commoditized and with a far broader market than the tejano-styled polca-ranchera. Although success did not come immediately, Mazz's strategy eventually would lead to the proverbial pot of gold.

El Grupo Mazz was formed in 1977 by vocalist Joe López and his boyhood friend, guitarist Jimmy González, in Brownsville, Texas, located in the lower Rio Grande Valley.[10] Both were born in that border city in 1950. Like most Texas-Mexicans of their generation, López and González initially were influenced by the rock stars of the sixties and seventies—the Beatles, Rolling Stones, and others. Thus, when López, a 1969 graduate of Brownsville High

School, formed his first band, Phases, "Hispanic songs were scarce in their repertoire" (Mazz publicity "bio"). Phases was a short-lived group, however; in 1971, López joined the U.S. Army. When he returned to his native city three years later, he turned to "Hispanic" music, singing with various groups, including the conjunto of a still-active Tony de la Rosa. González, meanwhile, also had been involved in various musical groups, including the Fort Brown Band. When he and López decided to join forces, the new group, named "Mazz," was on its way.

Grupo Mazz's first album, *Mazz,* appeared in 1978, followed in short order by *Más Mazz.* The publicity "bio" does not exaggerate by much when it claims, "A brilliant career was thus initiated, full of musical hits and continuous triumphs." By 1980, Mazz was beginning to challenge Onda Chicana bands for popularity. According to the Mazz "bio," the group's first big hit was "Laura ya no vive aquí," released in 1980. The song "sold in excess of 50,000 units" and was rated number one by *Billboard Magazine* "in Texas, Florida, and California Latin markets."

After 1980, Mazz's musical strategy, predicated on the now standardized formula of synthesized cumbias, baladas, and a sprinkling of accordion-backed polcas-rancheras, began to impress itself upon the tejano musical consciousness. The recently dominant Onda Chicana was fading rapidly from the social memory of the post-Chicano generation. The year 1980 also marked the inauguration of the Tejano Music Awards, an annual event that increasingly has served to make or break Tejano groups. The event has grown in size, commercial importance, and glitz over the years, and its bestowal of honors such as "Album of the Year" and "Vocalist of the Year" carries considerable prestige and media exposure, at least in the Tejano market.

In the mid-eighties, Mazz began to garner its share of awards. For example, in 1986, the group's *No. 16* LP captured the "Best Album Award" for setting a "benchmark in the industry with a winning mix of catchy polkas, melodic cumbias and sweeping ballads" (Mazz "bio"). Thereafter, Mazz would be one of the perennial winners at the Tejano Music Awards (it won six awards each year for 1991 and 1992), until it was eclipsed by Selena and Emilio Navaira in the mid-nineties.

The importance of Mazz in the history of Texas-Mexican music lies in its early decision to break from what was then a hegemonic form—the brass-heavy *polca* and its bimusical synthesis of swing-jazz and ranchero. Bucking a powerful trend, Mazz opted for what turned out to be la Onda's nemesis—

a downsized ensemble anchored by the synthesizer. Factors discussed earlier clearly aided Mazz and such contemporaries as La Mafia in their drive to supplant la Onda Chicana: a deep recession and new economic realities epitomized by "downsizing," a new generation, and movement along the dialectic of conflict itself. Of paramount importance were the moral economy of late capitalism and its inroads into the consciousness of Mexican Americans. Just as the highly symbolic compound bimusicality of the polca-ranchera powerfully articulated the ideology of a "centered" Texas-Mexican community, the performance style emerging in Tejano—choreographed with "lights, bombs and smoke," delivered by a diffuse, synthesized sound and missing the sharp bimusical edge of la Onda—perfectly reflected the emergent "decenteredness" of the post-Chicano cohort. In short, Tejano constituted a promiscuous mix of styles, rather than a synthesis. And Mazz was at the very center of these developments.

La Mafia: The Internationalization of Tejano

In 1980, Tony "Ham" Guerrero, the long-time trumpeter with Little Joe y la Familia, had been inactive as a musician for a spell, and he went to listen to a new group, for the purpose, he said, of "finding out what was new in tejano music." Here is Guerrero's account of the occasion: "I saw this little group, in 1980, '81, with long hair, singing, and a bunch of little girls out there in front of the band, and they're swinging their butts for the girls, and they were pretty boys. But, musically, they couldn't play their way out of a paper bag. They were horrible, and I said, 'If this is any indication of where tejano music is going, I don't want any part of it'" (Tony Guerrero interview, November 14, 1992).

The group Guerrero heard was La Mafia. And, despite Guerrero's disdain, La Mafia went on to become the first tejano-based group to gain large-scale international success—a success it attained on the strength of an increasingly non-tejano style and repertoire and, especially, a feel for what orquesta musician René Sandoval called "the MTV effect." Influenced by Music Television, La Mafia early in its career sought to capitalize on the "sparkle and glitter" of pop-rock and thus "bring back kids to Tejano music" (La Mafia "bio"). More than Mazz and other contemporaneous groups, La Mafia became known for its "pyrotechnics" (ibid.).

If Mazz represents the tejano entry into the world of the balada, then La

Mafia represents the cumbia. Throughout their careers, though, both groups continued to cultivate, if less frequently, the tejano-styled polca-ranchera. La Mafia was formed by Houstonians Henry Gonzales, Jr., and his two brothers, Oscar and Leonard, in 1979. Before becoming La Mafia, however, the group went through several names—all in Spanish—as the Gonzáleses seem initially to have been torn between catering to the familiar tejano market and reaching out to a more international one pointing toward Mexico. The brothers finally settled on a name that would "attract attention"—La Mafia (Marty Racine, "Zest" section, *Houston Chronicle,* March 4, 1993, p. 8).

Like most tejano groups, La Mafia struggled in the beginning, playing an endless string of jobs for "table scraps," (Racine, p. 9). Yet, the Gonzales brothers early recognized the potential for large-scale success beyond the confines of the tejano market, although they realized that a stylistic change would be necessary in order to pursue such success. Thus, while initially they did include a trumpet and two saxophones (mainstays of the Onda Chicana bands), by 1982 they had converted to the typical *grupero* instrumentation—electronic keyboards, electric guitar, bass, and drums. With this move, La Mafia (like Mazz, its budding rival in the emerging Tejano scene) had begun to distance itself from the brassy style of Onda Chicana bands.

Despite its more contemporary pan-latino style, La Mafia remained a regional Tejano act for some time. Although it was "criticized for doing cumbias" (Racine, p. 15), in the mid-eighties the group was still heavily dependent on the polca-ranchera for its repertoire—an index of its continuing link to earlier Texas-Mexican traditions. In fact, on the strength of the polca-ranchera, La Mafia was able to garner six Tejano Music Awards in 1985. By this time, La Mafia had released several hit LPs, among them *Mafia Mania* (1983), *Hot Stuff* (1984), and *15 Hits/15 Éxitos* (1984), all with Bob Grever's aggressive label, Cara Records. In 1986, the group signed a contract with CBS, and with the release of their LP, *La Mafia 1986,* which reached the number one spot on *Billboard*'s "Hot Latin Albums," the Gonzáleses had climbed to the top echelon of Tejano music.

In the mid-eighties, the Gonzales brothers made another strategic move designed to enhance their on-stage image. They adopted the "MTV effect"—a "sophisticated 36-channel multi-colored light system, a special effects–filled 'pyrotechnics show,' fog and smoke machines, and a dance segment" (La Mafia "bio"). Amid accusations that the pyrotechnics emphasized sight over sound and were a substitute for their "meager talents," group leader Henry Gonzales responded, "That was absurd and untrue. We initially got into elaborate stage shows because we wanted to do something different. Most [Tejano] groups were just stand-up bands and from the beginning we wanted to entertain our people not just musically but visually, too" (La Mafia "bio"). Gonzales added, "Some of the big acts we were opening for didn't even have the sound system we had, and we had better lights, better microphones" (Racine, p. 9).

But the Gonzáleses' ambition to "go international," to reach beyond their tejano base, remained frustrated. They yearned to tap into the larger latino market, especially in Mexico. They finally got their break in the late eighties, when La Mafia finally began to penetrate the larger Mexican market—something no tejano group except Freddie Martínez ever had managed to do. According to Racine, "La Mafia began working the border towns, then found a good booking agency and 'started going deeper'" (p. 9). Despite the usual troubles with Mexican customs and their demands for *mordida* (bribe), the group finally booked a performance in the important city of Monterrey. Because La Mafia was still relatively unknown on the other side of the border, the members "worked hard on our set for that one . . . we threw in everything we had" (keyboardist Armando Lichtenberger, quoted in Racine, p. 9).

The crowd responded enthusiastically, and from that moment on, La Mafia's popularity in Mexico increased exponentially, aided by the powerful sponsorship of CBS/Sony and its subsidiary, Sony Music Entertainment Mexico. Hit after hit followed, as the group's LPs, *Estás tocando fuego* (1991), *Ahora y siempre* (1992) and subsequent ones, all earned at least the "platinum" rating (sales of 250,000 units). With their internationalization, La Mafia's style changed, as it began to place less emphasis on the polca-ranchera and more on cumbias and baladas, which were characterized by lavish mixing done in La Mafia's new recording studio. Their 1996 LP, *Un millón de rosas,* with its "unique synthesizer bass sound," encompassed all the latest latino pop-music trends and offered a dazzling acoustical smorgasbord to complement the pyrotechnics of the group's light show.

Finally, while Tony Guerrero insisted that La Mafia's music "still sucks," in the glittering facility of its arrangements—the light pastiche blended from heterogeneous influences—the group evinced an instinctive grasp of the post-modern manipulation of surface effects. Yet, for all its eclecticism, La Mafia "considers itself a Tejano *grupo*"(Racine, p. 15). But, as lead singer Oscar Gonzales (now renamed Oscar de la Rosa) admitted, "We had to overcome that brand [tejano]" (ibid.). That is to say, while tejano in designation, La Mafia cultivated a transnational style. The outcome was a stylistic glaze of pop-rock, traditional tejano, balada, and cumbia.

Selena: The Queen of Tejano

The first time I saw Selena Quintanilla-Pérez perform live was at the Miller Outdoor Theater in Houston, Texas, on September 16, 1992. I had recently returned to my native Texas after a twelve-year residence in California, and I found the sensuous power of Selena's stage presence intoxicating. Her lusty voice and lissome movements mesmerized the pulsating mass of five thousand bodies in attendance. More than that, this was a tejano audience adulating one of their own. For these fans, Selena already was a glamorous star, a native tejana whose inspiring performances would inevitably launch her to the pinnacle of international stardom.

Yet, even as she exploited her sizzling sexuality on-stage, Selena, it is said, "was from the barrio . . . she still ate tortillas and frijoles" (disc jockey quoted in *People Weekly* 1995:7). The barrio girl-turned-star theme appears repeatedly in media discussions of the emerging diva. Again, *People Weekly,* in a "commemorative issue," put her star appeal in typical journalistic perspective: "She blazed and shimmered in the spotlight, but it was the fact that Selena was happily, proudly *del pueblo*—'of the people'—that forged a powerful, personal bond between her and her audience" (ibid.).

Adding to Selena's mystique was the steep trajectory of her rise to fame. Like many Mexican Americans, hers had been a perennial struggle to break out of the normative poverty of her working-class family. Her father Abraham— her business manager until her untimely death—once had led his own group, Los Dinos, in the 1960s, but, like many other would-be stars, he eventually was forced to seek more reliable employment. He got a job at a Dow Chemical plant in Lake Jackson, near Houston, as a shipping clerk (Patoski 1995: 34), and later opened a Mexican restaurant in Lake Jackson, where Selena got her first exposure as an entertainer. The restaurant failed, and Quintanilla spent the next few years drifting from job to job. Eventually he moved the family back to his hometown of Corpus Christi, where the Quintanillas remained until Selena's death.

The future Tejano diva was born in 1971, in Freeport, Texas, the last of three children born of Abraham, Jr., and Marcella Quintanilla. Much has been made of her father's relentless push to transform her into a star, but apparently Selena displayed singing talent from a young age. After some early disappointments, including a brief relationship with Freddie Records in 1983, she and the reincarnated Los Dinos finally signed on with a bigger and more active label, Cara Records, in 1985. The following year Selena y Los Dinos signed with Manny Guerra's GP Records, and shortly thereafter the group's first hit appeared, "Dame un beso" (flip side: "Con esta copa"). According to Patoski, "Dame un beso" made number three on the Tejano list in Dallas and number one in El Paso, and even earned Selena a "Record of the Month" award in New Mexico (1995:75).

The year 1987 was an auspicious one for Selena y los Dinos. The songstress won the Tejano Music Awards title, "Female Entertainer of the Year." It was a harbinger of things to come; Selena would become a perennial winner over the next several years. Meanwhile, Los Dinos' rendition of "La bamba," the traditional *son-huapango* from Veracruz, made it to the twentieth spot on *Billboard*'s Latin charts—a first achievement for the fledgling group. In April, Selena made her second appearance with fellow tejano Johnny Canales, whose increasingly popular television program, the "Johnny Canales Show," by then was reaching audiences throughout Latin America and the United States. On this occasion, Canales's show was taped in the Mexican border city of Matamoros. According to Patoski, at sixteen Selena was "filling out" and "there was a tinge of sexuality projected from the stage," while the youthful entertainer displayed a new level of self-confidence. In short, "the whole act had upgraded" (1995:78).

The year 1989 perhaps will be remembered as the turning point in Selena's quest for stardom. As had become almost routine for the budding starlet, she again swept the important Tejano Music Awards, being named "Female Entertainer of the Year" and "Female Vocalist of the Year." Los Dinos' contract with Manny Guerra had recently expired, and, as Patoski observed of activities backstage, the "reps" from the major labels were "schmoozing and sucking up" to Abraham Quintanilla, Jr. (1995:95). All were vying for Selena's next contract, now fully convinced that a major star was on the rise. Capitol/EMI, soon to be the dominant label in Tejano music, won the competition for Selena's talents. But more important for Selena and Tejano music generally were the comments of José Behar, an executive with the giant label. "We feel that Selena is not only a great Tex-Mex artist," he told the *Corpus Christi Caller-Times,* "but she can be a major star in Mexico and the South American market" (Patoski 1995:95). Selena's ties to her tejano roots were being loosened, even as she was being groomed for the international market.

Once Selena signed with Capitol/EMI, her rise to the pinnacle of the Tejano market was nothing short of meteoric. Her first CD with Capitol/EMI, *Selena y los Dinos,* was released in 1989, and the lead song, "Contigo quiero estar," eventually made it to eighth place on *Billboard's* Mexican Regional chart, the highest ranking yet for los Dinos. Most critical for Selena and Tejano music generally was the assiduous promotion of her records by Capitol/EMI. Utilizing methods reminiscent of those discussed above by Cameron Randle, the company's promotional staff "worked the radio stations as no independent producer had before" (Patoski 1995:96). Backed by Capitol/EMI, los Dinos' stock began to soar; as Patoski put it, "the traveling Quintanillas were pulling some decent change, with increasingly frequent five-thousand-dollar guarantees and advertising tie-ins" (ibid.: 98). It did not take long for Selena to reach a new landmark: her LP, *Selena y los Dinos,* reportedly became the first by a female tejana artist to sell 50,000 units.[11]

But Selena was reaching another important threshold; she rapidly was being transformed from the barrio girl-next-door into a merchant of sexuality. Patoski recognized this transformation: "When Selena turned eighteen [in 1989] . . . she became not only a woman, but also a full-blown commodity, signing with Capitol as well as Coca-Cola. . . . She had a voice that could growl ferociously, do a bedroom croon, or sound sweet, fragile, and totally wild all at once. . . . Her body was filling out with curves that added another potent weapon to her performing arsenal, a simmering, sensuous sexuality. Her flower was in full bloom" (1995:95–96).

In the ensuing years until her death in March 1995, Selena increasingly would capitalize on her "simmering sexuality." Indeed, commercial exploitation of her bursting nubility, as well as the "MTV effect" of bombs, smoke, and lights, by now *de rigueur,* cannot be underestimated in her meteoric rise to the pinnacle of Tejano music after 1989. While her voice did indeed possess the power and flexibility that impressed Patoski and other music journalists, the instrumental arrangements of los Dinos cannot, musicologically speaking, be judged as equivalent to the innovations of Little Joe y la Familia and other Onda Chicana groups—or even El Conjunto Bernal. Here Manny Guerra's comments are of some significance. While he may have had his own *machete* to grind (he lost Selena to Capitol/EMI), Guerra was not merely venting steam when he said of los Dinos: "What they're doing is bubble gum music" (Manny Guerra interview, November 27, 1992).

In the end, Selena followed the lead of the internationally oriented Mazz and La Mafia: she "played it safe" by adhering to the more or less standardized latino "flavor" built around the synthesizer. Moreover, while the young diva possessed considerable singing talent and a magnetic stage presence, she inevitably succumbed to market pressures and converted her voluptuous body into a commodity. It is precisely here that the paradox between use-value and exchange-value came to a head in the person(a) that was Selena Quintanilla. On the one hand, as *People Weekly* proclaimed, Selena was "happily, proudly *del pueblo,*" an attribute that, in true use-value fashion, "forged a powerful, personal bond between her and her audience" (p. 7). Everyone who knew her intimately praised her warmth and readiness to reach out and connect with other human beings. In many ways, she still played the role of the imaginary working-class Mexican American girl who obeyed her parents, practiced good manners, and endorsed the "wholesome lifestyle" of Mexican American culture. She was the simple barrio girl-next-door, as the movie *Selena* goes to great lengths to portray.

Yet, as *People Weekly* also recognized, Selena could be "smoldering" in her sexuality, particularly on stage. After 1989, Selena became a highly visible figure, an entertainer constantly in the public eye, and it became more and more necessary to manage her public image. More significant, directly in proportion to her burgeoning popularity, she seemed increasingly determined to exploit commercially her new image as sex icon. Thus, as *People Weekly* correctly observed, "On-stage, Selena was smoldering, flirtatious and passionate" (Spring 1995, p. 7). But the emphasis on her sexuality went beyond the stage; it clearly was part of a marketing strategy to create a Madonna-like latina sex queen.

For example, at a photo session for a new album, *Entre a mi mundo,* Selena chose a costume with a slinky, sequin-adorned black top with deep cleavage, a bare midriff, and skin-tight, curve-hugging black pants with a silver-buckled belt. The outfit was not vulgar—none of Selena's outfits were—but, like the purple spangled pantsuit she wore at her last concert (in Houston on February 26, 1995) and a stunning velvet pantsuit she wore at another photo session, this ensemble was "provocative," as her photographer observed (Patoski 1995: 117). Like all her costumes, this one clung tantalizingly to her full, curvaceous body. There could be no doubt, as Patoski recognized, that she aimed to titillate her "new type of fan: young males who saw the woman in the spotlight as a sexual animal" (ibid.).

In his biography, Patoski noted Selena's attempts to balance the demands of Mexican "traditional values," the pressures of the entertainment industry, and her determination to be the "new woman." She aimed to "carve out a career in a male-dominated, machismo-driven industry," while projecting an image suggestive of both sexuality *and* "family values" (1995:107). But a profound clash was being played out in Selena's public persona, an irreconcilable conflict between tradition-imbued working-class values and the sex-glamour-and-glitz world of the international music-commodity market. Ultimately, Selena represented the collision between two disparate cultural economies. One was based on use-value, with its associated web of personalized, reciprocal obligations; the other was based on exchange-value, with its impersonal exploitation of labor (or, in this case, sexuality). For the common people who adulated Selena, it was the image of the barrio girl, grounded in the principles of use-value, that filled them with pride and hope. For EMI Latin (Capitol / EMI) and the marketeers who continued to exploit Selena's sexuality after her death, it was her exchange-value that made her such a prized commodity.

While most dramatically manifested in the person of Selena, the clash between the cultural economies that animate Tejano music haunts every Tejano act. Most certainly it haunts the star whose career is highlighted next, Emilio Navaira.

Emilio: The King of Tejano

With Selena's disappearance from the scene, Emilio Navaira—or Emilio, as he came to be known—inherited her mantle as Tejano music's premier "superstar." Although he always had enjoyed considerable popularity in his own right, Selena's sizzling performance style had overshadowed the more sedate singer from San Antonio ("Tejano's low-key king," as Joyce Saenz Harris of the *Dallas Morning News* described him [December 3, 1995, p. 1E]). In the story from which this description is taken, Saenz Harris proposed, "In the absence of [Tejano's] late queen, Selena, he has become the artist most likely to succeed as a crossover solo act. Emilio is the Great Brown Hope, showcased on the same Nashville label that shot Garth Brooks to superstardom" (Saenz Harris, ibid.).

In fact, Selena, the "Queen of Tejano," and Emilio, the "King," formed a complementary pair. She was the sultry temptress, her flashy costumes emblematic of in-your-viscera female sexuality, as defined by a male-dominated entertainment industry. Yet she also was the demure, family-loving barrio girl. Emilio was her male obverse; while a dynamo on stage ("Audiences connect with his energy," wrote Saenz Harris, "and scream adoringly when he struts the stage" [p. 3E]), his performance was an exercise in controlled virility, his form-fitting western clothes casually symbolic of entrenched male power. And, as befits the King of Tejano, off-stage he was a "very down-to-earth star" (Saenz Harris, p. 3E). In sum, as defined by pop culture, the "Queen" and "King" of Tejano formed an iconic pair embodying idealized female and male roles: she a wanton yet wholesome sex goddess, he a low-key yet cocky embodiment of male dominance.

Despite certain parallels in their careers—she as "Queen," he as "King," both ambitious for crossover fame—Navaira's path to glory differed from Selena's. Unlike the slain diva, Navaira seems to have enjoyed a more mundane adolescence. Whereas Selena dropped out of school in the eighth grade to pursue her father's ambitions to make her a singing star, Navaira was quite successful as a student, particularly in relation to his singing talent.

Emilio Navaira was born in San Antonio on August 23, 1962. He reportedly sang at family gatherings "almost as soon as he began talking" (promotional "bio").[12] Navaira began singing in the school choir while still in elementary school, and he was talented enough to earn a voice scholarship to Southwest Texas State University in San Marcos. According to his publicity "bio," "After his third year, Emilio realized that his studies were leading to a career as a music teacher or choir leader, while his love of music involved performing. 'I went home from school that summer after my third year and I knew I wasn't going back,' he recalls. 'I didn't tell my Mom that.' Instead he tried out for a local Tejano band, led by David Lee Garza, and won the spot as lead singer."

This was in 1983, when Navaira replaced singer Ram Herrera, who had gone on to establish his own career leading another progressive conjunto, the Outlaws. Endowed with a flexible "down-home" tenor voice, Navaira fit readily into the Texas-Mexican conjunto tradition represented by David Lee Garza y los Musicales, despite its "progressive" label. Although trained in classical music, Navaira easily adopted the husky, somewhat nasalized tone typical of tejano conjunto singers. Since the conjunto singing style approximates the country-western, Navaira, who was bilingual, had no trouble moving back and forth between the two (he actually had sung country-western since he was a small boy, according to his "bio"). Navaira headlined los Musicales for five years, during which time the group was nominated for several Tejano Music Awards, in 1987 winning the "Album of the Year" award for the LP *Déjame quererte.*

In 1989, ready to establish his own identity (as had Ram Herrera), Navaira struck out on his own, forming a progressive conjunto, the Rio Band, which included his brother Raul as backup singer and all-around jester. Navaira's rise to "superstardom" in the Tejano market followed quickly. Signing with Cara/CBS in 1989, Navaira's career streaked to the zenith of the Tejano universe, along the way earning such honors as "Male Entertainer of the Year" and "Male Vocalist of the Year" in the Texas Music Awards, as well as the more important Grammy nomination for "Best Mexican American Performance." In 1992, Navaira switched recording labels, signing with the powerful EMI Latin. With the release of his LP, *Unsung Highways,* his supremacy in the Tejano field was confirmed; among male performers, he remained unchallenged for the better part of the nineties.

Like many before him, however, Navaira had dreams of success beyond Tejano. As a child he had been introduced to country music, and his desire always remained to "cross over" into that market. Thus, even while he was with David Lee Garza y los Musicales, he always included at least one country song in each LP. When he formed the Rio Band, the group mixed traditional polcas-rancheras with country songs, as well as a few cumbias. Eventually, Navaira (or "Emilio," as he came to be known in the country market) signed with Capitol/Nashville, a subsidiary of his controlling label, EMI, where he recorded his country-music debut, *Life Is Good.* As Navaira himself observed, "Doing a country album wasn't a drastic change for me. There's a real relationship between Tejano and country music. I certainly could have started with a country band, but David Lee Garza was my way of getting on stage, of making a living doing what I wanted to do, of reaching an audience in the beginning" (Emilio "bio").

Navaira is only partially correct in equating Tejano, especially conjunto, with country music. Historically they do share such attributes as class and song themes (see chapter 3). But country music long has been a thoroughly commodified musical form; Tejano has not yet completed that transformation. Fundamental stylistic (and symbolic) differences exist as well, not the least of which are embodied in the polca-ranchera and the elements that define it—

a particular accordion style, drumming techniques, and tempo. Nothing like it exists in country-western music. Stylistic differences also reflect divergent ethnic orientations and, historically, serve as markers for the social distance separating white and Mexican audiences. In short, country and conjunto represent distinct social realities; and, despite recognized affinities, a real gap exists between the two. Emilio's "spin down [the] country road," then (*Hispanic Magazine,* September 1995, p. 35), might represent the fulfillment of a lifelong ambition, but it was not without contradiction. In any case, as of the mid-nineties, his success in the country market had yet to be proven.

Conclusion: Tejano and the Collision of Moral Economies

The most fervent desire of major-label promoters of Tejano music since they entered that field has been to expand its commercial boundaries and thus convert it into a truly lucrative commodity. Sony Discos executive George Zamora expressed the prevailing sentiment in blunt terms: "We're very interested that the artists coming out of Texas aren't just strong in the Tejano market, but are able to be crossed over into Mexico and the U.S. mainstream as well, because that's where the big, big bucks are" (Burr 1994:32).

It is ironic that the goal of Zamora and other major-label executives received its greatest boost with the death of Selena. Indeed, the scramble to cash in on her posthumous fame, juxtaposed with the genuine grief expressed by her loyal supporters, stands as a testimonial to the clash of moral economies present in contemporary Tejano music. To Selena's fans, particularly women, a symbol of latina talent, wholesome sex appeal, and success in a male-dominated world had been senselessly snuffed out. It was as if their collective aspirations, embodied in this sultry, yet down-to-earth, barrio-bred *hermana* (sister), had been punctured just as surely as the bullet-shattered artery that killed the young diva. "She was a sister," said one tearful fan, "she was one of us." Fifty thousand mourners, most of them tejana women, kept a solemn vigil at a public wake held at the Bayfront Convention Center in Selena's ancestral city of Corpus Christi.

On the other side of the moral divide, entrepreneurs both connected and unconnected to Selena lost no time in mining the gold vein her death had opened up. Overnight, unauthorized biographies appeared, and *People Weekly* produced a commemorative Selena issue. A made-for-TV movie quickly was produced (on E! Entertainment Television), and a script for the big-screen

Selena was written and later filmed. Selena dolls and other memorabilia appeared. And, not surprisingly, EMI Latin capitalized on the fallen singer's new mythical status by aggressively promoting the "crossover" pop-music LP, *Dreaming of You,* which Selena was completing at the time of her death. Apparently oblivious to the incongruities involved, EMI Latin made the following promise in an advertisement appearing in *People Weekly's* commemorative issue: "We will do everything possible to ensure that Selena's legacy is never forgotten."

The irony in EMI Latin's promise lies not so much in its self-serving efforts to promote the mourned idol, but in the glaring contradictions surrounding Selena's death and subsequent memorialization. In many ways, a genuine culture heroine had been created in the Mexican American community, although unlike culture heroes of the past—figures like Gregorio Cortez, for example—Selena's heroification was unavoidably mediated by the mass market and its circulation of commodities. In other words, her use-value as an organic symbol of Mexican American female pride and solidarity immediately was overshadowed by her exchange-value as a marketable commodity. While sisters of the slain "Queen of Tejano" mourned, entrepreneurs plotted their next commercial venture. The "structure of feeling" (Williams 1977) generated in the Mexican American community by the disjunction between the two moral economies colliding in Selena's mythification found ready symbolic expression: alongside the grief and adulation, ugly little rumors circulated about the singer's relationship with her assassin, fan-club president Yolanda Saldívar, and other allegedly sordid activities.

But Selena was not the only performer dogged by the tension between the organic foundations of Tejano music and its superorganic transformation. Emilio Navaira, the other giant of Tejano, provides a less dramatic though equally poignant example. In his efforts to realize his dreams of "crossing over," and to prove his marketability in the world of country-western, he was compelled to de-ethnicize his name by dropping the giveaway to his Mexican origins—his last name. In the world of country-western, he was to be known simply as "Emilio." This may seem like a tactic driven purely by market forces—after all, "Navaira" is difficult to pronounce in English—but the discerning Cameron Randle offered a more compelling explanation. The following segment of our interview illustrates how deep-seated racism can complicate the workings of capitalist enterprise, while it sheds light on the dilemma facing ethnic artists like Emilio as they struggle to break out of a localized context and enter a "mainstream" market and its global circulation of commodities.

Randle and I were discussing the propensity of many Tejano performers, particularly in the "progressive" wing of conjunto, to mix country-western with Tejano. In acknowledging the ease with which artists like Emilio Navaira moved from Tejano to country-western, Randle nevertheless pointed to the difficulty in marketing a "bilingual" artist in the latter market. I asked:

MP: Does the language barrier have something to do with it?

CR: The language barrier—

MP: How about just, uh—you know, let's face it, there's always been conflict between—open conflict in the beginning and latent, you know—

CR: Sure.

MP: Does that, in any way, enter into the marketing strategies?

CR: Absolutely. Uh, you know, it's very unfortunate, but there are strains, uh, of very subtle racism. I think most—the most formidable obstacle that racism presents to us is, uh, in the context of country radio. In order for country artists of any ilk to succeed in today's market—it's not video, you know, it's not touring which makes a country artist. It's country radio exposure. And there is a tremendous distinction, I believe, between the audience for country music versus the core of radio programmers at country music stations who determine what those masses of millions of listeners will be exposed to. And the real challenge is getting an artist who doesn't conform to the conventional country standards, and by that I mean someone from Mexican American, you know, heritage.

MP: Like an Orozco [Rick Orozco, one of Arista's promising new country *and* Tejano performers].

CR: Like an Orozco. Uh, it's very difficult, just given the last name. Emilio dropped the use of his last name.

MP: Was that a, a, uh—

CR: That was a deliberate market strategy, and I say that, because [of] my former partner, Stuart Dill. When I left Refugee Management [Navaira's management agency], to set up Arista Texas, Stuart Dill continued as manager for Emilio. And it was a decision mutually arrived at between Stuart and Emilio to drop the last name. But that was [due to] Stuart Dill's knowledge that the problem with racism at country radio was going to prevent an artist like Emilio, with a name like Navaira, from ever being played.

(Randle interview)

Randle's remarks make it clear that, even in the later stages of an increasingly efficient system of capitalist production, distribution. and consumption, retrogressive ideologies driven by racism can "gum up the works," frustrating the best strategies of public-sensitive enterprises like the recording industry. It is still possible for a Hispanic name to be a liability in some music fields, such as country. This is not to say that a Mexican American cannot succeed in the country-western market. Rick Trevino (the last name is anglicized and pronounced without the "ñ") has been modestly successful, and even Emilio has made some inroads. But, as Randle suggests, the market is less than friendly to minority artists.

At times the "subtle racism" Randle recognized in country-western radio comes up in other, unexpected situations. The death of Selena herself provided such an occasion. Addressing the outpouring of grief from the Mexican American community over the tragedy of her death, the notorious radio talk-show host, Howard Stern, publicly aired an undercurrent of Anglo resentment at the "big fuss" raised over the singer's death (see *Corpus Christi Caller-Times,* March 31, 1996, p. A14). Regarding Selena, Stern was quoted as saying the following: "This music does nothing for me. Alvin and the Chipmunks have more soul. . . . Spanish people have the worst taste in music" (*Houston Chronicle,* April 6, 1995, p. A12). Stern's statement aroused considerable anger in the Mexican American community, and some leaders even threatened a boycott of businesses that advertised on the talk-show host's show. In Corpus Christi, meanwhile, "rancorous letters and telephone calls [from Anglos] flooded the *Caller-Times* complaining of endless media exposure and the city's push to memorialize Selena at a perceived cost to taxpayers" (*Corpus Christi Caller-Times,* March 31, 1996, p. A14).

Thus, at the end of the twentieth century, amid the intensive promotion generated by major-label budgets, Tejano had begun to reap the level of profits that had lured EMI Latin and other conglomerates to Texas in the first place. The music was showing signs—in its production, its performance (increasingly indistinguishable from pop-music spectacle), and its consumption patterns—of inevitable transformation from cultural icon defined by use-value to mass-market commodity driven by exchange-value. Yet, as both Anglo contempt for the memorialization of Selena and racist country-music programmers' resistance to Hispanic performers demonstrate, the relationship between the economy of music and its ideological manifestations is not a simple one. As I have tried to make clear, use-value and exchange-value are not simple antinomies but *dialectically* driven polarities in a complex, perpetual process of cultural *mediation.* The logic of commodity capitalism can be derailed, on the one hand, by actions motivated by use-value, such as Selena's mythification in the tejano community; and, on the other, by racist actions such as Howard Stern's.

Clearly, Tejano music, more than its orquesta and conjunto predecessors, continues to be caught in the gap between two disparate cultural economies. On the one hand, it is inescapably rooted in a residual but stubbornly active form of Texas-Mexican culture, still based on use-value and still at some distance from the dominant capitalist market-culture based on exchange-value. To reiterate Cameron Randle's observation, it is still "a blue-collar, secondary genre of music that is confined to a geographical area"—the organic artistic extension of a recognizable Texas-Mexican community. On the other hand, as Texas-Mexicans increasingly have succumbed to the pressures of "late capitalism" and its decentering effects (particularly as these are mediated through the atomistic patterns of consumption based on exchange-value) and as Tejano itself has come under the globalizing influence of mass marketing, the music increasingly has taken on the character of a superorganic commodity, with all the reifying tendencies inherent in that process.

Prediction is at best a form of speculation when it comes to musical evolution. Such is certainly the case when we attempt to peer into the future of Tejano and Texas-Mexican music in general. Despite its participation in the commercial frenzy unleashed by the large labels, the conjunto—especially the "traditional" branch—appears to have maintained a regional, tejano identity. Its "progressive" twin, meanwhile, vacillates between its organic identity and a massive deidentification brought on by the process of crossing over, especially as it merges with the already highly commoditized country-western music style. The other forms of Tejano—the balada and cumbia groups—maintain, at best, a tenuous relationship with their Texas-Mexican social base. Their transnational styles, highly standardized, commoditized, and increasingly stripped of any ideological substance (save, perhaps, a vague association with the latino masses), militate against the kind of esoteric appropriation experienced by the conjunto vis-à-vis its working-class constituents and by the orquesta vis-à-vis the tejano middle class (see chapters 3, 4, and 5).

Meanwhile, a potentially troublesome development has emerged for Tejano artists and their sponsors. The local market apparently has become saturated. In the early and middle 1990s, a bumper crop of new artists was harvested by the major labels, as they sought to cash in on an exploding field. The market was flooded with over a dozen new acts—La Diferenzia, Culturas, Shelley Lares, Los Chamacos, Elida y Avante, Bobby Pulido, and Inocencia, to name but a few. As the venerable Lalo Guerrero said about the old orquesta circuit, "Everybody was searching for the gold." But, as Ramiro Burr wrote of the bloated Tejano music scene, "Tejano musicians are suffering from a glut of artists and live performances that threaten to oversaturate the market. . . . More than a few concerts have bombed, and new artists trying to get a foothold are finding it hard to crack a flooded market" (*Billboard Magazine,* August 17, 1996, p. 38). In classic capitalist fashion, excess production had overtaken demand.[13]

Finally, in discussing the future of Texas-Mexican music, we must not forget the dialectic of conflict. Susceptible to the same mammoth contradictions that plague capitalism as it oscillates between the contesting play of crosscutting ideologies and economic forces, the dialectic is quite capable of accommodating forms of retrogressive ideology inimical to the *sine qua non* of late capitalism—the notion of "equaliberty" and its social indifference. Thus, as long as racism exists, however subtle, and as long tejanos perceive themselves as "Other" in the larger American social order (that is, as long as they maintain their sense of a differential identity based on persisting elements of a "residual culture"), we can expect Tejano and whatever succeeds it to remain in a state of tension between organic symbol and superorganic commodity.

Notes

1. See Flores (1994) for a cogent account of how the folk play *Los Pastores (The Shepherds)* articulates the "structure of feeling" (Williams 1977) of tejanos caught between the world of use-value and social reciprocity, and exchange-value and exploitation.

2. Unlike La Mafia, Navaira and his Rio Band are considered a "progressive" conjunto, probably because, early in his career, Navaira's claim to fame rested on conjunto-style polcas-rancheras.

3. Nonetheless, Selena considered herself "Tejano first and foremost" (Patoski 1996:94). "Although the band played a blend that mixed rhythm and blues, dance, and pop with strains of salsa and cumbia," added Patoski, "Selena had made her peace with Tejano long ago" (ibid.).

4. The synthesized violin-organ sound is ubiquitous; see almost any LP by Mazz, La Mafia, Selena, or any cumbia-balada group.

5. Cf. Negus: "At a general level globalization indicates a shift in thinking . . . towards . . . the relationships between geographical regions, and the economic, social and cultural movements across conventional boundaries which are becoming an increasing feature of the capitalist economy" (1992:6).

6. Reportedly, *Estás tocando fuego* eventually became the first LP by a Texas-Mexican group to reach the one-million plateau in sales (La Mafia "bio").

7. For example, while doing research on corridos, I once was told by a radio station executive in San Antonio that "his" disc jockeys did not play corridos dealing with "politics," especially those related to César Chávez's unionization efforts.

8. This is not to say that the major labels do not like diversity. On the contrary, like all mass producers, the majors are driven by an oxymoronic principle of late capitalism: have your diversity and standardize it, too. In the words of Fredric Jameson (Jameson speaks of change, but his statement applies equally to diversity): "The paradox from which we must set forth is the equivalence between an unparalleled rate of change on all the levels of social life and an unparalleled standardization of everything" (1994:15). Amplifying on this, Jameson adds, "It is crucial to distinguish between rhythms of change inherent to the system and programmed by it, and a change that replaces one entire system by another one altogether" (ibid.:17).

9. To be sure, Little Joe and Sunny were equally mesmerized by the big-money market, at least initially (see chapter 5 for Sunny's brush with the mass market). But the limits of the tejano market, coupled with the nativistic ideology of the Chicano Generation, wrought its effects on the two tejano icons, pulling them back into the world of use-value production that kept la Onda Chicana from making the leap from organic cultural performance to commercial spectacle.

10. Information on Mazz comes mostly from various "bios" available on the Internet.

11. Chelo Silva actually may have reached this milestone long before. I have no documentation of this, but she was popular enough in Texas and Mexico to have achieved the 50,000 plateau.

12. I am grateful to two friends—archivist Ramón Hernández and journalist Ramiro Burr—for sharing biographical information on Navaira and other contemporary Tejano performers with me.

13. As this book went to press, I was informed by disc jockey Rudy Treviño that the major labels were becoming increasingly disinterested in Tejano, and that the push for internationalization was faltering. Moreover, according to Treviño, there was talk of revitalizing the "indies," now that the majors seemed on the verge of abandoning Tejano. Should the "indies" take over, the music will have come full circle, and it is possible that the music may regain its organic place in Texas-Mexican culture.

Selected Discography

Alegres de Terán, los. *Corridos famosos.* Falcon FLP 4001 (LP).

Bernal, Conjunto. *Música tejana.* Bernal BELP-2035 (LP).

———. *Una noche en La Villita.* Bego 1015 (LP).

Bravos del Norte, los. *Ramón Ayala y los Bravos del Norte.* Freddie LP-1165 (LP).

Edward, Jimmy. *Jimmy Edward: Romántico.* Scorpio Productions 1008 SRP 209 (LP).

———. *My Special Album.* Texas Best Records TXB-LP 1001 (LP).

González, Balde. "No te preocupes por mí"/"Si no te amara tanto." Ideal 695 (78 rpm).

———. "Qué me puede ya importar"/"Oye, corazón." Melco 3950 (78 rpm).

Jordán, Steve. *Soy de Tejas.* Hacienda LP-7905 (LP).

———. *Steve Jordán.* Freddie Records FR-1058 (LP).

Latin Breed. *Más Latin Breed.* GCP Productions GCLP-108 (LP).

———. *Power Drive.* GCP Productions GCPLP 124 (LP).

Little Joe and the Latinaires. *Amor bonito.* El Zarape ZLP 1008 (LP).

———. *The Best of Little Joe.* El Zarape ZLP 1012 (LP).

———. *Por un amor.* El Zarape ZLP 1002 (LP).

Little Joe y la Familia. *Para le gente.* BSR 1038 (LP).

———. *Sea la paz la fuerza.* Leona Record Corporation LRC 019 (LP).

———. *Total.* BSR 1041 (LP).

———. *La voz de Aztlán.* Leona Record Corporation LRC 007 (LP).

López, Isidro, y su Orquesta. *Isidro López: El indio.* Arhoolie CD 363 (CD).

Mafia, La. *Estás tocando fuego.* Sony CDZ 80660 (CD).

———. *15 Hits/15 Éxitos.* Cara Records CA 0900 (LP).

———. *Honey.* Cara 043 (LP).

———. *La Mafia 1986.* CBS CRL-84320 (LP).

———. *Un millón de rosas.* Sony CDZ 81722/469800-2 (CD).

———. *Xplosiv.* CBS CRL-80072 (LP).

Mazz, El Grupo. *Command Performance.* Cara 031 (LP).

———. *Number 16/Número 16.* CBS CRL 84333 (LP).

———. *Solo para ti.* EMI Latin H4 7243 8 30913 4 8 (CD).

Mendoza, Lydia. *Flores de mayo.* Falcon FLP 4004 (LP).

———. *Lydia Mendoza: First Recordings, 1928–1938.* Folklyric Records 9023 (LP).

———. *Más Éxitos.* Falcon FLP 2029 (LP).

Navaira, Emilio. *Emilio and Rio Band.* CBS CRL 80140 (LP).

———. *Life Is Good.* Capitol Nashville.

———. *Quédate.* EMI Latin H4 7243 8 37705 4 2 (CD).

———. *Unsung Highways.* Capitol/EMI.

Ramírez, Agustín, y su Orquesta. *El barco chiquito.* El Zarape ZLP 1013 (LP).

Relámpagos del Norte, los. *Con la tinta de mi sangre.* Bego BG-1061 (LP).

———. *El disco de oro.* Alto Records Alto 1125 (LP).

Relámpagos del Norte, los, et al. *Las más alegres polkas.* Ideal ILP-127 (LP).

Selena y los Dinos. *Dreaming of You.* EMI Latin H2 72433 34123 2 7 (CD).

———. *Entre a mi mundo.* Capitol/EMI H242635 (CD).

———. *Selena Live.* EMI Latin H4 07777 42770 4 4 (CD).

———. *Selena y los Dinos.* Capitol/EMI H1E42144 (LP); H2Y42144 (CD).

Silva, Chelo. *Fichas negras.* Falcon FLP 4013 (LP).

———. *Mis favoritas.* Falcon GLP 14 (LP).

———. "Pedacito por pedacito"/"Te odio como te quiero." Columbia 4191C (78 rpm).

———. *La reina tejana del bolero.* Arhoolie 423 (CD).

Sunny and the Sunliners. *Amor de mis amores.* Key-Loc Records 3030 (LP).

———. *Los enamorados.* Key-Loc Records KL 3020 (LP).

———. *Grande, grande, grande.* Key-Loc Records 3028 (LP).

———. *Yesterday—and Sunny Ozuna.* Teardrop TD-2054 (LP).

Texas-Mexican Border Music. Orquestas Típicas: The First Recordings, (1926–1938). Arhoolie Records, CD 7017.

———. *Tejano Roots: Orquestas tejanas.* Manuel Peña, ed. Arhoolie Productions CD/C 36B.

———. Volume 2. *Corridos, Part 1: 1930–1934.* Arhoolie/Folklyric Records 9004 (LP).

———. Volume 3. *Corridos, Part 2: 1929–1936.* Arhoolie/Folklyric Records 9005 (LP).

———. Volume 4. *Norteño Acordeón, Part 1: The First Recordings.* Arhoolie/Folklyric Records 9006 (LP).

———. Volume 5. *The String Bands: End of a Tradition.* Arhoolie/Folklyric Records 9007 (LP).

———. Volume 9. *Cancioneros de Ayer, Part 3: Songsters from the Past, 1920s/1930s.* Arhoolie/Folklyric Records 9013 (LP).

————. Volume 9. *Cancioneros de Ayer, Part 4: Songsters from the Past, 1920s/1930s.* Arhoolie/Folklyric Records 9016 (LP).

————. Volume 10. *Narciso Martínez: El huracán de Valle.* Arhoolie/Folklyric Records 9017 (LP).

———— Volume 14. *The Chicano Experience.* Guillermo Hernández, ed. Arhoolie/Folklyric Records 9021 (LP).

———— Volume 17. *The First Women Duets.* Philip Sonnichsen, ed. Arhoolie/Folkyric Records 9035 (LP).

————. Volume 19. *Los Hermanos Chavarría.* Arhoolie/Folklyric Records 9037 (LP).

————. Volume 24. *The Texas-Mexican Conjunto.* Manuel Peña, ed. Arhoolie/Folklyric Records 9049 (LP).

Tigres del Norte, los. *El tahur.* Discos Fama 577 (LP).

Tortilla Factory. *Mis favoritas.* Falcon Records GLP 011 (LP).

————. *Tortilla Factory.* Falcon Records FLP-4063 (LP).

Villa, Beto, y su Orquesta. *Beto Villa.* Falcon FLP 108 (LP).

————. *Father of the Orquesta Tejana.* Arhoolie Productions 364 (CD/C).

————. "Mi cafetal"/"Adiós muchachos." Ideal 700 (78 rpm).

————. "Palco de honor"/"Victoria polka." Ideal 777 (78 rpm).

————. *Saludamos a Texas.* Ideal 104 (LP).

References

Abrahams, Roger D. 1977. Towards an Enactment-Centered Theory of Folklore. In *Frontiers of Folklore,* ed. William P. Bascom, 79–120. Boulder, Colo.: Westview Press.

Ackerman, James. 1962. A Theory of Style. *Journal of Aesthetics and Art Criticism* 20:227–37.

Acuña, Rudolfo. 1972. *Occupied America.* San Francisco: Canfield Press.

Alurista. 1979. "Mojologue." In *A'nque.* San Diego, Calif.: Maize Publications.

Alvarez, Rodolfo. 1973. The Psychohistorical and Socioeconomic Development of the Chicano Community in the United States. *Social Science Quarterly* 53(4):920–42.

Anaya, Rudolfo, and Francisco Lomelí, eds. 1989. *Aztlán: Essays on the Chicano Homeland.* Albuquerque: University of New Mexico Press.

Attali, Jacques. 1985. *Noise: The Political Economy of Music.* Minneapolis: University of Minnesota Press.

Bakhtin, Mikhail M. 1984. *Rabelais and His World.* Bloomington: Indiana University Press.

———. 1986. *Speech Genres and Other Essays,* trans. Vern W. McGee, ed. Caryl Emerson and Michael Holquist. Austin: University of Texas Press.

Balibar, Etienne. 1994. *Masses, Classes, Ideas: Studies on Politics and Philosophy Before and After Marx.* New York: Routledge.

Ballaert, William. 1956. *William Ballaert's Texas.* Norman: University of Oklahoma Press.

Baqueiro Foster, Gerónimo. 1964. *La música en el periodo Independiente.* Mexico City: Fondo de Cultura Económica.

Barrera, Mario. 1979. *Race and Class in the Southwest: A Theory of Racial Inequality.* Notre Dame, Ind.: University of Notre Dame Press.

Bauman, Richard. 1972. Differential Identity and the Social Base of Folklore. In *Toward New Perspectives in Folklore,* ed. Américo Paredes and Richard Bauman, 31–41. Austin: University of Texas Press.

————. 1985. The Mythmakers: Transmission of the Texas Myth. *Texas Humanist* 7(3):6–10.

Bell, Horace. 1927. *Reminiscences of a Ranger.* Santa Barbara, Calif.: Wallace Hibbert.

Ben Amos, Dan. 1972. Toward a Definition of Folklore in Context. In *Toward New Perspectives in Folklore,* ed. Richard Bauman and Américo Paredes, 3–15. Austin: University of Texas Press.

Blauner, Robert. 1972. *Racial Oppression in America.* New York: Harper and Row.

Bourke, John G. 1894. The American Congo. *Scribner's Magazine* 15:590–610.

Briggs, Charles L. 1988. *Competence in Performance: The Creativity of Tradition in Mexicano Verbal Art.* Philadelphia: University of Pennsylvania Press.

Burns, E. Bradford. 1980. *The Poverty of Progress: Latin America in the Nineteenth Century.* Berkeley: University of California Press.

Burr, Ramiro. 1993. Tejano Takes Off and Labels, Radio, Retail Catch On. *Billboard Magazine* (March 20): 41–42, 44, 46.

————. 1994. Luring Labels, Reawaking Radio and Securing Sponsorships, Tejano Is Burning Hot and Spreading Fast. *Billboard Magazine* (April 23): 30, 32, 34.

————. 1995. Growth of Labels, Radio and Mass Merchandizing Cap a Fifth Year of Phenomenal Growth. *Billboard Magazine* (September 2): 39, 42, 44, 46.

Cabral, Amilcar. 1979. *Unity and Struggle,* trans. Michael Wolfers. New York: Monthly Review Press.

Camarillo, Albert. 1979. *Chicanos in a Changing Society.* Cambridge: Harvard University Press.

Chabram-Dernersesian, Angie. 1992. I Throw Punches for My Race, but I Don't Want to be a Man: Writing Us—Chica-nos (Girls/Us)/Chicanas—into the Movement Script. In *Cultural Studies,* ed. Lawrence Grossberg et al., 81–95. New York: Routledge.

Chatfield, W. H. 1893. *The Twin Cities of the Border.* New Orleans: E. P. Brandon.

Clopper, J. C. 1929. J. C. Clopper's Journal and Book of Memoranda. *Texas Historical Quarterly* 13(1):44–80.

Curtis, Albert. 1955. *Fabulous San Antonio.* San Antonio, Tex.: Naylor Company.

Davis, William W. H. 1973 [1857]. *El Gringo; Or, New Mexico and Her People.* New York: Arno Press.

Debord, Guy. 1994. *The Society of the Spectacle.* New York: Zone Books.

De la Teja, Jesús Francisco, and John Wheat. 1991. Béxar: Profile of a Tejano Community, 1820–1832. *Tejano Origins in Eighteenth-Century San Antonio,* ed. Gerald C. Poyo and Gilberto M. Hinojosa, 1–24. Austin: University of Texas Press.

De León, Arnoldo. 1983. *They Called Them Greasers: Anglo Attitudes Toward Mexicans in Texas, 1821–1900.* Austin: University of Texas Press.

Dinger, Adele. 1972. *Folklife and Folklore of the Mexican Border.* Edinburg, Tex.: Hidalgo County Historical Museum.

Downs, Fane. 1971. The History of Mexicans in Texas, 1820–1845. Ph.D. diss., Texas Tech University.

Dunn, Si. The Legacy of Private Longoria. In *Scene,* Sunday magazine of the *Dallas Morning News,* April 6, 1975.

Erving, Susan, and Charles E. Osgood. 1954. Second Language Learning and Bilingualism. In *Psycholinguistics,* ed. Charles E. Osgood and Thomas A. Sebeok, 139–46. Bloomington: University of Indiana Press.

Etzkorn, K. Peter. 1973. *Music and Society: The Later Writings of Paul Honigsheim.* New York: John Wiley and Sons.

Evans, David. 1986. Structure and Meaning in the Folk Blues. In *The Study of Folklore,* ed. Jan Harold Brunvand, 563–93. New York: Norton.

Fanon, Frantz. 1965. *A Dying Colonialism.* New York: Grove Press.

Feld, Steven. 1990. *Sound and Sentiment: Birds, Weeping, Poetics and Song in Kaluli Expression.* Philadelphia: University of Pennsylvania Press.

———. 1994. From Schizophonia to Schizmogenesis: On the Discourses and Commodification Practices of "World Music" and "World Beat." In *Music Grooves,* ed. Charles Keil and Steven Feld, 257–88. Chicago: University of Chicago Press.

Flores, Richard R. 1994. Los Pastores and the Gifting of Performance. *American Ethnologist* 21(2):270–85.

———. 1995. *Los Pastores: History and Performance in the Mexican Shepherd's Play of South Texas.* Washington, D.C.: Smithsonian Institution Press.

Foley, Douglas E. 1988. *From Peones to Politicos: Class and Ethnicity in a South Texas Town, 1900–1987.* Austin: University of Texas Press.

———. 1990. *Learning Capitalist Culture: Deep in the Heart of Tejas.* Philadelphia: University of Pennsylvania Press.

Foster, Gerónimo Baqueiro. 1964. *La música en el perido independiente.* Mexico City: Fondo de Cultura Económica.

Franco, Jean. 1970. *The Modern Culture of Latin America.* Baltimore, Md.: Penguin Books.

Frith, Simon. 1988. Art, Ideology and Pop Practice. In *Marxism and the Interpretation of Culture,* ed. Cary Nelson and Lawrence Grossberg, 461–75. Urbana: University of Illinois Press.

Gamio, Manuel. 1971 [1930]. *Mexican Immigration to the United States.* New York: Dover Publications.

García, Mario T. 1981. *Desert Immigrants: The Mexicans of El Paso, 1880–1920.* New Haven, Conn.: Yale University Press.

——. 1989. *Mexican Americans: Leadership, Ideology and Identity.* New Haven, Conn.: Yale University Press.

García, Richard. A. 1991. *The Rise of the Mexican American Middle Class: San Antonio, 1929–1941.* College Station: Texas A&M Press.

Garrido, Juan S. 1974. *Historia de la música popular en México.* Mexico City: Editorial Contemporanees.

Geertz, Clifford. 1973. *The Interpretation of Cultures.* New York: Basic Books.

Goetzmann, William H. 1985. Anglo-American Dreams: Keep the White Lights Shining. *Texas Humanist* 7(3):30–32.

Gómez-Quiñones, Juan. 1990. *Chicano Politics: Reality and Promise.* Albuquerque: University of New Mexico Press.

González, Jovita. 1930. Social Life in Cameron, Starr and Zapata Counties. Master's thesis, University of Texas at Austin.

González, Nancie L. 1969. *The Spanish-Americans of New Mexico.* Albuquerque: University of New Mexico Press.

Gramsci, Antonio. 1971. *Selections from the Prison Notebooks,* trans. Quintin Hoare and Geoffrey Noel Smith. New York: International Publishers.

Gronow, Pekka. 1983. The Record Industry: The Growth of a Mass Medium. In *Popular Music,* volume 3: *Producers and Markets,* ed. Richard Middleton and David Horn, 53–76. New York: Cambridge University Press.

Gutiérrez, David G. 1989. The Third Generation: Reflections on Recent Chicano Historiography. *Mexican Studies/Estudios Mexicanos* 5(2):281–96.

Gutiérrez, Ramón A. 1991. *When Jesus Came, the Corn Mothers Went Away.* Stanford, Calif.: Stanford University Press.

Harris, Marvin. 1968. *The Rise of Anthropological Theory.* New York: Thomas Y. Crowell.

Hebdige, Dick. 1979. *Subculture: The Meaning of Style.* London: Methuen.

Hernández, Inez. N.d. *Con Razón Corazón.* N.p.

Herrera-Sobek, María. 1993. *Northward Bound: The Mexican Immigrant Experience in Ballad and Song.* Bloomington: Indiana University Press.

Howard, Raymond G. 1952. Acculturation and Social Mobility Among Latin-Americans in Resaca City. Master's thesis, University of Texas at Austin.

Hurston, Zora Neale. 1935. *Mules and Men.* Philadelphia: L. B. Lippincott.

Inkeles, Alex. 1979. Continuity and Change in the American National Character. In *The Third Century: America as a Post-Industrial Society,* ed. Seymour Martin Lipset, 389–416. Chicago: University of Chicago Press.

Jacobson, Rodolfo. 1978. The Social Implications of Intra-Sentential Code-

Switching. In *New Directions in Chicano Scholarship,* ed. Ricardo Romo and Raymundo Paredes, 227–56. La Jolla, Calif.: University of California at San Diego.

Jameson, Fredric. 1981. *The Political Unconscious: Narrative as a Socially Symbolic Act.* Ithaca, N.Y.: Cornell University Press.

———. 1984a. Foreword to *The Postmodern Condition,* by Jean-François Lyotard, vii–xxi. Minneapolis: University of Minnesota Press.

———. 1984b. Postmodernism; or, the Cultural Logic of Late Capitalism. *New Left Review* 146:59–92.

———. 1994. *The Seeds of Time.* New York: Columbia University Press.

Jansen, William H. 1965. The Esoteric-Exoteric Factor in Folklore. In *The Study of Folklore,* ed. Alan Dundes, 43–51. Englewood Cliffs, N.J.: Prentice-Hall.

Jordan, Rosan. 1972. Language Loyalty and Folklore Studies: The Mexican-American. *Western Folklore* 31(2):77–86.

———. 1981. Tension and Speech Play in Mexican-American Folklore. In *"And Other Neighborly Names": Social Process and Cultural Image in Texas Folklore,* ed. Richard Bauman and Roger D. Abrahams, 252–65. Austin: University of Texas Press.

Keil, Charles, and Angelica V. Keil. 1992. *Polka Happiness.* Philadelphia: Temple University Press.

Kendall, George W. 1935. *Narrative of the Texan Santa Fe Expedition.* Austin, Tex.: Steck Company.

Kenneson, Susan K. 1978. Through the Looking Glass: History of Anglo-American Attitudes Towards the Spanish-Americans and Indians of New Mexico. Ph.D. diss., Yale University.

Kirshenblatt-Gimblett, Barbara. 1995. Theorizing Heritage. *Ethnomusicology* 39(3): 367–80.

LaCappra, Dominick. 1983. *Rethinking Intellectual History: Text, Contexts, Language.* Ithaca, N.Y.: Cornell University Press.

Lambert, Wallace. 1978. Some Cognitive and Sociocultural Consequences of Being Bilingual. In *International Dimensions of Bilingual Education,* ed. James E. Alatis, 214–28. Washington, D.C.: Georgetown University Press.

León-Portilla, Miguel. 1972. The Norteño Variety of Mexican Culture: An Ethnohistorical Approach. In *Plural Society in the Southwest,* ed. Edward M. Spicer and Raymond H. Thompson, 77–114. Albuquerque: University of New Mexico Press.

Limón, José. 1978. Agringado Joking in Texas-Mexican Society: Folklore and Differential Identity. In *New Directions in Chicano Scholarship,* ed. Ricardo Romo and Raymundo Paredes, 33–50. La Jolla, Calif.: University of California at San Diego.

————. 1994. *Dancing with the Devil: Society and Cultural Poetics in Mexican American South Texas.* Madison: University of Wisconsin Press.

Lipsitz, George. 1990. *Time Passages: Collective Memory and American Popular Culture.* Minneapolis: University of Minnesota Press.

Lomelí, Francisco A. 1993. Contemporary Chicano Literature, 1959–1990: From Oblivion to Affirmation to Forefront. In *Handbook of Hispanic Cultures in the United States: Literature and Art,* ed. Francisco A. Lomelí, 86–108. Houston: Arte Público Press.

Lyotard, Jean-François. 1984. *The Postmodern Condition,* trans. Geoff Bennington and Brian Massumi. Minneapolis: University of Minnesota Press.

McLemore, S. Dale. 1980. *Racial and Ethnic Relations in America.* Boston: Allyn and Bacon.

McWilliams, Carey. 1948. *North From Mexico.* New York: Greenwood Press.

Madsen, William. 1964. *The Mexican-Americans of South Texas.* New York: Holt, Rinehart and Winston.

Malone, Bill C. 1985. *Country Music, U.S.A.* Austin: University of Texas Press.

Manning, Frank E. 1992. Spectacle. In *Folklore, Cultural Performances, and Popular Entertainments,* ed. Richard Bauman, 291–99. New York: Oxford University Press.

Manuel, Peter. 1995. *Caribbean Currents: Caribbean Music from Rumba to Reggae.* Philadelphia: Temple University Press.

Marx, Karl. 1977. *Capital.* Volume 1. New York: Vintage Books.

Mauss, Marcel. 1954. *The Gift,* trans. Ian Cunnison. London: Cohen and West.

Mayer-Serra, Otto. 1941. *Panorama de la música mexicana.* Mexico City: Fondo de Cultura Económica.

Meisenhelder, Susan. 1996. Conflict and Resistance in Zora Neale Hurston's *Mules and Men. Journal of American Folklore* 109(433):267–88.

Memmi, Albert. 1965. *The Colonizer and the Colonized.* Boston: Beacon Press.

Mendoza, Vicente. 1961. *La canción mexicana.* Mexico City: Fondo de Cultura Económica.

Mitchell, Tony. 1996. *Popular Music and Local Identity.* London: Leicester University Press.

Montejano, David. 1987. *Anglos and Mexicans in the Making of Texas.* Austin: University of Texas Press.

Montoya, José. 1972. La Jefita. In *Aztlán: An Anthology of Mexican American Literature,* ed. Luis Valdez and Stan Steiner, 266–68. New York: Vintage Books.

Muir, Andrew F. 1958. *Texas in 1837: An Anonymous Contemporary Narrative.* Austin: University of Texas Press.

Muñoz, Carlos, Jr. 1983. The Quest for Paradigm: The Development of Chicano

Studies and Intellectuals. In *History, Culture and Society: Chicano Studies in the 1980s,* ed. Mario García et al., 19–36. Ypsilanti, Mich.: Bilingual Press.

———. 1989. *Youth, Identity, Power.* London: Verso Press.

Murguía, Edward. 1975. *Assimilation, Colonialism and the Mexican American People.* Austin: Center for Mexican American Studies.

Negus, Keith. 1992. *Producing Pop: Culture and Conflict in the Popular Music Industry.* London: Edward Arnold.

Nettl, Bruno. 1985. *The Western Impact on World Music: Change, Adaptation and Survival.* New York: Schirmer Books.

Ong, Aihwa. 1996. Cultural Citizenship as Subject-Making. *Cultural Anthropology* 37(5):737–62.

Ortego, Phillip D. 1970. The Chicano Renaissance. In *La Causa Chicana: The Movement for Justice,* ed. Margaret M. Mangold, 42–64. New York: Family Service Association of America.

Padilla, Genaro M. 1989. Myth and Comparative Cultural Nationalism: The Ideological Uses of Aztlán. In *Aztlán: Essays on the Chicano Homeland,* ed. Rudolfo A. Anaya and Francisco A. Lomelí, 111–34. Albuquerque: University of New Mexico Press.

Paredes, Américo. 1958. *With His Pistol in His Hand.* Austin: University of Texas Press.

———. 1963. The Ancestry of Mexico's *Corridos:* A Matter of Definitions. *Journal of American Folklore* 76:231–35.

———. 1966. The Anglo-American in Mexican Folklore. In *New Voices in American Studies,* ed. Ray Browne, 113–27. Lafayette, Ind.: Purdue University Press.

———. 1993a. The Folklore of Groups of Mexican Origin in the United States. In *Folklore and Culture on the Texas-Mexican Border,* by Américo Paredes, ed. Richard Bauman, 3–18. Austin: CMAS Books.

———. 1993b. The Problem of Identity in a Changing Culture: Popular Expressions of Culture Conflict Along the Lower Rio Grande Border. In *Folklore and Culture on the Texas-Mexican Border,* by Américo Paredes, ed. Richard Bauman, 19–47. Austin: CMAS Books.

———. 1993c. Folk Medicine and the Intercultural Jest. In *Folklore and Culture on the Texas-Mexican Border,* by Américo Paredes, ed. Richard Bauman, 49–72. Austin: CMAS Books.

———. 1993d. The Mexican *Corrido:* Its Rise and Fall. In *Folklore and Culture on the Texas-Mexican Border,* by Américo Paredes, ed. Richard Bauman, 129–41. Austin: CMAS Books.

———. 1993e. The United States, Mexico and *Machismo.* In *Folklore and Culture on the Texas-Mexican Border,* by Américo Paredes, ed. Richard Bauman, 215–34. Austin: CMAS Books.

———. 1995 [1976]. *A Texas-Mexican Cancionero: Folksongs of the Lower Border.* Austin: University of Texas Press.

Patoski, Joe Nick. 1995. *Selena.* New York: Boulevard Books.

Peña, Manuel. 1980. Ritual Structure in a Chicano Dance. *Latin American Music Review* 1(1):47–73.

———. 1982. Folksong and Social Change: Two Corridos as Interpretive Sources. *Aztlan* 13:13–42.

———. 1985a. *The Texas-Mexican Conjunto: History of a Working-Class Music.* Austin: University of Texas Press.

———. 1985b. From *Ranchero* to *Jaitón:* Class and Ethnicity in Texas-Mexican Music. *Ethnomusicology* 29(1):29–55.

———. 1991. Class, Gender and Machismo: The "Treacherous-Woman" Folklore of Mexican Male Workers. *Gender and Society* 5(1):30–46.

———. 1999. *The Mexican American Orquesta.* Austin: University of Texas Press.

———. N.d. Folklore, Machismo and Everyday Practice: Writing Mexican-Worker Culture. Unpublished manuscript.

Peñalosa, Fernando. 1980. *Chicano Sociolinguistics.* Rowley, Mass.: Newbury House Publishers.

Richardson, Albert D. 1867. *Beyond the Mississippi.* Hartford, Conn.: American Publishing Company.

Robb, John D. 1980. *Hispanic Folk Music of New Mexico and the Hispanic Southwest.* Norman: University of Oklahoma Press.

Robinson, Alfred. 1925. *Life in California Before the Conquest.* San Francisco: Thomas C. Russell.

Robinson, Cecil. 1992. *No Short Journeys: The Interplay of Customs in the History and Literature of the Borderlands.* Tucson: University of Arizona Press.

Robinson, Deanna Campbell, Elizabeth R. Buck, and Marlene Cuthbert. 1991. *Music at the Margins: Popular Music and Global Cultural Diversity.* Newbury Park, Calif.: Sage Publications.

Rosen, Gerald P. 1975. *Political Ideology and the Chicano Movement.* San Francisco: R&E Research Associates.

Rubel, Arthur J. 1966. *Across the Tracks: Mexican Americans in a Texas City.* Austin: University of Texas Press.

San Miguel, Guadalupe. 1987. *Let All of Them Take Heed: Mexican Americans and the Quest for Educational Equity in Texas, 1918–1981.* Austin: University of Texas Press.

Sapir, Edward. 1949. Culture, Genuine and Spurious. In *Selected Writings of Ed-*

ward Sapir in Language, Culture and Personality, ed. David G. Mandelbaum, 308–31. Berkeley: University of California Press.

Saragoza, Alex M. 1987. The Significance of Recent Chicano-Related Historical Writings: An Appraisal. *Ethnic Affairs* 1:24–62.

———. N.d. The State and the Media in Mexico: The Origins of Televisa. Unpublished manuscript.

Sheridan, Thomas E. 1986. *Los Tucsonenses: The Mexican Community in Tucson, 1854–1941.* Tucson: University of Arizona Press.

Simmons, Merle E. 1963. The Ancestry of Mexico's *Corridos. Journal of American Folklore* 76:1–15.

Simmons, Ozzie. 1974 [1952]. *Anglo-Americans and Mexican-Americans in South Texas: A Study in Dominant-Subordinate Group Relations.* New York: Arno Press.

Slobin, Mark, and Jeff Todd Titon. 1996. The Music-Culture as a World of Music. In *Worlds of Music,* ed. Jeff Todd Titon, 1–16. New York: Schirmer Books.

Songs of the Homeland. 1995. Documentary film produced and directed by Hector Galán. 58 min. Austin: Galán Productions.

Spottswood, Richard K. 1990. *Ethnic Music on Records: A Discography of Ethnic Recordings in the United States, 1893–1942.* Urbana: University of Illinois Press.

Stallybrass, Peter, and Allon White. 1986. *The Politics and Poetics of Transgression.* Ithaca, N.Y.: Cornell University Press.

Steiner, Stan. 1970. *La Raza: The Mexican Americans.* New York: Harper and Row.

Stoeltje, Beverly. 1992. Festival. In *Folklore, Cultural Performances, and Popular Entertainments: A Communications-Centered Handbook,* ed. Richard Bauman, 261–71. New York: Oxford University Press.

Strachwitz, Chris. 1974. Una historia de la música de la frontera: Texas-Mexican Border Music. Volume 1. El Cerrito, Calif.: Arhoolie Productions.

Taussig, Michael. 1980. *The Devil and Commodity Fetishism in South America.* Chapel Hill: University of North Carolina Press.

Taylor, Paul S. 1968. *Mexican Labor in the United States: Migration Statistics.* New York: Jefferson Reprint Corporation.

———. 1971 [1934]. *An American-Mexican Frontier.* New York: Russell and Russell.

Thompson, E. P. 1965. *The Making of the English Working Class.* London: Victor Gollancz.

Titon, Jeff Todd, ed. 1996. *Worlds of Music.* New York: Schirmer Books.

Todorov, Tzvetan. 1984. *Mikhail Bakhtin: The Dialogical Principle,* trans. Wlad Godzich. Minneapolis: University of Minnesota Press.

Turner, Victor. 1969. *The Ritual Process.* Chicago: University of Chicago Press.

Vaid, Jyotsna, ed. 1986. *Language Processing in Bilinguals: Psycholinguistic and Neuropsychological Perspectives.* Hillsdale, N.J.: Lawrence Erlbaum Associates.

Valdez, Luis. 1972. "La Plebe." In *Aztlán: An Anthology of Mexican American Literature,* ed. Luis Valdez and Stan Steiner, xiii–xxxiv. New York: Vintage Books.

Vallejo, Guadalupe. 1890. Ranch-Mission Days in Alta California. *Century Magazine* 41(2):183–92.

Vizcaya Canales, Isidro. 1971. *Los orígenes de la industrialización de Monterrey.* Monterrey, Mexico: Librería Tecnológico.

Williams, Raymond. 1973. *The Country and the City.* New York: Oxford University Press.

———. 1977. *Marxism and Literature.* New York: Oxford University Press.

———. 1981. *The Sociology of Culture.* New York: Schocken Books.

Wilson, William A. 1973. Herder, Folklore and Romantic Nationalism. *Journal of Popular Culture* 6:819–35.

Zavalishin, Dmitry. 1973. California in 1824. *Southern California Quarterly* 55(4): 369–412.

Zea, Leopoldo. 1963. *The Latin-American Mind,* trans. James H. Abbott and Lowell Dunham. Norman: University of Oklahoma Press.

Index

superorganic, 3–8, 10–12, 24, 109, 181, 182, 184, 185, 211, 214, 215
Sutherland, Tom, 79

taco circuit, 95, 104
tambora de rancho, 44–46, 88, 90, 94
Tejano, xi, xii, 14, 15, 20, 24, 69, 84, 108, 178–82, 184–90, 192, 194–205, 207–15
Tejano Music Awards, 199, 201, 204, 209
Temerarios, 83
Texas Rangers, 20, 74, 80, 81
Texas Tornados, 107
Texians, 30, 69
Tex-Mex, 119, 133, 138, 204
Texo-centrism, 66, 68, 69
Tigres del Norte, 83, 105
tololoche, 90, 101
Tomás Núñez y su Orquesta, 124
Torero Records, 153, 154
Tortilla Factory, 176
Tovar, Rigo, 187
treacherous-woman theme, 53, 54–58, 61, 64, 70, 83
Treviño, Reymundo, 109, 134, 137, 138
Trevino, Rick, 213

Tropa F, 107, 186
Turner, Victor, 74

United Farm Workers, 79, 159

Valdez, Luis, 71, 160, 161
Valdez Leal, Felipe, 12
Vallejo, Guadalupe, 19
Vallejo, Mariano, 18
Vela, Rubén, 101, 150
victim *corrido*, 76, 77–82
Villa, Beto, 94, 119, 132–43, 154, 158
Villarreal, Bruno, 117
Vocalion Records, 11, 51, 123, 124

waltz, 28, 37, 55, 90, 101, 124, 125
war of maneuver, 16, 21
war of position, 17, 21, 74, 114
WEA Records, 107, 180, 189, 193
Williams, Raymond, 19, 25, 50, 51, 61–63, 114, 129, 162, 211, 215

Yonics, Los, 186

Zarape Records, 154, 155, 162, 177